The United States and the Origins
of the Cuban Revolution

JULES R. BENJAMIN

The United States and the Origins of the Cuban Revolution

An Empire of Liberty in an Age of National Liberation

PRINCETON UNIVERSITY PRESS
PRINCETON, NEW JERSEY

Copyright © 1990 by Princeton University Press
Published by Princeton University Press, 41 William Street,
Princeton, New Jersey 08540

In the United Kingdom: Princeton University Press, Oxford

Library of Congress Cataloging-in-Publication Data

Benjamin, Jules R.
The United States and the origins of the Cuban Revolution: an empire of liberty
in an age of national liberation / Jules R. Benjamin.
p.   cm.   Bibliography: p.   Includes index.
ISBN 0-691-07836-X
1. United States—Foreign relations—Cuba. 2. Cuba—Foreign relations—United States.
3. Cuba—History—Revolution, 1959—Causes. I. Title.
E183.8.C9B43 1990   327.7307291—dc20   89-34626

Publication of this book has been aided by the Whitney Darrow
Fund of Princeton University Press

This book has been composed in Linotron Times Roman

Princeton University Press books are printed on acid-free paper,
and meet the guidelines for permanence and durability of the
Committee on Production Guidelines for Book Longevity of the
Council on Library Resources

Printed in the United States of America by Princeton University Press,
Princeton, New Jersey

10 9 8 7 6 5 4 3 2 1

Designed by Laury A. Egan

TO MY STUDENTS

CONTENTS

LIST OF ILLUSTRATIONS

ACKNOWLEDGMENTS

I RECEIVED the financial and professional assistance of the following institutions: American Council of Learned Societies (Grant), American Philosophical Society (Grant), Eleanor Roosevelt Foundation (Grant), Truman Library Institute (Grant), F.D.R. Four Freedoms Foundation (Grant), American Historical Association (Beveridge Grant), University of Southern California (Center for International Studies Fellowship), and University of Pittsburgh (Center for Latin American Studies Fellowship).

The following persons reviewed early drafts of the manuscript: Harold D. Sims, Louis A. Pérez, Jr., David Green, Friedrich Katz, Fredrick Pike, Jorge I. Domínguez, Lloyd C. Gardner, Thomas J. McCormick, Robert L. Beisner, and David Healy. The final work is stronger for their efforts but still bears the stamp of its author. It is he who is responsible for what is written here.

JULES R. BENJAMIN
Pittsburgh, Pennsylvania
January 1989

The United States and the Origins
of the Cuban Revolution

INTRODUCTION

"We should do for Europe on a large scale essen-
tially what we did for Cuba on a small scale and
thereby usher in a new era of human history."

WALTER HINES PAGE
U.S. ambassador to
England, 1914

THIS BOOK is a study of the relationship between two states. It is not,
however, a traditional diplomatic history. It attempts to uncover not only
how the United States acted toward Cuba but also what deeper elements in
North American institutions and culture directed the use of its power. This
work is a study in the nature of hegemony. The tremendous influence exerted over Cuba by the United States serves, in this instance, as a point of
departure for studying the ways in which this power was understood by
those who wielded it and by those who contended with it.

The question of how North Americans and those in their government
understood their domination of Cuba has not received the study it deserves.
Perhaps this is because North Americans tend to define U.S. hegemony
over others as benign or as a phantom of hot-blooded nationalists and sinister subversives. By defining its own role in the world as anti-imperial, the
United States has made difficult any self-understanding of its acts of domination. North American scholars need to begin their study of U.S. expansion from a position outside the sway of this aspect of their culture.

ONE WAY of understanding the Cuban revolution is as the working out of
long-standing tensions in the relationship between the United States and
Cuba. From the early nineteenth century onward, the United States saw
itself as benefiting Cuba by exerting a powerful "Americanizing" influence on the island. Before the turn of the century the United States expected
to do so by annexing Cuba and after that date by modernizing her. In each
era the United States desired both to change Cuban society and also to keep
it stable. Leaders in Washington, however, never worked out a way of ac-

3

complishing the one desire that did not conflict with the other. In addition to this inner tension, North American influence clashed with a growing Cuban desire for independence. Even after Cuba gained her freedom from Spanish rule in 1898, that desire grew and eventually was defined in such a way that resentment of U.S. power became one of its central components.

Looked at from this perspective, the relationship between the two societies has a tragic aspect. Prior to 1959, Cubans were not able to work out political and economic structures that effectively integrated or, alternatively, resisted U.S. influence, nor could they accept that fact. For its part, the United States could not understand opposition to its influence by Cuba as other than immaturity or, at the end, alien subversion. Washington never seriously entertained the idea that its influence might represent an unbearable political and economic burden.

This book traces the tensions in the relationship, beginning its survey early in the nineteenth century and emphasizing the period between 1898 and 1961. It examines the Cuban republic, noting the growth of a frustrated nationalism, the lack of substance of the island's political order, and the imbalance of its economy. It also surveys the wide-ranging and often contradictory U.S. economic, political, and cultural influence that in important ways did ''Americanize'' Cuba but managed to do so only at the cost of presenting itself as the principal barrier to true independence. What the United States took to be the barometer of its success was, in the end, the source of its failure.

In 1959, when Cuban nationalism broke the old political system through which U.S. influence had been conveyed, the new government headed by Fidel Castro resisted the resurrection of that influence and, for the first time, did so effectively. The United States, unable to construe its role in Cuban history as other than benign, interpreted Castro's opposition first as impetuousness and then as a cloak for sinister designs. When the Cuban revolution adopted socialism, the latter suspicion was confirmed. As Washington moved to destroy the regime that had turned itself into a bitter ideological enemy, the United States once again confirmed itself, in Cuban eyes, as the ancient enemy of independence. The thesis of this work is that the relationship between the United States and Cuba broke down under its own weight; it could no longer bear the burden placed upon it by the antagonism between the U.S. desire to influence Cuba and the Cuban desire to fulfill the dream of true independence.

IN EXAMINING the relationship between the United States and Cuba, emphasis is placed upon the perspectives and actions of North Americans. A close examination of the Cuban side of the story is left to others. The analysis of North American behavior is built around the disparity between its broad historical orientation toward Cuba on the one hand and its actual impact upon the island on the other. A principal result of this disparity was the disorientation of U.S. policymakers. Because of the assumption of hegemony and benevolence that lay behind North American actions, policymakers expected to achieve the mutual enhancement of U.S. interests and Cuban welfare. Moreover, they assumed that Cuban society could be molded, or at least oriented, in a proper direction. Policymakers further assumed that *private* North American cultural and economic influence would play an important role in the process of orientation.

The evidence here indicates, however, that U.S. public policy and private influence did not complement each other. Market forces in the sugar industry and political pressures from the domestic sugar lobby, for example, were not bound by the overarching belief in the compatibility of United States and Cuban interests. Nor could U.S. cultural influence be neatly aligned with policy or with assumptions of benevolence. North American media and consumer goods saturated the island with the trappings of the Yankee middle class, helping to assure that many Cubans would be frustrated in their desire to consume and torn in their cultural orientation. In ways that threatened the social stability desired by the United States, the few Cubans who drove Cadillacs and gambled in the opulent casinos distanced themselves not only economically but culturally from their many countrymen whose floors were of dirt and roofs of palm.

Even foreign policy itself was often at odds with the long-run promotion of U.S. interests and with the assumption of benevolence. Pressure from Washington for Cuban conformity to North American political and economic norms created important internal pressures in Cuban society. While the extensive U.S. economic presence benefited those who integrated themselves into it or who learned to manipulate it, the larger effect was to exacerbate class and sectoral tensions. At the same time, the ability of Cuban leaders to contain or resolve such conflicts was undermined by their need to adhere to U.S. advice. The overall impact of the United States on Cuba was one that included structural and psychological damage of a significant and lasting kind.

United States leaders failed to notice these kinds of effects. For them, U.S. influence solved problems, it did not create them. In daily contact with Cubans who for the most part shared or aped their views, Washington officials had little reason to question their own assumptions. As a result, there was little recognition of the gap between the ideology of U.S.-Cuban relations and the actual structure of that relationship. Ignorance of this gap left the United States unprepared to deal with forces in Cuba that were intensified and antagonized by this disparity. Thus the tremendous power of the United States in Cuba produced challenges to its own influence at the same time that the North American worldview obscured the origins and nature of these challenges.

This study of the U.S. impact on Cuba differs in important ways from much of the existing literature on the origins of the revolution. From the perspective of this book, the Cuban revolution was neither betrayal nor deliverance, nor was it a U.S. policy failure in the ordinary sense of the term. It was rather a natural result of the flawed relationship between two states. While that relationship by no means made social revolution in Cuba inevitable, a study of its history does make the outcome more understandable.

IT MAY be argued that this work is negative, that it fails to suggest a way in which Washington might otherwise have used its power over Cuba. Such a critique suggests the belief that the United States can express itself in the world free from contradiction. It suggests that somehow the nation could have acted in Cuba so as to have promoted simultaneously U.S. interests, U.S. values, and Cuban independence. This work, however, assumes an inevitable tension between these goals. Acknowledgment of such tension would seem to be a necessary precondition for any less contradictory and less imperial relationship between Cuba and the United States.

No neat stroke of reason, power, or goodwill can erase the history of U.S.-Cuban relations. I have offered my reader the only advice I am able to give. I have attempted to show how closely the many strands of hegemony were woven and how tight a knot they made. Still, this work is not fatalistic. To loosen the knot requires only that both sides stop pulling so strenuously on the strands—as they have done these last thirty years. To unwind the knot, however, will be—as was its making—a long, painful process.

CHAPTER 1

THE ERA OF
INEVITABLE GRAVITATION:
THE UNITED STATES AND
COLONIAL CUBA

I

UNITED STATES interest in Cuba is almost as old as the North American nation itself. The earliest attraction was to the island's commerce, in which Yankee traders became important before the end of the eighteenth century and came to dominate as early as 1820.[1] By that time, the trading connection had given rise to a host of reasons for intense U.S. concern with Cuba. The best political minds of the new nation expounded on the strategic, economic, and ideological necessities that tied the island's fate to the empire of liberty being constructed in North America. Hopes and fears concerning Cuba's future abound in the writings of John Adams, Thomas Jefferson, James Madison, James Monroe, John C. Calhoun, and John Quincy Adams. Each in his own way expected Cuba to become either a part of the Union or an appendage to it.

Jefferson admitted toward the end of his life that "I have ever looked on Cuba as the most interesting addition which could ever be made to our system of states."[2] At several points during his administration Jefferson

---

[1] Robert F. Smith, *What Happened in Cuba?* (New York: Twayne Publishers, Inc., 1963), pp. 21–23; Jacques A. Barbier and Allan J. Kuethe, eds., *The North American role in the Spanish imperial economy, 1760–1819* (Manchester: Manchester University Press, 1984), pp. 15–22, 112–24, 141; Hugh Thomas, *Cuba: The Pursuit of Freedom* (New York: Harper & Row, 1971), pp. 66–71.

[2] Quoted in Smith, *What Happened*, p. 30.

seriously considered acts of diplomacy or even war that would result in "our receiving Cuba into our union."[3] James Madison wrote to Jefferson that "I have always concurred with you in the sentiment that too much importance could not be attached to that Island and that we ought, if possible, to incorporate it into our union."[4] As president, Madison sent William Shaler, a partisan of annexation, as United States consul in Havana and informed Britain that "the disposition of Cuba gives the United States so deep an interest . . . that they could not be a satisfied spectator at its falling under any European Government."[5] To these reasons for acquiring Cuba, John Calhoun added that of preventing slave rebellion on the island. As Monroe's secretary of war, he gave strong support to proposals of annexation that on several occasions came before the Cabinet. His fear of a black Cuba overrode concerns about the war with Britain that some felt annexation of the island might bring about.[6] In the end, it was Secretary of State John Quincy Adams, Calhoun's opponent in the Cabinet debates, who pronounced the most lasting verdict on U.S. relations with Cuba. Adams solved the contradiction between the North American desire for Cuba and her weakness at that point to fulfill it by declaring Cuba's fate to be ineluctable. As he explained in his often-quoted letter of instruction to Hugh Nelson, the United States minister to Spain:

> There are laws of political as well as physical gravitation; and if an apple severed by the tempest from its native tree cannot choose but fall to the ground, Cuba, forcibly disjoined from its own unnatural connection with Spain, and incapable of self-support, can gravitate only toward the North American Union, which by the same law of nature cannot cast her off from its bosom.[7]

While annexation was considered a natural fate for Cuba, independence was not. The dominant North American view throughout the nineteenth

[3] Smith, *What Happened*, p. 25. For U.S. interest in Cuba during Jefferson's administration see Philip S. Foner, *A History of Cuba and Its Relations with the United States* (New York: International Publishers, 1962), I, pp. 124–26.

[4] Thomas, *Pursuit*, p. 101; Foner, *History*, I, p. 147.

[5] Foner, *History*, I, p. 127.

[6] Calhoun's views are expounded in Arthur P. Whitaker, *The United States and the Independence of Latin America* (New York: W. W. Norton, 1964), pp. 399–404. The arguments of Henry Clay and James Monroe concerning U.S. interest in Cuba were often connected to the idea of geographical proximity. Monroe considered Cuba "as forming the mouth of the Mississippi." Clay held that "the law of its position proclaims that it should be attached to the United States." See Albert Weinberg, *Manifest Destiny* (New York: Quadrangle, 1963), pp. 65–66.

[7] Smith, *What Happened*, pp. 27–29. A general discussion of U.S. attitudes toward Cuba during the first quarter of the nineteenth century can be found in Lester D. Langley, *The Cuban Policy of the United States: A Brief History* (New York: John Wiley & Sons, 1968), ch. 1.

century was that, for reasons of geography, racial composition, and cultural heritage, the island was incapable of self-government. John Adams was among the most pessimistic. Reflecting a widely held view in Protestant North America that Roman Catholicism was hopelessly reactionary, Adams considered the establishment of democracy in Latin America as likely as its appearance in the animal kingdom.[8] Jefferson observed that history "furnishes no example of a priest-ridden people maintaining a free civil government."[9] Henry Clay, who held a more generous view of the possibilities of republican government in Latin America, nevertheless concluded in 1825:

> If Cuba were to declare itself independent, the amount and character of its population render it improbable that it could maintain its independence. Such a premature declaration might bring about a renewal of those shocking scenes, of which a neighboring Island [Haiti] was the afflicted scene.[10]

The twin perceptions—that Cuba could not stand on her own and that she would be drawn inexorably toward the United States—rendered the island's status as a colony of Spain almost congenial. Madrid was the weakest of the European imperial powers and hence constituted no strategic threat. Moreover, she was not a serious commercial competitor. United States trade with colonial Cuba, while harassed by Spanish mercantilism, was soon greater than that of the island with its mother country.[11] For much of the century, the view in Washington was that Cuba should remain under Spanish rule until the time came for her to be attached to the United States. The idea of an independent Cuba was one that did not gain serious consideration among North American leaders until the twentieth century, and, even then, many found it difficult to accept.

During the nineteenth century North American confidence about Cuba's destiny was periodically punctuated by fears that Spanish rule would be replaced by that of a more vigorous imperial power or that Madrid's legal but unenforceable commercial monopoly over the island might somehow be effectively established. Equally disturbing was the occasional trepidation that Cuba might attempt to gain the independence for which she was

---

[8] Whitaker, *Independence*, p. 37. This negative view was sometimes complemented by its opposite, which held that the inexorable march of freedom would break down Spain's tyrannical institutions in the New World.

[9] Whitaker, *The Western Hemisphere Idea: Its Rise and Decline* (Ithaca, N.Y.: Cornell University Press, 1954), p. 29.

[10] Foner, *History*, I, p. 155.

[11] Franklin W. Knight, *Slave Society in Cuba During the Nineteenth Century* (Madison: University of Wisconsin Press, 1970), pp. 43–45. By the 1830s, U.S. ships also dominated the slave trade with Cuba. Smith, *What Happened*, p. 36.

unsuited. When the mainland colonies of Spain revolted against Madrid in the second decade of the nineteenth century, many U.S. leaders expressed the fear that the liberation movement might spread to Cuba as well. Secretary of State Clay announced that "the United States are satisfied with the present condition of the Islands [Cuba and Puerto Rico], in the hands of Spain, and with their ports open to our commerce, as they are now open. . . . This Government desires no political change in that condition."[12] Clay's statement reflected the famous doctrine of President Monroe that "with the existing colonies or dependencies of any European power we have not interfered and should not interfere." Clearly the possibility of Cuban independence might call the law of gravitation into question. Nevertheless, in the period before the civil war, no liberation movement of serious proportions developed on the island, and as a result U.S. interests and expectations were not seriously challenged.

One group of North Americans, however, could not afford to be complacent. Slaveholders were attracted to the island as a natural field for expanding the peculiar institution. They were also moved by fear that a slave revolt there would create, as it had in Haiti, another black republic—this time just off the shore of Florida. As a result, many southern leaders promoted efforts either to purchase the island or even forcibly to remove Spanish control. Several unofficial military expeditions with the latter end in view were mounted from the southern United States in the 1850s.[13]

At times the intense southern desire to prevent the "Africanization" of Cuba was complemented by the generalized North American sense of its "manifest destiny" to spread its people and institutions. Stories of Spain's harsh rule in Cuba were common in U.S. newspapers and reinforced the view that Spain was a reactionary power whose command of the island would be swept away by the march of liberty from the north. Inspired by both southern fears and a broad expansionism, both the Polk and Pierce administrations offered to purchase Cuba, implying to Madrid the eventual loss of its colony if it refused to sell. There was widespread support in the United States for this means of acquiring Cuba. Purchase avoided the more militant schemes of the expansionist Democrats (which courted war with Spain or her protectors), and thus it was congenial even to some Whigs whose normal preoccupation was simply to keep Cuba out of British or French hands and its trade oriented toward the north.[14] The difficulty with

[12] Langley, *Struggle for the American Mediterranean, 1776–1904* (Athens: University of Georgia Press, 1976), p. 44. Also see Thomas, *Pursuit*, p. 104, and Langley, *Cuban Policy*, ch. 1. Clay took no note of the tension between U.S. predominance in Cuba's trade and Spanish political control of the island.

[13] Foner, *History*, II, chs. 2–10.

[14] Langley, *Cuban Policy*, ch. 2; Thomas, *Pursuit*, chs. 17 and 18. Polk noted in his diary

this neat solution was that no Spanish government, liberal or monarchist, could bring itself to give up the last remnant of its once great New World empire. This left North Americans in something of a box because Britain stood in the way of any forceful U.S. attempt to "free" Cuba.

By the 1850s this dilemma was being eclipsed by sectional controversy. Slavery and expansion were rapidly becoming incompatible, as northerners more and more saw Cuban annexation as a southern plot to preserve its peculiar institution and enhance its representation in Congress. The North American consensus about how to absorb Cuba was breaking down over the same issue that would soon rend the Union itself.

II

For its part, mid-nineteenth-century Cuba was moving in some ways toward and in others away from North American requirements for union. As always, the Spanish residents of the island clung to the authority in Madrid that was both the legal and structural basis of their economic and political power. On the other hand, the native elite, many of them slaveholders, had begun to turn toward North America, complementing the desire of the South for annexation. To complicate matters, liberal intellectuals began to promote an alternative to either Spanish or U.S. control. Reflecting the outlook of native whites of more modest means, they fleshed out the idea of Cuban nationhood.

The sugar boom of the late eighteenth and nineteenth centuries had created a new Creole elite based on ownership of land, slaves, and sugar mills.[15] This sugar aristocracy initially looked to Spanish power to protect it from slave revolt but grew nervous as such revolts (though suppressed) erupted in the 1840s. Moreover, the sugar barons grew impatient at Ma-

---

entry for May 10, 1848, that "I am decidedly in favor of purchasing Cuba and making it one of the states of the union." Quoted in Smith, *What Happened*, p. 38.

Southern annexationism is best illustrated by the well-known Ostend Manifesto, which concludes that it would be "base treason against our posterity, should we permit Cuba to be Africanized and become a second St. Domingo, with all its attendant horrors to the white race, and suffer the flames to enter to our own neighboring shores, seriously to endanger or actually to consume the fair fabric of our Union." Smith, *What Happened*, p. 67.

The Whig orientation toward Cuba is discussed in Lloyd Gardner, Walter LaFeber, and Thomas McCormick, *Creation of the American Empire* (Chicago: Rand McNally & Co., 1973), pp. 170–71.

[15] The sugar boom is described in Manuel Moreno Fraginals, *The Sugarmill: The Socioeconomic Complex of Sugar in Cuba* (New York: Monthly Review Press, 1976); Heinrich Friedlaender, *Historia económica de Cuba* (La Habana: Ed. de Ciencias Sociales, 1978), pp. 117–75; Julio Le Riverend, *Economic History of Cuba* (Havana: Book Institute, 1967), ch. 15; Ramiro Guerra y Sánchez, *Sugar and Society in the Caribbean* (New Haven: Yale University Press, 1964), pp. 42–54.

drid's inability and unwillingness to promote the healthy growth of their industry, which required access to African slaves and European and North American markets. Early in the nineteenth century Britain had begun a campaign to end the slave trade. Just as Cuba was in the midst of a sugar boom—an industry relying almost completely on slave labor—Britain pressured Spain (beleaguered by the attempt to control its rebellious American colonies) into outlawing the slave trade to her possessions.[16] Illegal traffic in slaves helped to sustain the Cuban sugar plantations thereafter, but the sugar aristocracy was frightened by the advance of abolitionist propaganda and especially by the possibility of slave rebellion on an island whose black population had rapidly risen to surpass that of the white by the 1820s.[17] Madrid's attempt to accommodate British pressure and still retain the loyalty of both the powerful Creole sugar oligarchy and the Spanish merchant class in Cuba was failing.

As Spanish power waned, elements of the Creole sugar aristrocracy began to look northward, to a state powerful enough to assure the security of the Cuban slave system and to provide the free trade that would sustain its economic health. Such a tie had its dangers, however. Political liberalism might accompany the economic liberalism of North America. As a result, the Cuban sugar aristocracy wavered between Madrid and Washington as the most effective guarantor of its interests. As part of the Union, slavery could be protected from British abolitionism, and unfettered access to the vital North American market would be assured. But the same threat of war that inhibited Washington—war with Britain to prevent U.S. control or with Spain to retain her colony—weakened the conviction of wealthy Cuban annexationists. War over Cuba, whatever its outcome, might destroy the plantations or, worse yet, liberate their servile labor force.[18] In one sense, Cuban slave owners were desperate for a change of political authority that might secure their valuable property. In another sense, however, they were inherently cautious, fearful of anything that might unravel the delicate social web holding slavery in place.

The outcome of the U.S. Civil War altered the context of Creole annexationism. Gone was the hope that ties to North America could protect the slave system in Cuba. United States policy would thereafter seek to absorb only an island free of slavery. Furthermore, slavery was weakened by the independence revolt that broke out on the eastern end of the island in 1868. The rebels eventually granted freedom to slaves who joined the uprising,

---

[16] David Brion Davis, *Slavery and Human Progress* (New York: Oxford University Press, 1984), pp. 235–39, 281–86.

[17] Knight, *Slave Society*, p. 22.

[18] For the worldview of Cuban slaveholders see Gordon K. Lewis, *Main Currents in Caribbean Thought* (Baltimore: Johns Hopkins University Press, 1983), pp. 140–60.

and their economic sabotage destroyed many of the sugar estates in the area. With slavery clearly on the wane, Spain had less to offer the sugar barons. Some of these wealthier Creoles had already begun to respond to the increasing competition from European beet sugar by accepting technical innovations in the milling and refining process so as to increase the amount and purity of their sugar output. These modernist Creoles now saw close ties to North America as a way of gaining access to advanced sugar technology and the rapidly growing U.S. market. However reluctantly, they began to turn from slave to contract labor and in doing so brought themselves into greater conformity with the newly triumphant free-labor doctrine in the United States.[19]

As some Creoles focused on the problems caused by outmoded systems of production and marketing, others identified the political barriers to economic progress. To solve this aspect of the problem, they began to agitate for autonomy under Spanish rule. Appeals were made to Madrid for greater economic and political rights (freer trade, lower taxes, and more political representation). As liberalism and positivism increased their hold on the Creole aristocracy as a whole, others of their class were moving beyond the idea of autonomy and toward independence. Though also fearful of black rebellion, and no more in search of a democratic Cuba than more conservative Creoles, they nevertheless concluded that Spain would not significantly loosen its control over their affairs. This group came to believe that only rebellion would remove her power and place the island under the rule of Creole politicians.

Liberal Creoles as a whole formulated the goal of independence, but the force that initiated the first independence war in 1868 was the smaller group of Creole landowners of eastern Cuba. This region was poorer, less technologically advanced, and distant from the center of Spanish economic power and political authority in Havana. It was also different in its racial composition. Unlike western Cuba, this area had in most places a white majority. Moreover, only a minority of its black population were slaves. Agriculture—which included coffee and cattle as well as sugar—was less dependent on slave labor, making the region less concerned about the growing philosophical assault on slavery and the consequent difficulty (and expense) of obtaining new slaves. Fear of black rebellion, which inhibited Creole initiative in western Cuba where blacks outnumbered whites, was

---

[19] Eugene Genovese, *The World the Slaveholders Made* (New York: Vintage, 1971), pp. 67–71; Rebecca J. Scott, *Slave Emancipation in Cuba* (Princeton, N.J.: Princeton University Press, 1985), pp. 119–20. Free-labor doctrine in the United States is discussed in Eric Foner, *Free Soil, Free Labor, Free Men: The Ideology of the Republican Party before the Civil War* (London: Oxford University Press, 1970), and David Montgomery, *Beyond Equality: Labor and the Radical Republicans, 1862–1872* (Urbana: University of Illinois Press, 1981).

less debilitating in the east. Finally, easterners depended less on the system of trade and credit controlled by Spain and received fewer benefits from it.[20]

The need to fight Spain meant the need to form a large army, and its only sources were the peasant and black masses. Such a mobilization required appeals to abolition and nationalism—ideas to which slaves and small farmers were ready to respond. These ideas frightened the rebellious Creoles as much as they emboldened them. Still, it was the power of these appeals that helped to sustain the rebellion (though mostly confined to the east) for ten years. That protracted guerrilla struggle failed to dislodge Spanish power, and it exposed the class, racial, regional, and political differences within a rebel army that consisted of Creole landowners, peasants, just-emancipated slaves and free blacks and mulattoes. Despite the internal divisions that eventually undermined the cause, however, the Ten Years War, as it was known, did much to establish the independence credentials (as much in romantic as in political terms) of a group of Creoles, along with the social dignity of the white, mulatto, and black underclass. The economic and political impact of the war also assured the demise of slavery—formally decreed by Spain in 1879 and fully terminated in 1886. Despite the defeat of the rebels in 1878, anti-Spanish republicanism and Cuban nationalism slowly came to form the core of political dissent in Cuba. They began to overshadow the autonomism and annexationism of the more cautious Creoles. Furthermore, the goal of independence, while still articulated by an elite, now became the property of large numbers of ordinary Cubans as well.[21]

III

The Ten Years War intruded upon the U.S. belief that Cuba would some day pass easily from Spanish to U.S. control. Just when the antagonism between free soil and slave expansionism was resolved by the Civil War,

[20] Knight, *Slave Society*, pp. 157–60; Scott, *Slave Emancipation*, pp. 45–47. Also see Francisco López Segrera, *Cuba: capitalismo dependiente y subdesarrollo, 1510–1959* (La Habana: Editorial de Ciencias Sociales, 1981), pp. 110–14. The proclamation of independence issued by the rebel landowners denounced the absence of political liberties, the exclusion of (white) Cubans from public office, excessive taxation, and governmental corruption. It called for the gradual emancipation of slaves with indemnification. See Foner, *History*, II, pp. 171–72.

[21] The Ten Years War is discussed in Thomas, *Pursuit*, chs. 20–22; Foner, *History*, II, chs. 14–16, 19, 21, and 22; and Knight, *Slave Society*, ch. 8. The evolving ideology of independence is discussed in Lewis, *Main Currents*, pp. 286–94. Also see Gerald E. Poyo, *With All and For the Good of All: The Emergence of Popular Nationalism in the Cuban Community of the United States, 1848–1898*, (Durham, N.C.: Duke University Press, 1989). References in these notes are to the manuscript of Poyo's work.

U.S. expectations about the island's future were disoriented by the rise of Cuban nationalism. At first, however, the complexity of North American ideology hid the difficulty. The Ten Years War was a war for independence and hence qualified as a just struggle in the minds of most North Americans. It easily took its place as part of the inevitable recession of European monarchy from the New World. Moreover, the Cuban rebels made the abolition of slavery part of their program—though less from conviction than necessity—thus endearing their cause to the Republican administration in Washington. As a result, President Grant, sustained by much of the public and press, favored recognition of the rebels' status as belligerents so as to be able to offer them assistance and assure their victory. The House of Representatives passed several resolutions to that effect.[22]

Some members of Congress, impressed by the analogy between the rebellion in Cuba and the forward march of liberty, wanted to recognize not only the belligerency of the rebels but their provisional government as well. The latter act, however, raised the issue of an independent Cuba, and few were comfortable with that particular outcome to the long-expected elimination of Spanish rule. In any event, the issue of independence rarely broke the surface of debate. While the rise of Cuban nationalism seemed to suggest the anomaly of an independent Cuba, it did not yet do so in a compelling manner. In fact, recognition of the rebels' belligerency—or even of their government—could still appear consistent with annexation because many of the anti-Spanish Creoles continued to seek it. While the idea was less popular among the fighting forces, many of the representatives of the republic-in-arms in the United States favored the substitution of United States for Spanish sovereignty.[23]

Cuban nationalism was not the only cloud on the horizon when North Americans once again surveyed the means by which the island might be absorbed. The racial perspective of white North Americans, while it invigorated expansion in some ways, inhibited it in others. From the viewpoint of Anglo-Saxon racism, the Ten Years War was a mixed signal. It foretold that a degenerate Spanish control was in decline, but it also suggested a Cuban attempt at self-rule that was doomed to failure. Initially the anti-tyrannical and abolitionist aspect of the struggle marked it as a healthy development. But as the war dragged on, it degenerated into a costly and bloody stalemate. To weaken the opposition, Spain reluctantly promised political reforms and even passed a law providing for the gradual emancipation of slaves. To muddy the waters further, toward the end of the conflict

---

[22] The diplomacy of the United States with Spain during the Ten Years War is described in Langley, *Cuban Policy*, ch. 3, and Foner, *History*, II, chs. 17, 18, and 20.

[23] Poyo manuscript, ch. 2; Langley, *Cuban Policy*, ch. 3.

Spain briefly had a republican government.[24] As a result, the progressive aspects of the insurrection receded, and it came to illustrate not only Spanish but Cuban inferiority as well.

This changing view of the war paralleled a declining confidence in the capacity of the freedman in the South. The "failure" of Reconstruction exposed a northern racial prejudice that had been obscured by the crusade against slavery.[25] In like manner emancipation in Cuba brought to the surface the long-held North American suspicion that the racially mixed population of the island could not chart its own future. As we have seen, John Adams raised this point early in the century. The logical solution was for North Americans—fit by culture, race, and religion—to absorb Cuba. But this logic was confounded by a reluctance to admit non-white peoples into the Union. This particular conflict within U.S. expansionism had appeared even in the heyday of Manifest Destiny in the 1840s. At the conclusion of the Mexican War, most North Americans favored taking the thinly settled portion of northern Mexico. When aggressive expansionist sectors raised the cry of taking "All Mexico," majority belief about the racial inferiority of the large population of central Mexico operated to limit U.S. territorial acquisition. In a typical comment, the editor of the Louisville *Democrat* praised the treaty that awarded northern Mexico to the United States because it provided "all the territory of value that we can get without taking the people. The people of the settled parts of Mexico are a negative quantity."[26]

The project of absorbing Cuba had encountered resistance of a similar sort. In addition to their suspicions that Cuba would be a field for the expansion of slavery, northern Whigs and Free Soilers doubted the possibility of absorbing the island's large and racially backward population. Free Soiler James Shepherd Pike opposed the acquisition of an island filled "with black, mixed, degraded, and ignorant, or inferior races." The Whig president, Millard Fillmore, told Congress, "Were this island comparatively destitute of inhabitants, or occupied by a kindred race, I should regard it . . . as a most desirable acquisition."[27]

---

[24] Stanley G. Payne, *A History of Spain and Portugal* (Madison: University of Wisconsin Press, 1973), II, pp. 467–70.

[25] For northern attitudes toward the freed slaves during Reconstruction see Kenneth M. Stampp, *The Era of Reconstruction, 1865–1877* (New York: Vintage, 1965), ch. 7, and Eric Foner, "Reconstruction Revisited," *Reviews in American History* (Dec., 1982), pp. 82–100.

[26] Quoted in Frederick Merk, *Manifest Destiny and Mission* (New York: Vintage, 1963), p. 151. Weinberg, *Manifest Destiny*, discusses the North American preference for "lands without inhabitants," (p. 164). The "All Mexico" movement is examined in Merk, *Mission*, chs. 5–8, and Weinberg, *Manifest Destiny*, ch. 6. The relationship of racial attitudes to expansion is examined in Reginald Horsman, *Race and Manifest Destiny: The Origins of American Racial Anglo-Saxonism* (Cambridge: Harvard University Press, 1981).

[27] Horsman, *Racial Anglo-Saxonism*, pp. 282–83.

Although inhibited by racial isolationism and abolitionism, the expansionists of the 1840s and 1850s had been sustained by a general optimism concerning the fecundity and aggressiveness of the Anglo-Saxon race. Secretary of State Buchanan sought to solve the problem of absorbing both the island and its people by assuming that Cuba could "be Americanized—as Louisiana had been."[28] The same racial degeneracy that made Hispanic, Indian, and black peoples (and their intermixtures) unsuitable for admission to the Union also made them too weak to resist displacement (physically or genetically) by North Americans. This prophecy seemed to be fulfilled as the Indians of North America receded and diminished in the path of white pioneers.[29] The Manifest Destiny of the era was generally sustained by racial optimism. The Anglo-Saxon race was destined not only to expand but to replace the weaker peoples surrounding it.

By the 1870s, when the Ten Years War brought the question of absorbing Cuba back into the political arena, the confident expansionism of the 1840s and 1850s was less in evidence. Now, more than before, the issue of race cut across the issue of expansion. North American opinion had been formed by decades of negative descriptions of each segment of the Cuban population. The Spanish rulers were papist, monarchist, and cruel. The Creoles had been annexationist allies of the southern slavocracy and in rebellion were unable to form a viable republican government or to defeat a decadent Spain. Black Cubans, according to the prevailing view of their race, were fit only for menial labor.[30] Incapable of overseeing its own affairs, this motley population also seemed unsuited to enter the North American republic.

This racial perspective informed an important part of the context in which the Grant administration pondered its response to the war. Within the Cabinet the debate seesawed between the president, whose hostility to Spain and desire to spread U.S. influence led him to favor recognition of the rebels' belligerency, and Secretary of State Hamilton Fish, whose belief that Spanish rule provided greater stability than would be found under a rebel government led him to oppose such an act.[31] Fish had visited Cuba in

[28] Ibid.

[29] The physical removal of the Indians is discussed in Weinberg, *Manifest Destiny*, ch. 3, and in Philip Borden, "Found Cumbering the Soil: Manifest Destiny and the Indian in the Nineteenth Century," in Gary B. Nash and Richard Weiss, *The Great Fear: Race in the Mind of America* (New York: Holt, Rinehart & Winston, 1970), pp. 71–97.

[30] Alice R. Wexler, "Sex, Race and Character in Nineteenth Century American Accounts of Cuba," *Caribbean Studies* 18: 3 and 4 (Oct. 1978/Jan. 1979), pp. 115–30. For the North American view of black people see Larry Kincaid, "Two Steps Forward, One Step Back" in Nash and Weiss, *The Great Fear*, pp. 45–70.

[31] Fish had other reasons for opposing recognition, including the avoidance of war with Spain and the possible impact of recognition on the U.S. monetary claims against Britain (the "Alabama" claims) for its unneutral actions during the Civil War. See Allen Nevins, *Hamil-*

1855 and, like many a North American traveler, had been, as he put it, "charmed with the climate, the scenery and the natural production of the island." He concluded, however, that "with its present population, the island of Cuba will be anything else than a desirable acquisition to the United States."[32] Allan Nevins, Fish's principal biographer, describes him as having "placed a low estimate upon the intellectual and moral qualities of much of the population; he doubted the aptitude of this conglomerate of Indian, [sic] Negro and Spanish blood for self-government and thought . . . that evolution under Spanish tutelage might be better than revolution."[33] It is not surprising, then, that Fish found the rebels unworthy of recognition, though he usually couched his arguments against doing so on the ground that they held no territory or seat of government. Despite this low opinion of Cubans, Fish embraced the thesis of absorption. His solution, as he informed the Cabinet, was to wait until the major powers—who might stand in the way of annexation—came "to regard the Spanish rule as an international nuisance, which must be abated, when they would all be glad that we should interpose and regulate the control of the island."[34]

To head off what he considered Grant's ill-advised proposal to recognize belligerency, Fish returned to an earlier solution—purchase. In formulating his proposal, he was influenced by the popularity of the rebels during the first years of the war. With the Cubans in the midst of a bloody struggle for liberty, buying the island outright was unseemly. Fish came up with a proposal whereby Cuba would buy its independence from Spain with bonds guaranteed by the United States that would use Cuban customs duties as security. The secretary of state also included a provision that "discriminating duties, prejudicial to American productions [are] to be abolished. All other duties (export and import) to remain unchanged unless with the consent of the United States."[35] The Spanish government considered this proposal but in the end, as with all previous offers, could not bring itself to accept it. Nonetheless, it stands as a milestone on the way to bringing the old assumption of U.S. dominance up to date, modernizing an annexation once tainted by southern filibusters and now inhibited by North American racial isolationism and the growth of Cuban nationalism. Unlike Grant's indiscriminate expansionism (illustrated by his clumsy attempt to annex Santo Domingo), Fish was moving toward a U.S. relationship with Cuba similar to the one actually worked out between 1898 and 1902.

---

ton Fish: The Inner History of the Grant Administration (New York: Dodd, Mead & Co., 1936), pp. 180–82, 226–27.

[32] William S. McFeely, *Grant: A Biography* (New York: W. W. Norton, 1981), pp. 197–98.

[33] Nevins, *Fish*, p. 180.

[34] Foner, *History*, II, p. 202.

[35] Nevins, *Fish*, p. 193, quoting from the proposal.

Growing U.S. influence in the internal Cuban economy in the last quarter of the century—complementing its long-standing predominance in Cuba's foreign trade—was establishing the basis for the kind of solution envisioned by Fish.[36] The large North American economic presence foreshadowed a form of U.S. dominance in Cuba that could circumvent the thorny issues of annexation, independence, and racial assimilation. Still, many difficulties remained, among them the atavistic state of U.S. public opinion.

If Fish worried about finding a way of ending Spanish rule that avoided anarchy on the island, the North American press concerned itself with Spanish atrocities and insults to U.S. citizens. On the popular level, patience for waiting for the ripe fruit of Cuba to fall from the tree seemed to be wearing thin. Like Cuban nationalism, the growing North American hostility to Spanish rule and the consequent desire to liberate Cubans from colonial domination were beginning to jostle the comfortable notion that the island would simply gravitate to the U.S. orbit. Unmindful of the contradictions, the same newspaper and magazine articles that called for U.S. intervention retained the old assumption that Cuba was unready for self-government. The remedy afforded was as often to "take" Cuba as to free her. Somehow North Americans managed to reconcile sympathy for the Cubans' aspiration to be free of Spanish rule with an unwillingness to concede that they were worthy of independence.

As North Americans struggled to fit a changing Cuba into the future that they had long prescribed for it, their own society was changing as well. The nature of U.S. expansionism was undergoing a broad shift. The motives and means of expansion were moving away from possession to control. The old continentalism, characterized by white settlers and territorial government, was giving way to a strategic-diplomatic-economic expansion that raised difficult questions about the relationship of the U.S. government to subject peoples.[37] As continental land-grabbing, race-exterminating, and union-building gave way to the expansionism of admirals, investors, and reformers, the simple idea of absorbing Cuba had to be brought up to date.

---

[36] The growing U.S. influence over the Cuban economy is discussed in Leland Jenks, *Our Cuban Colony: A Study in Sugar* (New York: Vanguard Press, 1928), ch. 3; López Segrera, *Subdesarrollo*, ch. 5; Thomas, *Pursuit*, chs. 23 and 24; Foner, *History*, II, ch. 23.

[37] The changing nature of U.S. expansionism is discussed in Richard Van Alstyne, *The Rising American Empire* (Chicago: Quadrangle, 1963); Robert L. Beisner, *From the Old Diplomacy to the New, 1865–1900* (New York: Crowell, 1975); Charles S. Campbell, *The Transformation of American Foreign Relations, 1865–1900* (New York: Harper & Row, 1976); Robert H. Wiebe, *The Search for Order, 1877–1920* (New York: Hill & Wang, 1967), ch. 9.

CHAPTER 2

THE CRUSADE AGAINST
AUTOCRACY: THE ENDING
OF SPANISH RULE

I

As LONG as Cuba had seemed to be gravitating inexorably into the North American orbit, it was for the most part assumed that the proper form of influence over the island would evolve naturally. However, once inevitability was brought into question by an increasing Cuban desire for independence on the one hand and growing U.S. concern about the undesirable consequences of annexation on the other, the question took on a much more perplexing form. Indeed, by the time the imminent demise of Spanish power forced the question, the complex interplay of interests and ideology in North America had created strong pressures both for the liberation *and* domination of Cuba. When the time came, there was no natural or ideologically comfortable answer, neither for Cuba nor for the United States.

UNNOTICED BY many North Americans, the structure of Cuban society was changing in the latter half of the nineteenth century. The sugar industry, dominant since its expansion at the turn of the century, went through another transformation. Production was revolutionized as advanced technology was applied to the milling process, increasing the amount and purity of the sugar squeezed from the cane. At the same time, expansion of the railroad system and port facilities modernized the means of bringing the product to market. These advances were necessary to keep Cuban cane sugar abreast of vigorous new competition producing both cane and beet sugar in the United States, Hawaii, and Europe. The effect of modernization was to concentrate the island's industry. An agricultural sector once characterized by many small holders raising a variety of products—sugar, tobacco, coffee, cattle, hogs—came to be dominated by a few large-scale producers. These were owners of *ingenios*, large steam-driven mill complexes that were in fact industrial facilities, tended by a large skilled and semi-skilled work force and consuming vast quantities of cane for processing into raw sugar and sugar by-products. The construction and overhead costs of the new *ingenios* were high, and only a few of the older class of sugar mill owners could make the necessary investment. Most of the remaining planters were reduced to the status of *colonos*, growers who owned cane land but not mills and who contracted to sell cane to the nearby *ingenio*. As concentration increased in the last third of the century, the number of mills declined steadily while the percentage of sugar output produced by the largest ones increased rapidly.[1] For the first time, a small number of Creole mill owners stood almost as high as the powerful Spanish businessmen and officials who ran the colony. By the same token, the gap between these very wealthy Cubans and the other natives—Creole, black, mulatto—was greater than it had ever been. The social distance between Creole and (Spanish-born) *peninsular* was now complemented by another between Cubans themselves. United States officials, instinctively drawn to the "whiter," well-to-do mill owners as the most talented and competent of Cubans, took little heed of the class tensions that might some day raise a challenge to rule by a Creole elite.

As the new elite of mill owners expanded their control of cane fields through purchase or contract with *colonos*, and as they integrated wage labor and advanced technology into their operations, they, too, began to suffer from a shortage of capital. The constant effort to increase output and purity to meet the growing world competition (and the lower market price it produced) forced the elite to turn increasingly to Spanish and particularly North American capital. When one of the periodic market slumps placed them on the verge of bankruptcy, many called upon the North American commercial houses that had traditionally financed the sale of their sugar in that market. In this manner, U.S. companies came to own a growing percentage of the stock in the largest mills. Long dependent on the U.S. market, the sugar elite now depended on U.S. capital as well. Indeed, many ceased to own their mills, becoming partners or administrators of U.S.-controlled companies. Some closed the circle by becoming U.S. citizens. Still too fearful to break with the Spanish rule that secured their property

[1] José R. Alvarez Díaz et al., *A Study on Cuba* (Coral Gables, Fla.: University of Miami Press, 1965), pp. 81–96; Lowry Nelson, *Rural Cuba* (Minneapolis: University of Minnesota Press, 1950), pp. 92–94; Friedlaender, *Historia económica*, II, pp. 534–53; Thomas, *Pursuit*, pp. 123–24.

rights, they nevertheless prepared themselves for the day when the viability of the old system might reach its end.[2] When that time came, however, the Creole elite would pass quickly from Spanish to North American hegemony. Unlike the landholding class of other Latin American states, they would never take the helm of their society.

The changing Cuban economy, now more than ever at odds with Spanish mercantilism, accompanied a secular economic decline that deepened the sense of Cuban nationhood and gave it new content. The expansion of cane lands to feed the huge *ingenios* had squeezed the small landholdings of the peasantry and had created a rural proletariat out of former slaves and farmers.[3] Caught between a high U.S. tariff and controls by Spain, the cigar industry came to the point of collapse during this period. Large numbers of cigar workers followed their almost equally desperate employers as they set up shop inside the North American tariff wall in Key West and later in Tampa.[4] As the island's working class increased and faced growing uncertainty of employment in the depressed island economy, it became influenced by the anarchism that many immigrant Spanish workers brought with them. This was a time of bitter strikes by Cuban cigar workers. By the 1890s, the ranks of the alienated underclass from which a rebel army might be drawn had grown quite large. Land hungry peasants and just plain hungry cane cutters, urban workers facing both a depressed economy and a colonial regime that barely tolerated workers' organizations, were ready not simply for a change of authority but for a new social order. Their sense of being Cuban was growing at the same time as their grievances against both the Spanish and Cuban elite.[5]

Despite the increasing class tensions, the island's Creoles, including portions of the downwardly mobile planter class, were also becoming more influenced by *Cubanidad*. Perched upon a mountain of debt or reduced to the status of *colonos*, the planters were more desperate for relief than ever. After the defeat of the 1868–1878 rebellion, most had returned to the politics of reform. They established the Liberal Party and demanded represen-

[2] Myra Wilkins, *The Emergence of Multinational Enterprise* (Cambridge: Harvard University Press, 1970), p. 151; Jenks, *Colony*, pp. 29–35; Louis A. Pérez, Jr., "Toward Dependency and Revolution: The Political Economy of Cuba between Wars, 1878–1895," *Latin American Research Review* 18:1 (1983), pp. 132–34.

[3] Pérez, "Vagrants, Beggars and Bandits: Social Origins of Cuban Separatism, 1878–1895," *American Historical Review* 90:5 (Dec. 1985), pp. 1100–2.

[4] Alvarez Díaz et al., *Study*, pp. 108–10; Louis A. Pérez, *Cuba Between Empires, 1878–1902*, (Pittsburgh: University of Pittsburgh Press, 1983), p. 95. The movement of portions of the Cuban cigar industry to Florida had begun in the 1860s. See Fernando Ortiz, *Cuban Counterpoint: Sugar and Tobacco*, (New York: Vintage, 1970), pp. 79–80. The politics of these communities of Cuban cigar makers in Florida is discussed in the Poyo ms., ch. 6.

[5] Pérez, "Vagrants, Beggars and Bandits," pp. 1118–20.

tation in the Spanish parliament, the Cortes. But blocked yet again by Madrid's need to tax and control Cuba so as to ease the burdens of her own economic decline and by the refusal of the *peninsulares* to see their privileges sacrificed on the altar of autonomy, some Creoles began to despair of the possibility of reform. Of those who moved away from the colonial tie, however, different elements drifted toward separate positions. Some Creoles returned to their earlier annexationism; others foresaw the island tied to the United States in a condition of autonomy similar to the one Spain would not grant. Much moreso than in 1868, Creole elements accepted (however nervously) armed rebellion as the only means of clearing the way for a northern orientation. A minority even embraced war with Spain as the path to full sovereignty, the lofty status justified by decades of costly struggle against foreign domination. Even among those Creoles dedicated to independence, however, some saw it as a means rather than an end.[6] While peasants and workers (white, mulatto, black) became more willing to embrace rebellion as a means of freeing up the social hierarchy, certain of the Creoles with property and position cast about for a form of political and economic liberation from colonialism that would not threaten their status. Even these liberal Creoles, following the racial doctrines accepted among educated whites and the elitist heritage from Spain, presumed the non-Hispanic elements of their society to be unfit for leadership (and perhaps even citizenship) and favored a republic run by a native oligarchy. A few, however, drawn in the main from professionals and intellectuals, harbored a more democratic vision of *Cuba Libre*.

II

By the 1890s, the differing goals among Creoles, between Creoles and the masses and among the masses themselves, had risen to a point where they threatened to undermine the anti-Spanish cause or even to turn anti-colonial conflict into civil war. The fact that the disparate native groups cooperated during the independence revolt of 1895–1898 owes much to the work of José Martí, the most revered figure in Cuban history. Martí, acting both as an intellectual and a political actor, fashioned a vision of a free Cuba that broke through class and racial barriers. He endowed the cause of independence with a program of social justice. In the republic to be won, all Cubans would share not simply the franchise but dignity and economic welfare. Love of country was tied to love of one's neighbors in a way that bound together cultural nationalism and moral egalitarianism.[7]

[6] Pérez, *Cuba Between Empires*, chs. 1 and 2.

[7] Martí's ideas are described in John M. Kirk, *José Martí: Mentor of the Cuban Nation* (Tampa: University Presses of Florida, 1983), esp. chs. 4–6.

Beginning in the early 1880s, working amidst the large exile population in the United States, Martí confronted the divisions within the nationalist community. In contrast to those who defined independence solely in political terms, Martí appealed to the Cuban underclass to see the future republic as one in which its voice would be heard. In place of the filibustering bands and the charismatic rebel chieftains characteristic of the earlier period, Martí and others helped to base the new rebellion upon a constituency-based political party, the Partido Revolucionario Cubano (PRC). This organization took root particularly in exile working-class communities. Unlike earlier Cuban liberation "juntas" composed of well-to-do, educated Creoles (often self-appointed), workers and others of humble origin rose to leadership in the PRC. Worker support became crucial, as the financial contributions to the cause, especially of the Florida-based cigar makers, became an important source of party funds.[8]

Martí's success in integrating workers into the nationalist cause was not easy and took a decade to accomplish. Significant numbers of Cuban workers had been attracted to Spanish anarchism and syndicalism and were suspicious of any anti-colonial program that made no mention of the relationship of capital to labor in a free Cuba. These workers—especially those in the cigar industry, many of whose employers were Cuban—were tempted to place class before national struggle. Martí's inclusive nationalism, which pointed the way beyond class conflict in a society dedicated to fortifying social bonds that transcended material conditions, enabled workers attracted to a materialist utopia to combine it with a nationalist one.[9]

While bridging the gap between nation and class, Martí and his allies worked also to overcome the barriers between black and white Cubans. The emancipation of slaves in the 1880s had left them in a state quite distant from true freedom. After navigating a long period in which they "compensated" their former owners with their labor, they were thrust, as free workers, into a severely depressed economy. In the main, they continued to work on the sugar plantations, where their labor was hardly needed except for a brief three- or four-month harvesting and milling orgy (the *zafra*) during which the ripened cane had to be cut and ground as rapidly as possible. Beyond that, the society seemed to have little use for them. However, though impoverished as always, they were no longer subject to the tight control that had characterized slavery. Among their new freedoms was the freedom to join in rebellion.[10]

---

[8] Foner, *History*, II, ch. 25; Pérez, *Cuba Between Empires*, pp. 16–17; Thomas, *Pursuit*, pp. 301–2; Poyo ms., pp. 160–63, 248–54, 261–65, 283–87.

[9] Gerald E. Poyo, "The Anarchist Challenge to the Cuban Independence Movement, 1885–1890," *Cuban Studies* 15:1 (Winter 1985), pp. 29–42.

[10] Scott, *Slave Emancipation*, pp. 285–88.

Martí addressed himself to Afro-Cubans as he did to workers. He understood the racism that added a heavy social burden to their existing economic plight. In 1890 he helped to found a school for black Cubans in New York. There he lectured weekly, pointing out that the Negro had to be treated "according to his qualities as a man." He helped instill in his pupils a pride in being Cuban and in doing so helped them to assert their dignity as black people. With the nation as the ideal, blacks clearly stood as the equal of other Cubans. Though Spain continually raised the specter of race war (as she had once raised that of slave rebellion) to divide her enemies, the PRC was able to attract Afro-Cubans, as did the 1895 rebellion itself. Indeed, in that conflict a majority of the rebel soldiers were black, as were almost 40 percent of senior commissioned officers.[11]

It is important to note that, despite its mass base, the PRC did not have a revolutionary program. As Martí expanded the idea of nationhood to embrace the grievances of poor Cubans, he was careful not to alienate those well-to-do Creoles who committed themselves to the armed struggle for independence. Martí's moralistic, pan-class view of nationhood embraced both the Cuban masses and patriotic members of the elite as well. By dignifying the anti-colonial struggle in humanist terms, Martí helped to channel underclass anger onto a higher plane where it might blend with elite conceptions of society derived from the Enlightenment. On a practical level, planters and professionals could contribute their money and skills to a movement that, while it armed the masses, served, in some measure, as insurance against social revolution. Martí's role—one that has made him the hero of both radical and conservative chroniclers of Cuban history—was to inject social issues (some of them quite radical in their day) into the idea of independence while containing their explosive force within the spacious vision of a "pure" republic.

Though the ideas that underlay the new rebellion were not revolutionary, they did represent a major shift in the nature of Cuban nationalism. As the mass base of the movement grew, it challenged the elitism and annexationism of those Creoles who had chosen to break with Spain. The idea of a popular republic also contradicted assumptions held by many North Americans concerning the capabilities of Cubans. Moreover, the new elements of the nationalist constituency were for the most part anti-annexationist. Martí had long opposed annexation, not simply as a poor alternative to independence but as a denial of all he wished the movement to stand for. He lived in New York City from 1881 to 1895 and left in his voluminous writings his astute critiques of U.S. politics and culture. At first he was

[11] Philip S. Foner, ed., *Our America by José Martí* (New York: Monthly Review Press, 1978), pp. 17–18; Pérez, *Cuba Between Empires*, p. 106; Thomas, *Pursuit*, pp. 300 and 306.

ambivalent about North American society, attracted to its republicanism and its freedoms but repelled by the materialism of the Gilded Age and the concentration of wealth and power. By the late 1880s, Martí had become an uncompromising anti-expansionist. He concluded in 1889 that "the republic was becoming plutocratic and imperialistic." To those who argued that U.S. power was necessary to remove that of Spain he replied: "And once the United States is in Cuba, who will drive it out?"[12]

III

In the United States, much of this broad change in Cuban society and ideology went undetected. The question posed by most North Americans, even as late as 1895, was the unhurried one of how to get a decadent Spain to run Cuba properly or, if she failed to do so, how to remove her dead hand. The growing demand for independence on the island did not discomfit North Americans because only the more conservative formulations of it were noted in the media and the government. Many presumed that even an independent Cuba would be drawn into the North American orbit. In fact, the rising anti-colonialism of Cubans fit so well with assumptions concerning the inevitable displacement of Spanish by North American influence that nothing seemed amiss. Soon to think of themselves as embarked on a mission to "free" Cuba, most North Americans would have been surprised to discover that their conception of the island's future was decidedly less progressive than that of most Cuban nationalists.

By the late nineteenth century, however, absorbing Cuba was not turning out to be natural at all. It was becoming complicated not only by Cuban nationalism and North American isolationist racism but by a major shift in U.S. society as well. The issue of what to do about Cuba resurfaced just as the long-gathering impact of industrialization and centralization on an agrarian and local order was cresting in the form of acute class tensions. In this context, taking Cuba came not as an opportunity to conservative leaders in the Democratic and Republican parties but as a potentially dangerous complication. Because of the social turmoil, there arose in the mid-1890s somewhat distinct mass and elite solutions to the Cuban "problem." In its plight, the underclass reached out to embrace the Cuban rebels, while the new industrial elite was concerned to control events in Cuba. Though the principal concerns of the People's or Populist Party were domestic and economic—currency, railroads, land, election reform—its national platform in 1896 included a special section in which the party announced to the

---

[12] Philip S. Foner, ed., *Inside the Monster: Writings on the United States and American Imperialism by José Martí* (New York: Monthly Review Press, 1975), p. 45; Foner, *Our America*, p. 26.

Cuban people its "deepest sympathy for their heroic struggle for political freedom and independence" and called on the U.S. government to "recognize that Cuba is, and of right ought to be, a free and independent state."[13] By comparison, the *Journal of Commerce*, representing business interests in the Northeast, declared in May 1897:

> The infant States, States suffering from aggravated attacks of Populism and cheap money, and statesmen given over to crazes of various sorts, the faith healers of politics, the financiers who desire to force bankruptcy on the country as a means of breaking down the gold standard . . . are all boiling over with sympathy with the Cuban insurgents and are doing their utmost to goad this country and Spain to a war.[14]

The debate over Cuba was complicated not only by differing class orientations but also because it took place at a time when the old continentalist and Manifest Destiny justifications for expansion were being reworked to make them serviceable to the growing North American need for customers rather than land. The Monroe Doctrine was being transformed by the growing power of the United States from a way of preventing European interference in the New World to a warrant for spreading North American influence within it. When Latin America was sprouting "sister republics" early in the century, the great republic in the north had preferred to see itself as protector of this flowering of freedom. By the end of the century, however, the sister republics were viewed as unstable, uncivilized, debtor states whose mixed and dark races explained their failure to maintain republican decorum. The Anglo-Saxon racism that once sustained the removal of people who stood in the way of the "empire of liberty" was now elevated to a scientific doctrine that consigned whole cultures to dependent existence.[15] The problem now for North America was how to protect inferior peoples from external domination without accepting their equality or appearing to dominate them herself.

The matter would have been simplified if the Cuban rebels of 1895 had been seen as a black rabble in the fashion of the Haitian revolutionaries of the early nineteenth century. However, hostility toward Spain and foreign domination caused the Cuban rebels to be pictured in North American jour-

---

[13] Donald Johnson and Kirk Porter, comps., *National Party Platforms, 1840–1972* (Urbana: University of Illinois Press, 1975), p. 106.

[14] Joseph E. Wisan, *The Cuban Crisis as Reflected in the New York Press, 1895–1898* (New York: Octagon Press, 1977), p. 301.

[15] Few studies examine this transition. See Weinberg, *Manifest Destiny*; Merk, *Manifest Destiny and Mission*; Van Alstyne, *The Rising American Empire*; and Horsman, *Race and Manifest Destiny*.

nals as white warriors, neatly ranked behind the banner of liberty.[16] As armed republicans challenging colonial rule, mass opinion in the United States took a fraternal rather than a paternal attitude toward them. North American imperialists tried to get around this positive image of the rebels by focusing not on the rebellion or its aims but on the territory itself. The island—long cherished, as we have seen, as a "natural appendage to the North American continent," as John Quincy Adams had put it, or as a dangerous foreign-controlled bastion threatening her coasts[17]—had been transformed by the imperial thought of the late nineteenth century into a valuable naval outpost from which the United States could secure the stability of the Caribbean and control the approaches to the interoceanic canal that was now considered necessary. By simultaneously stimulating the North American desire for liberty, markets, and empire, the Cuban rebellion forced the tensions among these goals to the surface.

Fashioning a new ideology of expansion took several decades to accomplish and was never without its critics. By the second decade of the twentieth century, however, the contours of the new expansionism were clear. By that time, the angry emotions of the era of continental expansion (land-grabbing, race-exterminating) had been separated from the loftier aim of expanding the realm of republican citizenship and liberty. The base motives and their accompanying acquisitiveness, once the propelling force of the classic agents of civilization (the pioneer, the family farmer), now sustained the extension of North American corporate enterprise. Dollars and U.S. Marine platoons spread this component of the North American system, first in its entrepreneurial and commodity form and eventually in its reformist and managerial aspect.[18] By offering an opportunity to attach the lofty aim of Cuban independence to market expansion and empire, the war with Spain in 1898 helped ease the transition.

The new expression of U.S. expansion grew out of the changes that had taken place in North American society since the Civil War. The industrial sector of the economy had grown rapidly; it had become dependent on a national market containing large oligopolies and suffered from periodic de-

---

[16] Gerald F. Linderman, *The Mirror of War: American Society and the Spanish-American War* (Ann Arbor: University of Michigan Press, 1974), pp. 128–33.

[17] Smith, *What Happened*, p. 27. Daniel Webster declared in 1826 that "Cuba . . . is placed in the mouth of the Mississippi. Its occupation by a strong maritime power would be felt, in the first moment of hostility, as far up the Mississippi and the Missouri, as our population extends." Smith, p. 35.

[18] This subject is discussed in Jules R. Benjamin, "The Framework of United States Relations with Latin America in the Twentieth Century," *Diplomatic History* 11:2 (Spring 1987), pp. 91–112.

pression.[19] This shift in structure caused reactions in each social class. The gentry and the old middle class who had been bypassed by this change were alienated by the rampant materialism of the new industrialists and feared that this new elite would corrupt politics and drive the masses into rebellion against law and order. Indeed, the increasingly bitter strikes that punctuated the 1880s and 1890s seemed to many a sign that hopelessness and radical ideologies were infecting the working class. This class was on the margins radical but was subtly reactionary as well in that workers' hostility to employers was tinged with resentment over the loss of their former autonomy as husbandmen, tradesmen, or mechanics.[20] Farmers reacted to the more impersonal, regional economic forces as well. Many of them fashioned a view that those in the large urban centers who commanded the system of credit and transportation were creating a society in which ties to the land would be broken and earnings from it spirited away to banking and railroad metropolises.[21]

These tensions seemed to peak in the 1893–1896 depression, the most severe of the century. Farmers organized formidable political power beneath the banner of silver currency and the deeper commitment to agrarian community. By the election of 1896, they had formed their own party (the People's Party) and momentarily turned the Democratic Party in their direction.[22] Workers also organized by craft, by industry, and with ideologies of class interest and even class struggle. Bitter strikes in coal, railroads, iron and steel often led to clashes between workers and police or federal troops.[23] The gentry and the old middle class, fearful of both the new industrial oligarchy and working-class radicalism and egalitarianism, called for constitutional order and political reform. The new industrialists and the politicians whom they bought (literally) or influenced through economic power in constituencies cast about for a way to hold together the new national financial and economic order by which they prospered.

[19] This development is examined in Samuel P. Hays, *Response to Industrialism, 1885–1914* (Chicago: University of Chicago Press, 1957); Glenn Porter, *The Rise of Big Business, 1860–1910* (Arlington Heights, Ill.: Harlan Davidson, 1973); Wiebe, *Search for Order*.

[20] The reaction of workers to rapid industrialization is examined in Herbert Gutman, *Work, Culture and Society in Industrializing America* (New York: Vintage, 1977). The reaction of established classes is described in Richard Hofstadter, *The Age of Reform* (New York: Vintage, 1955), pp. 135–43. Wiebe, *Search for Order*, chs. 1–4, examines the tensions of the period.

[21] Lawrence Goodwyn, *The Populist Moment: A Short History of the Agrarian Revolt in America* (New York: Oxford University Press, 1978) paints the farmer's perspective.

[22] Goodwyn, *Populist Moment*, ch. 8; Hofstadter, *Age of Reform*, chs. 1–3.

[23] Melvyn Dubofsky, *Industrialization and the American Worker, 1865–1920* (Arlington Heights, Ill.: AHM Pub. Co., 1975), focuses on workers' organizing efforts during this period.

Each class cast the problems of social change in foreign as well as domestic terms. The gentry and old middle class hoped for a realm of international law and peaceful commerce to provide a calm environment within which social tensions might be eased. Workers focused on the shoreline with its tariffs that seemed to protect their jobs and its immigration laws that seemed to endanger them (but also united families). When questions of freedom and tyranny arose in other lands, workers often directed their own growing hostility to domination against the policies of the imperial powers. Farmers held even stronger views about the tariff (for industrial goods) and immigration (especially of foreign capital). Like workers, their view of world affairs was colored in part by their declining welfare at home. But they faced the world not only as an oppressed class but as agricultural businessmen, and in this regard they were as fervent promoters of foreign markets as any industrialist facing similar "overproduction."[24]

However, while industrialists saw market expansion in terms of integrating themselves into the existing system fashioned by the great powers, farmers, reflecting hostility to their own oppressors, wished to challenge the tariff and colonial structure of those powers. This perspective often made them partisans of a morally justified expansion that still had roots in the era of Manifest Destiny. The new business class, for its part, was becoming committed to a program of market expansion but preferred to buy rather than fight its way into the world market. Since the tendency for democratic crusading came from their domestic opponents, businessmen were nervous about international tensions. Moreover, as the owning class in an era when armed combat still rested more upon mass armies than mechanized weaponry, there seemed to be little profit and great potential loss in taking the country into war.[25]

The problems caused by the social tensions of the 1890s were so deep that they were diagnosed in cultural as well as economic terms. Intellectuals, religious leaders, and influential professionals raised fears that society had become decadent, effeminate, plutocratic, claustrophobic, or racially and ethnically polluted. Alarms were struck announcing that the landed frontier was closing, that the strength of the race (Anglo-Saxon) and its religion (Protestant) were being undermined, that powerful foreign states were fencing in America, that unassimilable peoples were pouring into her cities, that barbarian races were threatening the extension of her civilization, that her leaders had become corrupt, aimless, or soft.[26]

[24] 24. On the farmer as businessman see William A. Williams, *The Roots of the Modern American Empire* (New York: Random House, 1969).

[25] On the attitude of businessmen toward international conflict see Julius W. Pratt, *Expansionists of 1898* (New York: Quadrangle, 1964), ch. 7.

[26] The cultural crisis of the 1890s is discussed in David Healy, *US Expansionism: The*

If concern with the imperfections of her social order was typically North American, so was her assertive response. Cultural malaise was to be overcome by personal manliness, religious decline by evangelism, the challenge of powerful states and backward peoples by "democratic" expansion, and a "defensive" navy. Social Darwinism required the United States to compete with other states and peoples or be left behind. The concept of the "white man's burden" gave what seemed an ethical imperative to the domination of non-white cultures.[27] The most confident response came from imperialists, who called for a powerful navy and for the strategic bases that would enable it to protect the sea-lanes for U.S. commerce and to project national power. They desired to control foreign lands and peoples to assure that the United States would take her rightful place among the great industrial powers.

Assertiveness raised problems of its own. The creation of colonies and protectorates clashed with the still potent self-image of the North American republic as the enemy of colonial empires. In the canon of the old Manifest Destiny, while one could do violence to (uncivilized) people, rule over an alien population was both immoral and destructive of the health of the republic. Moreover, as the new imperialism of the end of the century was by and large an elitist doctrine, mass sentiment preferred liberation of subject peoples and the destruction rather than replacement of tyrants. A conservative version of the popular hostility to empire was expounded by an articulate segment of the old elite, which turned to anti-imperialism as a defense of the Constitution, the purity of the republic and the race, and the avoidance of costly, emotionally wrenching military conflict.[28] This latter concern did not engage the masses, who were willing to challenge colonial powers and were often even less cautious than the imperialists, who generally confined their stronger threats to declining imperial states.

As domestic tensions increased in the wake of the panic of 1893 and began to take on a zero-sum quality, solutions that lay outside the system, however controversial, became attractive. A society that had always been expanding—in wealth, population, and territory—quite naturally looked beyond its present bounds for solutions to the new domestic problems.

Imperialist Urge of the 1890's (Madison: University of Wisconsin Press, 1970), esp. chs. 5 and 7; Jackson Lears, *No Place of Grace: Antimodernism and the Transformation of American Culture, 1880–1920* (New York: Pantheon, 1981), ch. 3; Walter LaFeber, *The New Empire: An Interpretation of American Expansion, 1860–1898* (Ithaca, N.Y.: Cornell University Press, 1964), ch. 2.

[27] Healy, *US Expansionism*, ch. 1.

[28] Robert L. Beisner, *Twelve Against Empire: The Anti-Imperialists, 1898–1900* (Chicago: University of Chicago Press, 1968 and 1985); E. Berkeley Tomkins, *Anti-Imperialism in the United States: The Great Debate, 1890–1920* (Philadelphia: University of Pennsylvania Press, 1970), chs. 1–7.

Growth in the size of the republic, in its foreign commerce, and in its influence upon surrounding territories had been hallmarks of North American history. Many of the contemporary economic and cultural critiques, even opposing ones, envisioned expansion as a solution to the transition from agrarian to industrial America. To the extent that consensus was achieved, it rested on market expansion (for goods, capital, and eventually services) with the attendant widening of U.S. political, religious, and cultural influence.[29] This consensus did not extend to the *means* of market expansion, however. Was it to be achieved by market forces or by government action; by cooperation, competition, or even in conflict with other trading nations; by means of international law, tariff agreements, political pressure, or even colonial empire?

Because of the peculiar mix of capitalist and republican values in North American ideology, the most compelling idea of market expansion was one that envisioned the spread of both U.S. goods and individual freedoms. However, given the classic imperial designs of some North Americans, the widely held racist notions of the day, and the need to protect the lives, goods, and property of businessmen, it was easier to proclaim an anti-empire of liberty than to create one. Whenever in practice it became apparent that the new expansionism failed to convey pure North American values, domestic opponents arose—usually for domestic reasons—to denounce it. In the end, such debates had a greater effect on the form rather than the content of expansion, but they could delay and distort its expression until North Americans once again convinced themselves that theirs was an unsullied enterprise.

IV

As the method of North American expansion shifted, replacing the pioneer with the investor and the cavalry with the gunboat, and containing mass and elite conceptions at greater distance from one another than in the past, the old project of absorbing Cuba had become outmoded. Few were willing to foresake the historic goal, but the island's fate as a colonial possession or a state in the union was now highly problematic. Indeed, because of the conflicting aspects of the new North American expansionism, Cuba's future was far from settled when rebellious islanders once again pushed the question to the foreground.

By 1895, changes in the economic structure of North America had also affected her ties to Cuba. The century-old trade connection was now reinforced by U.S. ownership of major productive assets on the island: mines,

[29] LaFeber, *New Empire*, ch. 4.

sugar mills, plantations.[30] As a result, the older, broadly held North American concern over its "right" to trade with Cuba had expanded into a concern, on the part of investors, with the protection of property and the promotion of production. Dissatisfaction with Spain's protectionism was now complemented by a critique of her colonial administration as a whole. As some North Americans became producers in Cuba, they adopted the long-standing economic grievances of the wealthy Creoles. To some degree, Washington also acquired the Creole perspective. United States officials concluded that the island could attain social peace and prosperity and could adopt its proper relationship with North America only if Madrid freed it from the economic burdens and restrictions that were built into Spanish colonial policy.

Just as Creole requests for autonomy had, over the years, foundered on the rock of Spanish colonialism, so the official U.S. desire for rational administration of the island was doomed as well. In fact, as Spanish power declined rapidly in the century, reform of her rule in Cuba became less rather than more likely. In the last third of the century, political instability in Spain, the growing intransigence of the *peninsular* population of the island, and the uncompromising position of the deepening Cuban nationalism each pointed away from reform and toward war. By the time the planter elite and Washington officials began to realize that Spain could not release her grip, the middle-range solutions (to their dismay) had vanished. It would fall to the McKinley administration to find its way around the unattractive choice between independence and annexation and toward an acceptable manner of exerting U.S. influence over Cuba.

The new rebellion in Cuba broke out about halfway through the administration of Grover Cleveland. Initially the president treated the matter casually. Washington did not seem to suspect that the apple, finally, was about to fall from the tree. Indeed, had the Spanish effort to subdue the rebellion not become so protracted, destructive, and brutal, the question of U.S. intervention might not even have arisen. Despite the greatly increased economic and military strength of the United States by the 1890s and despite the imperial perspective growing in certain circles, Washington did not initially see in renewed rebellion the opportunity to extend its control to Cuba. At the outset, Cleveland and his secretary of state, Richard Olney, were more concerned to end the fighting than to terminate Spanish rule.[31]

The Cleveland administration stood by its obligations to respect Spanish sovereignty and made an effort to prevent arms from reaching the rebels

---

[30] Jenks, *Colony*, ch. 3.

[31] Philip S. Foner, *The Spanish-Cuban-American War and the Birth of American Imperialism* (New York: Monthly Review Press, 1972) I, ch. 10.

through U.S. territory. The initiation of the revolt had almost been stymied in January 1895 when U.S. officials confiscated three boatloads of arms gathered over three years of painful fund-raising by the PRC.[32] The administration's correct treatment of Spain was based on the assumption that the rebels could not overcome Spanish power and that Madrid would soon defeat them, restore order, and then begin to address the grievances of the moderate Creoles. This was also the expectation of those Creoles not associated with the revolt and of North Americans with large economic interests on the island. However, when the rebellion expanded in scope and intensity, U.S. policymakers were forced to take a more assertive stance.

Unlike the 1868 rebellion, which had been confined for the most part to the isolated and backward eastern end of the island, rebel forces now attacked Spanish outposts and productive facilities in all areas, including the wealthy western provinces. In desperation, Spain sent a massive army to hold onto her most valuable colonial possession. She sent a new commander, General Valeriano Weyler, a veteran of the Ten Years War, who extended the conflict to the civilian population. His policy of "reconcentrating" the rural population in the Spanish-held cities not only separated them from the guerrillas but also overwhelmed Spanish ability to care for them. Huddled together in large numbers, without money, adequate provisions, or proper sanitation, many succumbed to disease or starvation.[33] This tragedy, together with the brutal guerrilla warfare of the rebels and the more brutal Spanish response, spread death and destruction throughout the island. Such a bitter conflict was not propitious for pursuing a policy of colonial reform and the gradual replacement of Spanish by U.S. influence.

The widening and costly war on the island worked against moderate solutions among Cuban factions and also injected a divisive influence into the North American political arena. News of the carnage, relayed to the United States by the exile community, reinvigorated the long-standing hostility to Spain and Spanish control of Cuba. As the fighting intensified, popular opinion in North America sided overwhelmingly with the rebels, whose daring exploits (real and invented) against a powerful foreign master resembled the now mythic struggle against British rule. In any event, as Spain was evil, surely her enemies in the field must be serving the cause of justice.[34] Farmers and workers, sensitive to their own oppression by powerful forces, found reasons to identify with the Cuban rebels as well. Many U.S.

[32] Foner, *Spanish-Cuban-American War*, I, pp. 2–3.

[33] Langley, *Cuban Policy*, p. 96; Campbell, *Transformation*, pp. 242–43.

[34] Linderman, *Mirror of War*, pp. 120–27, describes the negative image of Spain in the United States. The activities of the Cuban exiles is treated in George Auxier, "The Propaganda Activities of the Cuban Junta in Precipitating the Spanish American War," *Hispanic American Historical Review*, 19 (1939), pp. 268–305.

newspapers reflected and, by their biased and often sensational reporting, deepened this feeling.[35] By 1896, this mass sentiment spread to Congress, which passed numerous resolutions (but nothing binding) calling on the president to make manifest U.S. sympathy by recognizing the belligerency of the rebels.[36] Some editors and congressmen went further and called for recognition of Cuban independence, although the tone of these declarations was usually more anti-Spanish than pro-Cuban. Unlike the older era of Manifest Destiny, there was little talk of annexing Cuba, only of "freeing" her.

President Cleveland and, after him, McKinley resisted pressure from Congress to give any sort of recognition to the rebels. Neither believed the independence forces capable of establishing a responsible government. They held that recognition would only encourage the guerrillas to continue the struggle and make them less willing to compromise with Madrid—the solution that the U.S. executive preferred and for which it continued, almost to the end, to see some possibility. Furthermore, as overseers of a Cuban policy whose goal now included the defense of U.S.-owned property, they opposed recognition of belligerency, as this would relieve Spain of her legal obligation to compensate North Americans for their economic losses due to the conflict.[37]

Opposition to belligerency was also the stance of North Americans with economic interests on the island. Despite their losses, early in the war U.S. investors saw no alternative to Spanish protection, however inadequate. Like Washington, they had no confidence in the rebels, whose inability to defeat the large Spanish army in the field led them to a scorched-earth policy that they hoped would make the island an unbearable economic burden to Madrid. Following their Creole counterparts, U.S. property owners saw autonomy as the safest way out of the unsatisfactory choice between Spanish mercantilism and the rebels' war taxes.[38]

The perspective of the property-owning class in Cuba was influential in Washington since much of the information from the island came through U.S. consuls, whose contacts other than Spanish officials were wealthy Creoles and North American businessmen. One of the largest U.S. landowners, Edwin Atkins, had written to Secretary of State Olney in May 1896 that "I found a very general feeling both among Spanish residents and native Cubans favoring autonomy (home rule). . . . The most intelligent of

---

[35] Reporting of the war in U.S. newspapers is examined in Wisan, *The Cuban Crisis*, and in George Auxier, "Middle Western Newspapers and the Spanish American War, 1895–1898," *Mississippi Valley Historical Review* 26 (March 1940), pp. 523–34.

[36] Foner, *Spanish-Cuban-American War*, I, pp. 185–90.

[37] LaFeber, *New Empire*, p. 287.

[38] Thomas, *Pursuit*, p. 332.

these people expressed a wish that the United States might use its friendly services to such end."[39] This opinion was, of course, solicited from the narrow spectrum of acquaintances that a wealthy man like Atkins would have. What is noteworthy is that his perspective—employing U.S. pressure to move Spain toward a moderate outcome to the anti-colonial struggle— was the one adopted by the Cleveland and McKinley administrations. The popular cry of "Cuba Libre" was not taken up at the White House.

The cautious policy emanating from Washington was sustained for the most part by the business community in the United States. Though few members of this community had direct interests in Cuba, they, too, were concerned about the outcome of the rebellion. They were understandably opposed to the rebels, whose strategy included the destruction of property and whose propaganda—though in this instance directed to poor Cubans rather than potential North American patrons—announced that land confiscated from those loyal to Spain "shall be divided among the defenders of the Cuban Republic."[40] The business press in general supported a policy of ending the conflict without U.S. intervention.[41] The *United States Investor* held that war was "never beneficial from a material standpoint,"[42] and even those interests directly harmed by the war called only for Washington's help in achieving an honorable reconciliation between the parties in conflict.[43]

So cautious was the approach of businessmen and policymakers that it left them vulnerable to the charge that they were insensitive to the suffering and the republican aspirations of the Cubans. Leaders of the Populist and Democratic parties, sensitive to grass-roots or to ethnic communities that sympathized with the rebels, had berated Cleveland's inaction and thereby weakened the gold-standard wing of the Democratic Party, which he led. After Inauguration Day in 1897, the Populists and silver Democrats had an even more suitable target: McKinley and the high-tariff industrial magnates of his wing of the Republican Party. The strongly pro-rebel New York *Journal* (Hearst's sensationalist newspaper) had earlier denounced Cleveland's efforts to mediate the conflict as "conspiracy with the Spanish government,"[44] and now warned the new president that the people "will never forgive him the betrayal of Cuba."[45] Such attacks worried businessmen and

---

[39] Edwin F. Atkins, *Sixty Years in Cuba* (Cambridge, Mass.: Riverside Press, 1926), pp. 235–36.

[40] Pérez, *Cuba Between Empires*, p. 136.

[41] Pratt, *Expansionists of 1898*, p. 235.

[42] Ibid., p. 240.

[43] Ibid., p. 248.

[44] Wisan, *The Cuban Crisis*, p. 246.

[45] Ibid., p. 281.

the leaders of the Republican Party, which was associated with such interests. Inaction might hurt the party at the polls and give the forces of inflation, recently defeated in the presidential election of 1896, a new lease on life.[46]

The problem for business interests and industrial-oriented politicians was that their policy of ending the war and promoting autonomy by means of quiet pressure on Spain was not producing results. An official ultimatum to Madrid might hasten autonomy, but it might, instead, lead to war. Those at the helm of the new industrial economy (just climbing out of its deepest depression) were working themselves into a corner. Their failure to end the war was providing ammunition for their domestic political enemies. In the unease with which Republican businessmen and McKinley's Cabinet viewed the idea of an independent Cuba, Democrats detected a chink in their opponents' armor. But war might frighten the nervous stock market and end the economic recovery that had begun in 1897.[47] In such a context, the next electoral round with farmers, workers, or gentry might go against them. At first merely annoyed by the war in Cuba, business interests were becoming disturbed by its ramifications. The old question of absorbing Cuba was taking on unexpected class attributes.

V

Unprepared to exert U.S. influence in a precipitate manner, the Cleveland administration fought simply to retain its room for maneuver. For the two years remaining to it, the administration resisted popular pressure to intervene while hoping that Spain would end the fighting and thus remove the source of agitation in North America. In the absence of a Cuban "crisis" that stirred mass passions, a quiet and gradual program for replacing declining Spanish influence might be worked out. But preoccupied by its effort to resist popular pressure for liberating Cuba, the administration never discovered a safe way of intervening.

Hoping that Spanish military power or political flexibility would remove U.S. leaders from their dilemma, diplomatic notes to Madrid stressed the importance of ending the rebellion and responding to Cuban grievances. The only initiative taken in them was to offer U.S. mediation of the conflict. Beyond that, Olney's correspondence with the Spanish government simply noted—though with an increasing tone of frustration—the North American sympathy for efforts to achieve "freer political institutions," the brutality of the conflict, and the fact that it was "utterly destroying Amer-

[46] Linderman, *Mirror of War*, pp. 6–8.
[47] Pratt, *Expansionists of 1898*, pp. 237–42.

ican investments.''[48] The secretary hoped that these references to U.S. concern over the war would spur a Spanish attempt to resolve the conflict.

Another way of ending the war was, of course, a rebel military victory. Few if any U.S. policymakers thought this possible. More significantly, they opposed such an outcome. Olney wanted peace in Cuba, not an insurgent victory. He told the Spanish minister that "once Spain were withdrawn from the island . . . a war of races would be precipitated."[49] Given his low estimation of Cubans, a product of the racial beliefs of his day (and especially of his class), Olney saw the proper solution to the Cuban "problem" in a reform of the colonial relationship. He was willing, he told Madrid,

> to cooperate with Spain for the immediate pacification of the island, on the basis of such a plan as, leaving Spain her rights of sovereignty, shall yet secure to the people of the island all such rights and powers of local government as they can reasonably ask.[50]

Cleveland shared Olney's view of the insurgents, referring to them—in private correspondence—as "the most inhuman and barbarous cutthroats in the world."[51] In the absence of a Spanish victory or a political compromise, the belief in Washington that Cubans could not govern themselves led, logically, toward the intervention that it still abhorred.

Even less desirous of North American intervention than was Washington, Madrid attempted to mollify U.S. concerns by continually promising that it would soon put down the rebellion. Despite its fear of U.S. power, however, Madrid would not accept the North American offer of mediation, fearful of any formal act that might undermine its claim to sovereignty.[52] When Spanish efforts failed to defeat the rebels, both Madrid's and Washington's room for maneuver narrowed. By the time Cleveland sent his annual message to Congress in December 1895, he was forced to conclude that neither Spain nor the rebels seemed capable of controlling Cuba and that the stalemated conflict was ruining "the industrial value of the island."[53] Since a rebel victory was undesirable, a Spanish victory now unlikely, and continued warfare destructive to U.S. interests, the president called upon Spain to grant "genuine autonomy." Because of his narrowing options, however, he had to note that failure on her part to do so might, at some point, force the United States to act.[54]

[48] LaFeber, *New Empire*, p. 292.
[49] Foner, *Spanish-Cuban-American War*, I, p. 194.
[50] Ibid., p. 195.
[51] Ibid., p. 181.
[52] Pérez, *Cuba Between Empires*, pp. 70–71; Thomas, *Pursuit*, p. 333.
[53] LaFeber, *New Empire*, p. 296.
[54] Ibid.

Unlike many of his predecessors, Cleveland was a confirmed anti-imperialist. He would not accept political rule over alien peoples. He opposed war with Spain because he abhorred its likely fruit: a territory occupied by U.S. forces and—so he believed—incapable of ordering its own affairs.[55] But Cleveland was also an economic expansionist, and he vigorously defended the Monroe Doctrine in 1895 when Great Britain attempted to expand the boundary of its British Guiana colony at the expense of Venezuela. The tough talk by both Cleveland and Olney during the boundary dispute made clear that they were committed to a growing U.S. sphere of influence in the Caribbean.[56] It was Olney who, in warning the British, declared in July 1895 that "today the United States is practically sovereign on this continent, and its fiat is law upon the subjects to which it confines its interposition."[57] Cleveland's difficulty was that his anti-imperialism in the Cuban case prevented him from acting against Spain. Not only was inaction becoming very unpopular at home, it was becoming counterproductive. Without strong U.S. action the war might not end. In that event, the large U.S. trade with Cuba, the growing North American investment there, and the generally accepted proposition that her influence would prevail not only on the island but in the surrounding sea as well would all be placed at risk. The decline of Spanish imperialism was removing the last impediment to the goal of absorbing the island. The rapidly growing Cuban nationalism, however, left the United States little time to settle its domestic differences over what to do with the Cubans who came with it.

VI

President-elect McKinley, having just emerged from the bitter electoral campaign of 1896 with William Jennings Bryan in which the silver issue symbolized a host of deep social tensions, hoped, as had Cleveland, that the war would end. The tariff, the depression, the currency issue, the problems of overproduction and export expansion all pressed for attention. Anarchy in Cuba or war with Spain were assumed to work against or at best interfere with conservative solutions to these pressing problems.[58] But McKinley could not ignore the fact that Cuba was one of the largest U.S. export markets.[59] As an ally (some would say representative) of big business, McKinley and his wing of the Republican Party were strongly com-

[55] Campbell, *Transformation*, pp. 65–66; Beisner, *From the Old Diplomacy to the New*, pp. 95–96.

[56] LaFeber, *New Empire*, pp. 256–59. Williams, *Roots*, pp. 293–95, 300–2, 304–7, 309–16, and 387–88, describes Cleveland's formulation of U.S. economic expansion.

[57] LaFeber, *New Empire*, p. 262.

[58] Williams, *Roots*, p. 410.

[59] Langley, *Cuban Policy*, pp. 84–86; Jenks, *Colony*, p. 21.

mitted to export expansion and, unlike Cleveland, the new president was a willing expansionist, though not an aggressive one. If conflict with Spain became the only alternative to the loss of the large U.S. stake on the island and the political initiative at home, McKinley was better oriented to face the prospect of war.[60]

Many in the new president's own party had taken the partisan opportunity of chastising Cleveland for allowing the bloodletting to continue. The Republican platform of 1896 had called for the United States to "actively use its good offices to restore peace and give independence to the Island."[61] As we have seen, this cry was taken up by the popular press. By the beginning of McKinley's term in the spring of 1897, that press had begun to turn from editorial advocacy of recognition of the rebels' belligerency to calls for some kind of U.S. intervention.[62] The papers were vague about possible outcomes—annexation, protectorate, independence—but they were clear in their sympathy for the anti-colonial cause (if not precisely for the rebels themselves) and in their hatred for Spanish tyranny. McKinley now came under even greater pressure to act than had his predecessor.

Initially, like Cleveland, McKinley worried as much about war with Spain as about chaos in Cuba. But as time went on, he began to pressure Madrid more insistently to offer autonomy. He also began to formulate the means and ends of U.S. intervention, should that become necessary. In doing so, the president tried to keep his options open. He resisted domestic calls for intervention while pressing Spain for reforms that would end the rebellion and allow the natural growth of U.S. influence in the island to resume. Unlike Cleveland, he did not in private exclude the idea of annexing Cuba, though his public statements rejected this alternative. Like Cleveland, however, he was not impressed by the rebels because he considered them unable to govern properly and because an independent Cuba might obstruct the process of gravitation.[63] In July 1897 the State Depart-

[60] LaFeber, *New Empire*, pp. 327–32. McKinley's approach to expansion was positive but not doctrinaire. He was not an anti-imperialist and favored the annexation of Hawaii. On the other hand, he did not espouse the need for colonial empire. McKinley could best be described by Goren Rystad's term "informalist." He had no consistent belief (economic, constitutional, strategic, racial, etc.) about the propriety of controlling foreign lands. He approached the use of U.S. power abroad in terms of the interests that seemed involved in each particular situation. See Goran Rystad, *Ambiguous Imperialism* (Lund, Sweden: Scandinavian Books, 1975), pp. 25–34.

[61] Johnson and Porter, *National Party Platforms*, p. 108.

[62] Wisan, *The Cuban Crisis*, pp. 280–82.

[63] McKinley's purposiveness and initiative with regard to Spain are now accepted by most scholars. They eschew the earlier idea that the president was passive and pushed into war by domestic forces. See Joseph Fry, "William McKinley and the Coming of the Spanish-American War: A Study of the Besmirching and Redemption of an Historical Image," *Diplomatic*

ment informed Spain that the war would have to stop because its continuation "injuriously affects the normal functions of business, and tends to delay the condition of prosperity to which this country is entitled."[64] For the first time, the United States was taking the position not only that the war harmed U.S. economic ties with Cuba but that it affected U.S. prosperity itself. This reflected the change taking place in business opinion which, though still opposed to war, was beginning to conclude that the rebellion, because of its political ramifications *within* the United States, was a barrier to the restoration of healthy economic conditions. In the words of the State Department's note to Spain, the war "keeps up a continuous irritation within our borders."[65] The tail was beginning to wag the dog—not the outcome foreseen by John Quincy Adams.

By the fall of 1897, Spanish forces had made some headway against the rebels, although they were no closer to defeating them. Then in October the Spanish Liberal Party, long in favor of reform of the administration of Cuba, gained the prime minister's office in Madrid. The new premier, Práxedes Sagasta, rescinded the reconcentration order, removed Weyler from command, and proclaimed a program for achieving Cuban autonomy.[66] These actions briefly revived Washington's hope that the rebellion could be ended without social upheaval in Cuba or war between the United States and Spain. Nevertheless, in his message to Congress in December, McKinley seemed to be preparing the way for some kind of U.S. involvement. The president said that Spain should be given time to make her reforms effective but that if they did not bear fruit soon, the United States would have to take action. The nature of such action was not hinted at, though McKinley did make clear that he opposed most of the initiatives being suggested: recognizing insurgent belligerency, recognizing independence, or annexation.[67] The president's distrust of the insurgents, combined with the unpopularity of annexation among a people keen to liberate the island, narrowed his choices significantly.

VII

Options were narrowing in Cuba as well. Sagasta's reform effort, sniped at by conservative opponents in Madrid and Havana, was able to produce only

---

History 3:1 (Winter 1979), pp. 77–97. Also see Beisner, *From the Old*, ch. 5. McKinley's unpublicized interest in purchasing or annexing the island and his opposition to its independence are documented in Foner, *Spanish-Cuban-American War*, I, chs. 11 and 12.

[64] 64. LaFeber, *New Empire*, p. 336.

[65] Ibid.

[66] Payne, *A History of Spain and Portugal*, II, p. 512.

[67] LaFeber, *New Empire*, p. 341.

a Cuban assembly that had little or no real authority. Once again Creole hopes that autonomy would secure their status and their fortunes were dashed. Spain could neither place political power in their hands nor could it defeat the rebels. In the circumspect manner that befit their station, Creoles began to turn toward the United States.[68] The antagonists of the Creoles, the *peninsulares*, were frightened into action by the same autonomy that seemed so hollow to the natives. The loyalist element on the island, longtime opponents of the Spanish Liberals, felt betrayed by Sagasta's attempt to take their monopoly of political power from them and by the new military commander's unwillingness to pursue the rebels as vehemently as had Weyler. They mounted a series of demonstrations against the autonomy decree. Pro-Weyler officers declared their refusal to fight for an autonomous Cuba. In January 1898 the *voluntarios*, volunteer regiments formed from among Spaniards resident in Cuba to help defend Spanish sovereignty, rioted in Havana, destroying the offices of pro-autonomist newspapers. In their desperation, pro-Spanish elements were also forced to think of the possibility of a Cuba without Spain. Many left the island; others, contemplating their future in an insurgent-ruled or a U.S.-dominated Cuba, began to seek out North Americans to whom they could confide their fears and hopes.[69]

Polarization of the island's politics seemed to open the way for the insurgents. At the beginning of 1898 they stood unconquered by the largest army that Spain had ever sent to the New World. Madrid's forces, undermined by years of irregular combat, by recurring epidemics of yellow fever, and now by its officers' disdain for fighting anything but a colonial war, had lost all offensive capacity. Though not on the verge of victory, the military position of the rebel forces (the Liberation Army) had become unassailable. Throughout much of the countryside they held the field, though that terrain was by now denuded of most of its economic assets.[70] The political structure of the independence forces was less solidly established, however. Their unity had not survived the battle death of Martí in the first months of the insurrection. Martí had feared the consequences of a long, bloody struggle and had hoped for a quick victory leading to generous treatment for the vanquished. The brutal, three-year stalemate following his death not only embittered the combatants, it reopened the divisions within the independence movement. That portion of it based on the island—composed of the Council of Government and the Liberation Army—was uncompromisingly committed to independence, but its main elements

[68] Pérez, *Cuba Between Empires*, pp. 137, 154–56.

[69] Ibid., pp. 158–62.

[70] Ibid., pp. 167–68.

had long quarreled with one another. The military wing blamed the provisional government for hampering the war effort, while the civilian officials feared the Caesarism of certain commanders. The exile portion of the movement, based largely in the United States, was itself divided. Much of the PRC remained committed to independence (and to Martí's lofty vision of it), but as Spain's power eroded and as autonomy collapsed, the landed and professional elements of the party were joined by new exiles of similar status who tended to see independence as a stage that would succeed a U.S. protectorate or precede U.S. annexation.[71]

VIII

The failure of autonomy combined with the intransigence of both the *peninsulares* and the insurgents spelled the end of McKinley's hope for a moderate conclusion to the rebellion. The president now had to formulate a North American program for bringing peace to Cuba. He had to define the nature of the now almost inevitable U.S. intervention and prescribe the proper form of North American influence in Cuba. Given the public and congressional mood, the president's program would have to end the fighting, remove Spanish control, and demonstrate both U.S. power and benevolence. McKinley's program had to meet other standards as well. As the leader of the political party that represented sizable portions of the urban, industrial, commercial, and banking interests—and the political, professional, and media elites associated with them—the president had to formulate a program that would open the island fully to U.S. trade and investment, provide a suitable government there, and demonstrate that the United States was a responsible world power. He also had to separate his program from that of the imperialists who sought to annex Cuba, as well as from that of the pro-rebel sympathizers who sought a binding U.S. recognition of the Cuban republic. The imperialist position was unpopular because it was seen as immoral and/or unconstitutional and thus could not serve as a basis for taking the nation into war. The pro-rebel position, while popular, was held by most North Americans of wealth and influence to be confining and even dangerous. Moreover, it was flawed because it was inconsistent with historic North American assumptions about the fate of Cuba. Finally, the president had, for his own purposes, to ignore the Cuban independence movement, though he could ill afford a direct confrontation with it.

Fortunately for the president and his allies in the business and power-expansionist communities, opposing forces suffered from important internal weaknesses. The small band of North American anti-imperialists were

---

[71] Insurgent politics is examined in Pérez, *Cuba Between Empires*, ch. 5.

tainted by their upper-class origins and by their unwillingness to use U.S. power either to rule or serve other peoples. The Cuban independence movement, as we have seen, contained division (especially among Creoles) that promised to deliver important segments of the nationalist leadership to a program of U.S. hegemony. For their part, many Spaniards on the island were now quietly awaiting the Yankees. Perhaps most important, behind the popular anti-colonialism of North Americans lay a racism that might undermine the faith if Cubans were discovered to be undeserving of sovereign status. Moreover, the pro-rebel sentiment contained an ethnocentrism that might easily brush aside those that it once wished to liberate. Here, too, the president might find allies, though unpredictable ones.

In the wake of the riots by the *voluntarios* in January, McKinley had sent the battleship *Maine* to Havana, ostensibly on a courtesy call but actually to demonstrate U.S. concern over the deteriorating situation. The remainder of the fleet had been assembled at Key West.[72] About the same time, McKinley repeated the old offer of U.S. mediation, this time in more vigorous terms. The United States would now have to play the stabilizing role that had been cast for autonomy. Indirect approaches to exerting U.S. influence would have to be abandoned. One of these indirect methods had been to secure clear access to the island's economy. The U.S. minister to Madrid, Steward Woodford, had been negotiating a new commercial treaty with Spain that was to have complemented autonomy. Indeed, Woodford judged that "such a treaty should obtain for us the practical control of the Cuban market."[73] When the failure of autonomy rendered the treaty irrelevant, Woodford turned to a more direct vehicle and suggested to the Spanish colonial minister that the United States purchase Cuba. For a time, McKinley placed his own hope in such a direct solution. He asked Whitelaw Reid, a close ally and owner of the New York *Tribune*, to prepare for negotiations with Madrid. The president also sent a private letter to the queen of Spain offering to pay $300 million for Cuba.[74]

McKinley even entertained—though he did not officially endorse—the unusual purchase plan of John J. McCook, a Republican leader close to the president. McCook and an important Wall Street banker, Samuel M. Janney, planned to buy Cuban independence from Spain with capital raised by a U.S. banking syndicate they had formed. The syndicate would be com-

---

[72] LaFeber, *New Empire*, p. 344.

[73] Ibid., p. 346.

[74] Efforts to purchase Cuba during this period are discussed in LaFeber, *New Empire*, p. 393; Thomas, *Pursuit*, p. 367; Foner, *Spanish-Cuban-American War*, I, pp. 241, 247, 249n; Pérez, *Cuba Between Empires*, p. 172. McKinley was attracted to McCook's plan but did not like the fact that it involved recognition of Cuban independence. See Foner, *Spanish-Cuban-American War*, I, p. 247.

pensated—handsomely it hoped—with bonds of the brand-new Cuban republic, payment of which would be guaranteed by a lien on future Cuban customs receipts, with the U.S. government as financial trustee.[75] These efforts would founder on Spanish unwillingness to sell that which it had spent so much to keep. What is interesting about them is their entrepreneurial conception, illuminating the distance between a business view of the island as an asset and the public passion to liberate Cuba.

McKinley continued to increase the pressure on Spain. Diplomatic notes now threatened Spain with U.S. intervention and the loss of Cuba if she did not stop the fighting quickly and prepare an acceptable form for her departure.[76] The president's difficulty was that it would take time to see if Spain would meet this demand and events were outracing him, threatening to precipitate a war whose purpose he might not control. On February 9 Horatio Rubens, an ally of the independence leadership based in New York, gave the press a private letter from the Spanish minister in Washington, Dupuy de Lôme, that the exiles had taken from the files of the minister's correspondent. De Lôme's insulting remarks about McKinley forcefully struck the public as an example of the personal, palpable Spanish villainy that formed the core of their understanding of the conflict. The letter disturbed the administration for different reasons. In addition to the disparaging remarks, the letter made clear that Madrid did not intend to find a way out of the war acceptable to the United States and that it still hoped, somehow, to prevail.[77]

The popular image of Spanish treachery was more powerfully reinforced just a few days later when a great explosion sank the *Maine* in Havana harbor. More than 250 U.S. sailors were killed. The pro-Cuban press now had, despite lack of evidence, "proof" of Spanish wickedness.[78] Again, the administration was impressed, too, but not by the belief that the Spanish had sunk the vessel. Such an act contradicted Madrid's consistent efforts to avoid provoking a U.S. intervention. Washington was disturbed by Spain's inability to prevent such an act by those who *did* desire intervention—certain of the rebels or peninsular opponents of reform. Here was evidence that even in her administrative center on the island Spain had lost control of events. The administration had to be careful that it did not lose control as well.

The public outcry over the *voluntario* riots, the De Lôme letter, and the

---

[75] David Healy, *The United States in Cuba: 1898–1902* (Madison: University of Wisconsin Press, 1963), pp. 13–14; Foner, *Spanish-Cuban-American War*, I, pp. 220–22. Note the similarity of McCook's proposal with that of Hamilton Fish described in ch. 1.

[76] LaFeber, *New Empire*, pp. 336, 341–42.

[77] Campbell, *Transformation*, p. 253; Beisner, *From the Old*, p. 111.

[78] Wisan, *The Cuban Crisis*, ch. 20.

sinking of the *Maine* raised the possibility that Congress would force the president into war with Spain on its own terms. The administration still preferred to avoid war and had not given up all hope of definitive action from Spain. But now its principal concern was to retain the ability to define the purpose (and results) of war should it become inevitable.

The pressure on the president was now at its highest level. Much of the press favored intervention, some to avenge the *Maine*, others to "pacify" Cuba. References to the dignity and exploits of the rebels were replaced by hatred of Spain among the more warlike papers and discussions of Cuba's future status by more "respectable" ones.[79] The less sensationalist *Sun* declared that U.S. sympathy for Cuba "cannot be appeased by anything short of Cuban deliverance from the Spanish Yoke," that America was under "obligation to stop Spanish barbarity in Cuba and to deliver Cuba from the Spanish transatlantic domination."[80] The more aggressive *World* called for Cuban independence but pointed out that "Cuba as the scene of a remorseless and barbarous war of extermination is a constant menace to us and a standing reproach to our civilization,"[81] indicating that liberation was not a selfless act.

As war approached, the idea of annexing Cuba, little in evidence in the pro-Cuban press during the early part of the war, made an appearance but as a Cuban rather than a North American desire. The *World* correspondent reported that, faced with the possibility of independence, many wealthy Cubans and *peninsulares* preferred annexation.[82] The press had discovered what the administration had known for many months. McKinley's special agent in Cuba, William H. Calhoun, reported in June 1897 that "Cuban planters and Spanish property holders are now satisfied that the island must soon slip from Spain's grasp, and would welcome immediate American intervention."[83] In November Consul Fitzhugh Lee reported that "all classes of the Spanish citizens . . . would prefer annexation to the United States or some form of American protectorate."[84] While headlines called for a free Cuba, allies of U.S. hegemony were gathering in the wings.

While waiting for Spain to respond to his demands, the president had not been inactive. Early in March he asked Congress for a $50,000,000 emergency military appropriation. The battleship *Oregon* was ordered to the

---

[79] Ibid., p. 398.

[80] Ibid., p. 401.

[81] Ibid., p. 402.

[82] Ibid., pp. 338, 376.

[83] Pérez, *Cuba Between Empires*, pp. 157–58. Calhoun's report also reinforced the administration's mistrust of the insurrectionists. It concluded that independence would lead to class and race war and that Cubans could not establish a republican form of government. See Foner, *Spanish-Cuban-American War*, I, pp. 213–14.

[84] Pérez, *Cuba Between Empires*, p. 159.

Caribbean from its dock in Bremerton, Washington.[85] The administration was also preparing for war in the Pacific, reflecting the larger strategic interests of those in the Cabinet like Assistant Secretary of the Navy Theodore Roosevelt. Three months earlier the Navy Department had ordered the Pacific Fleet under Commodore George Dewey to prepare to attack the Spanish-held Philippine islands in the event of war with Spain.[86] The "coastal defense" ironclad navy that had been built in the late 1880s and early 1890s was now ready to challenge a rapidly declining imperial power.

As policymakers moved toward war, they were encouraged by the slow but steady shift in business opinion in that same direction. Leaders of the business community finally came to the conclusion that continued agitation for intervention and continued uncertainty about the possibility of war were more unsettling to economic recovery (which had begun late in 1896) than war itself.[87] These men strongly favored market expansion and were particularly concerned about the apparent division of China into colonial fiefdoms in 1898. But their preference was for "open door" diplomacy rather than realpolitik as the best way to expand U.S. exports and protect U.S. foreign investments.[88] The economic journals had opposed intervention in Cuba because the cry for action arose from domestic forces that they distrusted and because war was unpredictable; it might become protracted or drag the nation into conflict with a powerful state, precipitating a financial panic. Indeed, the pacific tone of the business press had led both pro-Cuban papers and imperialist spokesmen to talk of the softness of the capitalist class.[89] Now, spurred on by those among them with interests in Cuba, the bourgeoisie proved willing to adapt its form of expansionism to the requirements of the moment.

The momentum toward war increased on March 28 when the report of the U.S. naval board investigating the *Maine* disaster was made public. The board did not fix responsibility but concluded that a submarine mine rather than an internal explosion had sunk the ship. Renewed condemnations of Spain filled the press and, again, Congress echoed with resolutions calling for intervention.[90] Even congressional moderates joined the call for action. An influential convert was Senator Redfield Proctor, just back from a trip to Cuba, who painted a bleak picture to his Senate colleagues of conditions

---

[85] Margaret Leech, *In the Days of McKinley* (New York: Harper, 1959), pp. 168–69.

[86] Leech, *McKinley*, p. 162; LaFeber, *New Empire*, p. 361.

[87] Pratt, *Expansionists of 1898*, pp. 143–49; LaFeber, *New Empire*, pp. 385–90; Williams, *Roots*, pp. 43–44, 410–11, 415.

[88] Pratt, *Expansionists of 1898*, pp. 257–59.

[89] Wisan, *The Cuban Crisis*, pp. 282–83; Lears, *No Place of Grace*, pp. 101–2, 108, 112, 115–17; Richard Hofstadter, *The American Political Tradition* (New York: Vintage, 1961), pp. 206–15.

[90] Wisan, *The Cuban Crisis*, pp. 422–29.

there. He was an opponent of annexation and saw a better future for Cuba after the war as a self-governing state helped toward prosperity and stability by a ''large influx of American and English immigration and money.'' A millionaire marble-quarry owner, Proctor, with his reference to the ''surpassing richness'' of the island, reflected the businessman's recognition that war for Cuba held promises as well as dangers.[91] Neither an imperialist nor an anti-imperialist, Proctor merely observed that autonomy had failed and that the war had devastated the island. He expressed confidence that with help from the United States, the island's problems could be solved and its economic opportunities exploited. His position was very different from that of imperialists like Senator Henry Cabot Lodge, who felt that Washington had to establish direct control over Cuba as a strategic and economic appendage of the United States. Positions were converging, however. By March senators like Proctor and Lodge were in agreement that the situation in Cuba was intolerable and that the United States had to end the war. This consensus caused congressional leaders to inform McKinley that Congress would act on its own if the president did not do so. Even the business press now agreed that war to end the uncertainty resulting from unending turmoil in Cuba was necessary.

McKinley, too, was now ready for war. On March 20 the State Department had made a final effort to move Spain. Madrid was told in forceful terms that she had to end the conflict in a matter of weeks. Again, Washington indicated its desire to act as mediator. But Spain, loath to take any action that smacked of surrender, requested time to go through the formality of placing the question of peace before the not yet convened Cuban assembly, its decision to be ratified in turn by the Cortes. The procedures of empire were irrelevant by now and Washington refused to consider any delay. Spain was informed that an armistice must be declared by the end of March, just a week away.[92] But Spain could not produce the desired armistice. She wanted the rebels to ask for it first, thus avoiding the image of Spanish defeat. The rebels, steeled by years of hardship and buoyed by the prospect of U.S. intervention, would not consider anything but a grant of independence.

On April 4 Assistant Secretary of State William Day told U.S. Minister Woodford that the Spanish offer of an armistice only if the rebels requested it was unacceptable. On that day McKinley prepared his message to Congress asking for authority to make war. He delayed sending the message so that North Americans could be quietly evacuated from Cuba. Frightened

---

[91] Ibid., pp. 414–15; Linderman, *Mirror of War*, pp. 37–46.
[92] LaFeber, *New Empire*, pp. 394–95.

by the imminence of conflict, Spain agreed on April 9 "to arrange and facilitate peace on the island" by suspending hostilities.[93]

Madrid's action was too vague, and Spain's ability to act effectively was no longer believed in Washington. On April 11 McKinley addressed Congress and, for the first time, disclosed the kind of intervention on which he had decided.

McKinley's message was a proposal not only to end the war and remove Spanish sovereignty—points on which all but a handful of anti-imperialists now agreed—it was an effort to assure that outmoded, dangerous, or naive solutions to the problem of absorbing Cuba would not prevail. The president's task was to take the formidable and divergent North American ideas about Cuba—anti-imperialism, annexation, market expansion, protection of property, strategic control, the spreading of liberty, the white man's burden—and forge them into an effective national will while at the same time placing them in a hierarchy of influence that assured primacy to the politically conservative, economically expansionist aims of the administration. As the president's speech made clear, his war was not to be the war for empire of the jingoes nor would it be the war of liberation of the anti-colonialist, anti-plutocratic masses. McKinley's would be a war for markets and stability. To accomplish that, the president had to call for a conflict that enabled North Americans to see themselves in a noble posture while assuring that this self-flattery did not cause the real prizes of the conflict to slip from their minds or their grasp.

The president's speech struck all the right chords: the Cubans were "a dependent people stirring to be free"; the island was "a once prosperous community reduced to comparative want, its lucrative commerce virtually paralyzed." "Our trade has suffered," he said, "the capital invested by our citizens in Cuba has been largely lost," and "our people have been so sorely tried as to beget a perilous unrest among our own citizens." After describing the unhappy three-year conflict, he concluded that Spain could not defeat the rebels, that home rule could not work, and that the war and its baneful effects on North America had no end in sight. He then revealed, finally, the basis on which he intended the United States to intervene. The president said that the goal should be to "pacify the island," and to that end the United States need not recognize the independence of the "so-called" Cuban republic "at the present time." He recommended instead "the forcible intervention of the United States as a neutral" to stop the war. This would be done "in the cause of humanity," to assure U.S. citizens "protection and indemnity for life and property," and because of the "very serious injury to commerce, trade, and business of our people. . . . The

[93] Ibid., p. 396.

only hope of relief and repose from a condition which can no longer be endured," he concluded, "is the enforced pacification of Cuba."[94] In his only reference to a longer term goal, the president said:

> When it shall appear hereafter that there is within the island a government capable of performing the duties and discharging the functions of a separate nation, and having, as a matter of fact, the proper forms and attributes of nationality, such government can be promptly and readily recognized and the relations and interests of the United States with such a nation be adjusted.[95]

To accomplish his task, the president asked Congress for authorization to "use the military and naval forces of the United States as may be necessary for these purposes."[96] He proposed a reasoned, businesslike conflict, imperial enough to assure its economic goals in the face of rival states and unruly natives yet sufficiently in harmony with the idea of liberating colonized peoples to retain the allegiance of those who would have to fight it.

In the House, some Democrats wanted to attach to the authorization requested by the president a resolution recognizing the Cuban republic. Republican Party control of the body led to its defeat, and the president was authorized merely to establish "a stable and independent government"— phrasing that still gave McKinley the flexibility he required. The Senate, however, did inhibit the president's freedom of action. It passed several resolutions, one of them recognizing the Cuban republic[97] and another, the famous Teller Amendment, stating:

> That the United States hereby disclaims any disposition or intention to exercise sovereignty, jurisdiction, or control over said island except for the pacification thereof, and asserts its determination when that is accomplished to leave the government and control of the island to its people.[98]

McKinley was prepared to veto the Senate resolutions, but in the conference with the House to prepare the final joint resolution, recognition of the Cuban repubic was dropped, although the less restrictive Teller Amend-

---

[94] The speech is contained in Arthur Link and William J. Leary, Jr., eds., *The Diplomacy of World Power: The United States, 1898–1920* (New York: St. Martín's Press, 1970), pp. 15–25.

[95] Ibid., p. 22.

[96] Ibid., p. 25.

[97] This was known as the Turpie-Foraker Amendment. See Smith, *What Happened*, pp. 111–12.

[98] Ibid., p. 112.

ment was retained to remove any taint of imperialism. The president accepted the resolution in this form and signed the more important declaration of war, which simply gave him the authority to make war on Spain.[99] What form of U.S. influence in Cuba the Teller Amendment might be compatible with was left for another day.

[99] Ibid.

CHAPTER 3

THE SEMI-SOVEREIGN
REPUBLIC OF CUBA

I

THE STRANDS out of which were woven the interventionist consensus of 1898 were diverse and, in some instances, contradictory. North American interventionists hoped to strike a blow against a brutal and anachronistic Spanish colonialism, or against a mercantilism that stifled the economic health both of Cuba and her northern neighbor, or against the prospect of chaos, race war, and the "Africanization" of the island. Others saw war against Spain as adding a new state to the Union, or as fulfilling a moral commitment to spread liberty, or as gaining strategic control of the Caribbean, or, finally, as shouldering the white man's burden and thereby placing the United States among the ranks of responsible imperial powers. Once Spanish resistance had been brushed aside—in a "splendid little war" of only fourteen weeks—the very different implications of a war to "take" and a war to "free" Cuba had to be sorted out.

President McKinley had adroitly sidestepped the contradictions between realpolitik, economic expansion, moral mission, and radical republicanism when he took the country into war. Fortunately for him, the experience of the war itself significantly altered the balance between liberation and domination in North American motivation. It also broke down the barriers between elite and mass approaches to Cuba. In defeat Spain ceased to appear reactionary or brutal. Her officers surrendered graciously to the U.S. commander, making way for what they presumed were the new defenders of property and privilege on the island. The rapid removal of the Spaniard brought North Americans face to face with the weary Cubans and their war-ravaged land. Upon closer inspection, the once-potent image of the rebels

52

as gallant, republican warriors vanished. That image had begun to recede from the moment U.S. forces landed near Santiago at the eastern end of the island. There they encountered Cuban guerrilla forces who were dark-skinned and whose dress and manner reflected the great poverty of the Oriente region and the even greater privations resulting from three years of difficult warfare.

Just as McKinley had been unimpressed by the rebels' provisional government and had refused to grant them the official recognition that would have made them a formal political ally, so U.S. officers quickly concluded that the ragged, poorly armed rebel force could not serve as a proper military ally. The U.S. military considered them unfit to serve except as guides and bearers. North American soldiers for the most part saw them as unfit in moral and racial terms as well. The disparity in provisions between the United States and rebel forces led to thefts of U.S. supplies by the almost starving Cubans. Soon it was common for North Americans to conclude that the Cubans could never be the agents of their own liberation. When rebel forces reacted to this treatment with resentment, they were pronounced ungrateful. So little respect now seemed due them that the U.S. commander, General William R. Shafter, excluded them from the formal ceremonies after the Spanish surrender of Santiago. After the war, as U.S. soldiers returned home with stories of lazy, cowardly, thieving Cubans, the once-discredited Spanish view of their incompetence gained currency and was reinforced by the social Darwinism and racism with which most North Americans already viewed ''tropical'' peoples.[1]

As popular attitudes toward the rebels became less generous, wider scope was provided those forces which had approached the conflict with greater self-interest. Imperialists, market expansionists, and moral reformers now had the opportunity to broaden the meaning of ''pacification'' in the Teller Amendment. Redefining the U.S. aim in Cuba from independence to control was, of course, consistent with the old idea of North American hegemony on the island and thus came about quite rapidly. Indeed, it had begun as soon as war was declared. In the first weeks of the conflict Whitelaw Reid, like many influential people around McKinley, told the president that he ''deeply regretted'' passage of the Teller Amendment and advised him that war against Spain meant that ''we are making ourselves morally responsible for decent government in Cuba. . . .'' Reid's paper, the New York *Tribune*, editorialized, ''By casting out Spain this government takes upon itself the burden of insuring to Cuba a more civilized sufferable government than Spain has provided.'' Prophetically, the Chicago

---

[1] Linderman, *Mirror of War*, pp. 132–33, 137–39, 141. For a discussion of the importance of the rebel forces to U.S. victory see Foner, *Spanish-Cuban-American War*, II, ch. 15.

Tribune editorialized that the Teller Amendment "expresses the present intentions and feelings of the people of the United States. . . . It is far from being the intention of the American government or people to drive out the Spanish devil and then allow the devils of disorder, misrule and anarchy to govern Cuba."[2] Business interests, which had been wary of war with Spain, became strong supporters of the move away from liberation and toward control. Before the war ended, the New York *Journal of Commerce* joined the voices questioning the Cubans' capacity for self-government and called for a reinterpretation of the Teller Amendment, as did other business journals.[3] Adding to the chorus were annexationists like Henry Cabot Lodge who, having been constrained to speak of "our duty to Cuba" before 1898, could now return to their true position.[4]

The popular war against Spain produced an outpouring of books whose changing titles illustrate the evolution of U.S. attitudes toward Cuba. Henry Houghton Beck's *Cuba's Fight for Freedom* and Murat Halstead's *The Story of Cuba: Her Struggles for Liberty* were typical of the popular works that appeared during the war. In the wake of the conflict, as North Americans began to sum up the results of the crusade, a typical title was Trumbull White's *Our New Possessions: A Graphic Account, Descriptive and Historical, of the Tropic-Islands of the Sea That Have Fallen Under Our Sway.* . . . Demonstrating that support for Cuban independence did not preclude annexation, Halstead had begun his book with a confident prediction: "With Cuba's destiny in the hands of her own people, she will obey the irresistible attraction of our Union to be one of the United States." White began his own discussion of Cuba by noting, "It is manifest destiny that the commerce and the progress of the island shall follow American channels and adopt American forms."[5]

The prevailing racial perspective in North America also helped to define the meaning of "pacification." Before the war, both moral and imperial expansionists had kept a decent distance from the race issue because Spain used the specter of "Africanization" to prevent U.S. support for the rebels

[2] Wisan, *The Cuban Crisis*, p. 450; Foner, *Spanish-Cuban-American War*, I, p. 279.

[3] Pratt, *Expansionists of 1898*, pp. 274–75.

[4] E. Berkeley Tomkins, *Anti-Imperialism in the United States*, pp. 70–71, 86; Healy, *US Expansion*, pp. 52–54.

[5] Henry Houghton Beck, *Cuba's Fight for Freedom and the War with Spain* (Philadelphia: Globe Bible Pub. Co., 1898); Murat Halstead, *The Story of Cuba: Her Struggles for Liberty* (Akron, Ohio: Werner Co., 1898), 6th ed., p. 9; Trumbull White, *Our New Possessions: A Graphic Account, Descriptive and Historical, of the Tropic-Islands of the Sea That Have Fallen Under Our Sway* . . . (n.p.: Trumbull White, 1898), p. 461. During the war White had written *Our War with Spain for Cuba's Freedom*. Another influential postwar work was Robert Porter's *Industrial Cuba* (New York: G. P. Putnam's Sons, 1899). Porter was McKinley's "Special Representative" in Cuba.

Cuba Libre!
William Allan Rogers, *Harper's Weekly*, April 30, 1898

Uncle Sam's New Class in the Art of Self-Government
William Allan Rogers, *Harper's Weekly*, August 27, 1898

and because the inferiority and unassimilability of "backward" peoples
were an influential argument of the anti-imperialists. After the defeat of
Spain, imperialists and expansionists rediscovered the black component of
the island's population. Many of them now argued that the inferiority of
that race made necessary continued U.S. rule over the island. In this way,

Miss Cuba Receives an Invitation
MISS COLUMBIA (to her fair neighbor):
"Won't you join the stars and be my forty-sixth?"
Chicago Record-Herald, 1901

it was now the expansionists who tied their argument to the widely held conviction that Cubans were not competent to run a republic.[6]

The changed attitude toward Cuba appeared in magazine illustrations and political cartoons as well. Prior to the war, the principal pictorial image of Cuba had been that of a helpless maiden (often Lady Liberty herself) in mortal danger. After 1899 the most common image of the Cuban was that of an ignorant or unruly brat. Miss Liberty had been white and graceful; the brat was black and ungainly.[7]

The drift toward control of Cuba was also sustained by the fact of imperial possession itself. The military strategy of the war had been to destroy Spanish forces based in the Caribbean and Asia. It was this strategy that produced not only the "liberation" of Cuba but the attacks on Puerto Rico and the Philippines as well. The military strategy had drawn upon the lesser, imperial motive for the war. North American imperialists saw the war as an opportunity to carve out a U.S. sphere of influence in the Caribbean and the Far East, toward which the nation's growing economic and military power had been "naturally" directed by a century of continental expansion to the south and west. The revival of European colonialism in the 1890s had heightened the claustrophobia of North American expansionists who saw strategic areas (like the isthmus of Panama) and markets (like China) being preempted by aggressive European states. Power expansionists seethed with the knowledge that these states were no wealthier or more powerful than the United States. They merely displayed the political will to overcome the remaining geographical and cultural barriers to control of the world by industrial states. But the desire of North American expansionists to play the game of power openly had been thwarted to a great degree by popular opposition to territorial expansion beyond the North American continent. Public opinion (with a few exceptions) frowned upon ruling or assimilating "backward" peoples and opposed as well the powerful government or military apparatus needed to do so. Such acts were deemed feudal, royal, or colonial—ways of life against which American republicanism had been set.

The war with Spain took North American thinking across an important threshold and created an opening for power expansionists. Now the fruits of imperial war were in North American hands; she must rule these lands or set them free. The logic of North American anti-colonialism led toward liberation of oppressed peoples, but in the Hobbesian world of clashing empires liberation seemed to mean throwing the fish newly plucked from

[6] Rubin F. Westin, *Racism in U.S. Imperialism* (Columbia: University of South Carolina Press, 1972), pp. 54, 139–41, 144.

[7] John J. Johnson, *Latin America in Caricature* (Austin: University of Texas Press, 1980), pp. 80–95, 161–75, 209.

the imperial net to the nearest shark. Just as North American imperialists had faced the problem of getting the United States to do that which she had never done, now the anti-imperialists had to argue for undoing that which had been done. As President McKinley responded to his critics: "It is no longer a question of expansion with us; we have expanded. If there is any question at all, it is a question of contracting; and who is going to contract?"[8]

Despite the change in mood caused by the war, one anti-imperialist argument still carried weight. This was the idea that rule over alien peoples overseas would debase American republicanism and lead to inglorious foreign wars. Indeed, such a war had broken out in the newly acquired Philippines in 1899. Seen in perspective, this conflict was clearly one of imperial subjugation of a native rebellion and produced the kinds of atrocities on the part of U.S. forces that had so incensed North Americans when earlier attributed to Spanish troops in Cuba. The Philippine insurrection lasted four years and was very costly. Nevertheless, in the end even this undisguised colonial war was pursued and rationalized. As with the alternative to keeping the Spanish islands, the alternative to subjugating the rebellion was the surrender of the U.S. position in Asia. An even more effective argument was McKinley's claim that the United States had to stay in the Philippines "for the protection of the vast majority of the population who welcome our sovereignty against the designing minority."[9] Despite such efforts to reconcile liberation and domination, however, the insurrection raised troublesome questions even among expansionists and helped to assure that clear violations of the consent of native peoples would always be unpopular at home.[10]

The course of the U.S. military occupation of Cuba, which lasted from 1899 to 1902, was influenced to some degree by the concern that if it were too severe, Washington might have another native rebellion on its hands. Nevertheless, the principal barrier to overbearing U.S. control was the pledge of independence contained in the Teller Amendment. The resolution narrowed Washington's options in Cuba as compared with the Philippines. On the other hand, North American influence in Cuba, unlike its new po-

[8] The imperial aspects of the war with Spain are discussed in LaFeber, *New Empire*; Ernest R. May, *American Imperialism* (New York: Atheneum, 1968); Pratt, *Expansionists of 1898*; Marylyn Blatt Young, "American Expansionism, 1870–1900: The Far East," in Barton Bernstein, ed., *Toward a New Past* (New York: Vintage, 1969). The quotation from McKinley is in Margaret Leech, *McKinley*, p. 544.

[9] Rystad, *Ambiguous Imperialism*, p. 46.

[10] The response to the Philippine insurrection is discussed in Henry Graff, ed., *American Imperialism and the Philippine Insurrection* (Boston: Little Brown, 1969); Thomas G. Paterson, *American Imperialism and Anti-Imperialism* (New York: T. Y. Crowell, 1973); and Robert Beisner, *Twelve Against Empire*.

sition in the Philippines, had long been identified with the growth of the great North American republic. Some expansionists, like former Secretary of State Richard Olney, favored annexation of Cuba as strongly as they opposed taking the Philippines.[11] As a result, while annexation and war in the Philippines produced significant controversy, "pacification" of Cuba stirred much less debate. Even those who now felt free to raise the old issue of annexation could gain an audience simply by making it clear that they foresaw a natural rather than a forced process at work. Nobody spoke of ruling the island (for very long) without the consent of its people. The trick was to obtain that consent.[12]

Slowly, as the occupation progressed, the very different goals of "taking" and "freeing" Cuba found common ground in the project of "Americanizing" the island. Again, Senator Proctor reflected the new consensus. He had opposed annexation before the war and had even considered the Cubans capable of self-government, though he felt this to be more likely after the "whitening" of the island's population by North American immigration. Soon after the war, he, like others, regretted the pledge of independence but acknowledged that such a promise now stood in the way of forceful annexation. As he surveyed Cubans, he discovered that they were "far inferior" to North Americans, and he began to speak of the need to "manage" their affairs.[13] Proctor's views stood midway in the short spectrum between those North Americans who saw "Americanization" as a natural stage of the gravitational pull leading to annexation and those who saw it as a means of preparing Cuba for the rigors of independence. Even Senator Henry M. Teller, the author of the famous independence amendment, joined the new consensus. He, too, concluded that Cuba was not ready for independence. In fact, he expected that when she was mature enough her people would see the wisdom of annexation.[14]

The nineteenth-century idea that Cuba was not viable outside the U.S. orbit made the island's deficiencies quite apparent to North Americans as they now surveyed the possibility of its independence. While this view led imperialists to call for formal control of the island, it led reformers to save Cuba from her own weaknesses. The U.S. military governor, General Leonard Wood, told McKinley that "we are dealing with a race that has steadily been going down for a hundred years and into which we have to infuse new life, new principles and new methods of doing things." The emotive terms "duty," "right," and "destiny" had, in the decades before

[11] Rystad, *Ambiguous Imperialism*, pp. 246–47.

[12] Beisner, *Twelve Against Empire*, p. 184, notes that even anti-imperialists made exceptions when it came to Cuba.

[13] Linderman, *Mirror of War*, pp. 50–51.

[14] Healy, *The United States in Cuba*, p. 85; Rystad, p. 28.

1898, carried most weight as obligations to defend peoples against powerful states. In the wake of war with Spain, they would help to justify overseeing these people's affairs to protect them from their own backwardness as well as from predator nations. In the words of Senator Albert Beveridge, "If it is our business to see that Cubans are not destroyed by any foreign power, is it not our duty to see that they are not destroyed by themselves?"[15] Beveridge hoped that duty would lead to annexation, but moral and cultural expansionists could avoid difficult constitutional issues and fulfill their duty with good works. Protestant evangelists established almost ninety schools (*colegios*) in Catholic Cuba between 1898 and 1901. Public school reformers built a new instructional system on the island with organization and texts imported from Ohio. In 1900 Harvard brought 1300 Cuban teachers to Cambridge for instruction in U.S. teaching methods. Eventually, serious efforts would be made to "Americanize" the systems of justice, sanitation, transportation, and trade as well.[16]

What the new balance of imperial, reformist, and liberationist forces and arguments implied for Cuba was not colonial rule or independence but tutelage. The danger that she would fall prey to European colonialism or internal inadequacy could be averted by remaking her society. In Cuba's case, the promise of independence eliminated the colonial option for the United States and led toward a substitute form of control that depended upon healthy doses of North American influence.

II

The mood in the United States was a self-confident one when Spain signed the treaty that transferred the island in December 1898—a document that bore the mark of no Cuban signatory. By this time, the United States saw itself as the sole victor over Spanish colonialism and oppression, a feat it presumed the Cubans to have been incapable of achieving. The rebels' thirty-year role in draining Spanish power and authority was ignored. This view found expression in the almost universal reference in North American literature to the "Spanish-American" War. Buoyed by the rapid success of her arms and by the old presumption that her influence over Cuba was inevitable, Washington began military occupation of the island with great expectations. The U.S. administrators wished to establish gradually in

[15] The quotations are from Healy, *The United States in Cuba*, p. 179, and Louis A. Pérez, Jr., *Cuba Under the Platt Amendment: 1902–1934* (Pittsburgh: University of Pittsburgh Press, 1986), p. 50.

[16] Margaret Crahan, "Religious Penetration and Nationalism in Cuba: U.S. Methodist Activities, 1898–1958." Paper presented to the Yale conference on Cuban history and society, Seven Springs, Conn., Oct. 1977; Healy, *The United States in Cuba*, ch. 15.

Cuba the open economy and republican machinery whose absence had been, in their minds, the flaw in Spanish rule. The presence of these elements, they believed, would assure the stability, conservative administration, and rational economic order that would create the soil in which U.S. influence could flourish. Since most of these U.S. officials were annexationists,[17] they believed that eventually, under moderate leaders chosen by Washington, and with an economy made robust by close ties to the United States, Cubans would discover union with North America to be the only assurance of their continued prosperity and safety from racial and political turmoil. Those North Americans who objected to annexation differed principally in viewing the result of U.S. influence to be a North American-style republic with close ties to her northern sister.

While the question of whether U.S. influence in Cuba would in the end be more or less formal was held in abeyance, the U.S. military government set about establishing the basis for such influence. The institutions of the Cuban independence movement—the Liberation Army, the Provisional Government, the Cuban Revolutionary Party—never having been recognized by Washington, were now ignored and eventually disbanded. The impoverished rebel soldiers were paid seventy-five dollars each to disarm and return to their homes. A U.S.-created and directed rural guard took its place. Leaders of the Cuban army and government who accepted the occupation regime were given subordinate posts in the U.S. military government. United States investments were encouraged, and major revision of the Spanish tariff—a goal Washington had sought for over a century—was set in motion. Teams of North American experts examined the mineral, agricultural and human resources of the island to determine the proper means of exploiting its wealth.[18]

Any attempt to control the affairs of Cuba had to be made without pronouncing a formal policy of colonial rule or forceable annexation. Fortunately, the process of "Americanization" could be pursued without a particular status for Cuba as its conclusion since almost all North Americans believed that an increase in U.S. influence was necessarily good. Nevertheless, the genius of the expanding North American republic had to express itself to some degree through the fostering of popular institutions. Hence, the "Americanization" of Cuba required that Cubans be helped to hold elections and write a constitution. Since almost all of the U.S. divisional commanders (who administered the several zones of occupation) consid-

---

[17] Pérez, *Cuba Between Empires*, pp. 271–74.

[18] Jules R. Benjamin, *The United States and Cuba: Hegemony and Dependent Development, 1880–1934* (Pittsburgh: University of Pittsburgh Press, 1977), pp. 6–12. The origins of the Rural Guard are discussed in Louis A. Pérez, Jr., *Army Politics in Cuba* (Pittsburgh: University of Pittsburgh Press, 1976), pp. 9–16.

ered Cuba unready for self-government and expected annexation to be the result of growing North American influence, they intended to oversee the process of republic-building quite closely. The primary task was to control the election process as much as possible. United States officials realized that the Spanish and Cuban upper classes were most favorable to annexation and that the peasantry was least so. This fact, and their own elitism, led them to place restrictions on suffrage that discriminated against the poor. Despite these precautions, however, representatives of the elite fared badly in the local elections of June 1900 and in the later vote to elect a constituent assembly to write a constitution.

Despite the disenfranchisement of the majority without property or literacy, nationalists connected with the struggle against Spain were generally successful candidates.[19] Surveying the result, the U.S. military governor, Leonard Wood, wrote to Senator Orville Platt that "the dominant party in the [constitutional] convention today contains probably the worst political element in the Island and they will bear careful watching."[20] Annexationists like Wood were loath to turn the government over to such people, but the McKinley administration could not safely undo the republicanizing process it had set in motion. The earlier opposition by Cubans to the franchise restrictions made it clear that they would react vehemently to any attempt to overturn the election results. The North American consensus allowed Washington to direct the affairs of Cuba but not in a manner that made manifest Cuban opposition.

United States officials in Washington and Havana pondered their dilemma and, goaded by the opposition party in the U.S. Congress, which asked why pacification was taking so long, eventually discovered a way out. The solution arrived at was to trade North American acceptance of the electoral outcome for guarantees that a sovereign Cuba would conduct itself in a manner consistent with U.S. interests. This required that the vague assumptions of U.S. hegemony, incubated for over a century, finally be spelled out. If the island had to be handed over to Cubans who might not be sensible enough to desire union with North America, then conformity with U.S. desires would have to be secured at the outset. Secretary of War Elihu Root had begun the process in January 1901 shortly after the Cuban constitutional convention began its meetings in Havana. He suggested to Secretary of State Hay the "advisability of requiring the incorporation into the fundamental law of Cuba of provisions to the following effect." Root then named the points that history has since recorded as the Platt Amendment: the right of the United States to intervene in Cuba, consent by the

---

[19] Healy, *The United States in Cuba*, pp. 129–32; Pérez, *Cuba Between Empires*, p. 311.
[20] Pérez, *Cuba Between Empires*, p. 316.

United States before Cuba could enter into a treaty with another state giving that state special rights, and naval bases for the United States on the island. To these, Senator Orville Platt's Committee on Relations with Cuba later added a U.S. veto over the extent of the Cuban government debt. In that form it was passed by both houses of the U.S. Congress.[21]

The Cubans were shocked by the tightness of the bonds decreed by the U.S. Congress. Public demonstrations across the island registered their strong dissent. In the deferential language they had already learned, the convention delegates responded to Washington that "some of these stipulations are not acceptable, inasmuch as they modify the independence and sovereignty of Cuba."[22] The Cuban argument carried little weight with the administration, which felt that even with these guarantees it was forgoing a degree of control over Cuba that it had a right to expect. Secretary of War Root felt that the restrictions represented the "extreme limit of this country's indulgence in the matter of the independence of Cuba."[23] Indeed, U.S. officials found nothing contradictory in a document infringing Cuban sovereignty, whose first article stated: "Cuba shall never enter into any treaty or other compact with any foreign power or powers which will impair or tend to impair the independence of Cuba."[24]

When the members of the constitutional convention refused to make the Platt Amendment a part of their constitution as required by the United States, Washington threatened to extend the military occupation until they did so. Root emphasized to McKinley that "no constitution can be put into effect in Cuba . . . until they have acted upon this question of relations in conformity with this act of Congress."[25] However, as noted above, McKinley could not be openly imperial. Such a stance would challenge the belief in North America that the provisions of the Platt Amendment were for the good of Cuba. More immediately, a public ultimatum by Washington would provoke the anti-imperialist minority in the U.S. Congress, an unattractive prospect in view of the damage inflicted upon the expansionist foreign policy of the administration by the ongoing rebellion in the Philippines. These domestic considerations led Root to appease the Cubans, though he held fast to the U.S. demands. He privately informed representatives of the convention delegates that the right of intervention would not be employed indiscriminately and only as a last resort. After much threat-

---

[21] Healy, *The United States in Cuba*, pp. 153–54, 162–64, 166. Opposition to the Platt Amendment in the United States is surveyed in Foner, *Spanish-Cuban-American War*, II, ch. 26.

[22] Smith, *What Happened*, p. 127.

[23] Pérez, *Cuba Between Empires*, p. 322.

[24] Smith, *What Happened*, p. 125.

[25] Pérez, *Cuba Between Empires*, p. 325.

ening and cajoling behind the scenes, a majority of the convention was finally induced to approve the special rights that the United States demanded. Several months later, after the assassination of McKinley had elevated Theodore Roosevelt to the presidency, Leonard Wood acknowledged to the new chief executive that "there is, of course, little or no independence left Cuba under the Platt Amendment."[26] Placing the defense of U.S. interests within the core statute of the Cuban republic assured that Cuban independence would not challenge—indeed, that it would express—the hegemony that North Americans had long expected to enjoy on the island.

ANOTHER ASPECT of North American hegemony was the belief that Cuba served as a natural market for U.S. goods. By the turn of the twentieth century, when the movement of U.S. capital had become as natural and beneficent as the cargoes of the clipper ships had been, hegemony in Cuba included unimpeded access for U.S. investments as well as goods. Moreover, powerful North American corporations were being put together to exploit the opportunities opened by the removal of Spanish control and the new assurance of long-term U.S. influence.[27] Under the tenure of the U.S. military government, an economic relationship that would gain access for U.S. capital to the unexploited resources and devastated plantations of the island was set in motion. Governor Leonard Wood promulgated decrees that facilitated construction of railroads and ownership of plantations by North Americans.[28]

All did not run smoothly with the plan to open Cuba to a flood of North American capital. Washington ran into trouble with anti-monopoly forces in the U.S. Congress. Just as some North Americans wielded the weapon of anti-colonialism to press for a narrow interpretation of "pacification," others used popular opposition to the trusts in an attempt to prevent powerful U.S. corporations from exploiting Cuba under the protection of military occupation. Having had to work its way around the Teller Amendment, Washington was faced with another act of Congress—the Foraker resolution—which forbade the occupation authorities from granting franchises or concessions. The author of the bill, Senator Joseph Foraker, feared that these favors would go to North American monopolists who would then press for an indefinite continuation of U.S. rule in order to protect their

---

[26] Healy, *The United States in Cuba*, p. 178. Promise of closer trade ties to the United States were used by Wood to make the Platt Amendment more acceptable to Cubans. See Foner, *Spanish-Cuban-American War*, II, p. 620.

[27] Benjamin, *Hegemony*, p. 8.

[28] Pérez, *Cuba Between Empires*, p. 359.

interests.[29] Governor Wood strongly opposed the ban on concessions because he held that U.S. capital was necessary to bring political stability to the island and draw it eventually into the Union. Wood went so far as to define the elusive state of "pacification" as one in which capital was free to invest and secure in the fruits of its investment. With the help of the War Department, Wood managed to evade the ban, issuing revocable permits and employing other devices. In the final analysis, however, U.S. investors found security less directly through the Platt Amendment, which seemed to guarantee that Cuba would respect the rights of U.S. capital after independence.[30]

The administration's plan for close trade ties between the United States and Cuba also ran into opposition in Congress, in this instance from protectionists worried about a flood of cane sugar. North American beet-sugar growers and refiners also availed themselves of the weapon of anti-monopolism, pointing out that the principal beneficiary of such imports would be the East Coast cane-sugar refiners, most of whom had been gathered into Henry O. Havemeyer's American Sugar Refining Company. Havemeyer's company controlled almost ninety percent of the U.S. market for refined sugar. Protectionists had an easy target when they attacked the "sugar trust." As a result, the key element of the trade program—reduction of the tariff on Cuban cane—was delayed until 1903, by which time Havemeyer had eliminated the objections of the beet-sugar refiners by buying them out, too. Havemeyer did not have the last word, however. Pressure from the Justice Department forced him to sell off most of his beet-sugar holdings in 1913.[31]

By and large, the removal of Spanish control and the works of the U.S. occupation cleared the way for the rapidly expanding U.S. economy to extend itself throughout the island without the hindrance of Spanish mercantilism or Cuban sovereignty. Nevertheless, the industrial and capital exporters' plans for an economic protectorate in Cuba would come under periodic assault by agricultural protectionists with influence in the U.S. Congress. The massive U.S. sugar investments on the island were arranged by large New York banking houses in conjunction with the major eastern-seaboard sugar-refining interests. However, the door to the U.S. sugar market that alone made this investment profitable was guarded by congressional committees under pressure from beet-sugar growing and refining interests in the Midwest and West. It was these committees that set the level

[29] Foner, *Spanish-Cuban-American War*, II, pp. 468–71.

[30] Healy, *The United States in Cuba*, pp. 82–84, 191–93.

[31] Benjamin, *Hegemony*, pp. 11–12; Jenks, *Colony*, p. 29. Also see Alfred S. Eichner, *The Emergence of Oligopoly: Sugar Refining as a Case Study* (Baltimore: Johns Hopkins University Press, 1969); Foner, *Spanish-Cuban-American War*, II, ch. 29.

of the sugar tariff and (after 1934) of the sugar quota. The clash between these two economic interest groups highlighted one of the most frustrating aspects of Cuba's economic dependency. Full cooperation with the eastern interests—and the loss of control over her economy that it entailed—did not even assure her of a just reward. The beet interests periodically sought to break the system of economic integration devised by Wall Street. During these contests, the outcome of which were vital to them, the Cubans stood as mere spectators. Thus the Cuban republic would become dependent not simply upon North American corporations but upon the unpredictable outcome of tariff contests in the U.S. Congress between representatives of farmers and sugar refiners.[32] While a particularly painful aspect of Spanish rule had been that it was weak, a special burden of U.S. hegemony would be that it contained internal conflicts.

If North American economic hegemony failed to solve the problem of differing U.S. economic interests, its political hegemony failed to solve the problem of Cuban nationalism. The heroes of the liberation movement were deemed by the mass of Cubans to be their natural leaders. These were usually military men, generally darker in skin color and more militant in their nationalism than the Creole leadership as a whole. They were more popular than the moderates, who had for the most part spent the war years in exile, lobbying for U.S. intervention. It was the latter group that contained those Creoles who had hoped at one time for autonomy under Spain or annexation to the United States. Quite naturally, Washington looked to these moderates in its efforts to find responsible leaders for the island.[33] But as the North Americans discovered, these moderates could not compete at the polls with the more uncompromising *independentistas* unless they, too, spoke the emotive language of Cuban nationalism. As a result, Washington eventually resigned itself to having its hegemony mediated by an elected Cuban government. What it never figured out was how to trust nationalistic officeholders or, alternatively, how to give moderate officeholders enough leeway to make them appear credible to Cuban voters.

At a deeper level, Washington's problem was not simply that it had little confidence in Cuban leaders. It had removed the base from which autonomous leaders might arise. Though impeded by its republican ideology, Washington had used its tremendous wealth and power to bully, bribe, and lure each of the institutions of the long liberation struggle into its hegemonic design. The Cuban Revolutionary Party, the Provisional Government, and the Liberation Army, drained by the unequal contest with Spain, were finally undone by a removal of Spanish rule that left political power

---

[32] Benjamin, *Hegemony*, pp. 6, 24–25.
[33] Foner, *Spanish-Cuban-American War*, II, pp. 456, 458, 462.

and public office in the hands of North Americans. Each of the organizations of the independence rebellion, already at odds with one another over the conduct of the war, turned to Washington in the hope that cooperation would give it advantage over its domestic rivals and eventually primacy in the state structure being built by the occupation authorities. Instead of competing for state power as elements of a victorious independence movement, they competed for the favor of the U.S. military governor.[34] The once-powerful planter elite was absorbed into U.S. hegemony as well. As their war-ravaged and heavily mortgaged properties were sold to North American investors, they, too, turned to Washington for an alternative path to social and economic mobility. By fostering the demobilization of the opponents of colonial rule—the army and the party of liberation and the Creole elite—Washington helped to sever each from its crucial identification with Cuban nationhood. Thereafter, neither the government, the army, nor the economic elite could be effectively nationalist, while over the years nationalism came to reside in movements against the state, the military, and the bourgeoisie.

III

The Cuban republic began its life on May 20, 1902, without any institution of its own making. Her state and her army were now North American creations, her social structures those molded by Spanish hands over the centuries. This alien framework rested upon a fundamental statute modeled after that of the United States and bearing the stigma of the Platt Amendment, which gave the United States the right to intervene. In language blending North American innocence and hypocrisy, this right of intervention was to be exercised "for the preservation of Cuban independence."[35] Tension was built into this system because most Cubans considered intervention and independence incompatible.

The weaknesses of the system were hidden to some extent by the revival of the Cuban economy after 1900. Washington had sweetened the pill of the Platt Amendment by the trade treaty that gave Cuban sugar privileged access to the North American market. The Cubans had made such access one of their principal requests, even though Washington obtained in return the practical elimination of Cuban barriers to the entry of U.S. goods. Few of them heeded Martí's admonition: "Whoever says economic union says political union. The nation that buys, commands. The nation that sells,

[34] The divisions within the independence movement and its reaction to the U.S. occupation are described in Pérez, *Cuba Between Empires*, chs. 12, 13, and 15. Much of the discussion here is based upon Pérez's account.

[35] Platt Amendment, 1902, article III, cited in Smith, *What Happened*, p. 125.

serves."[36] The trade bond was sealed on the U.S. side as well since more and more of the sugar entering from Cuba was coming from U.S.-owned mills. The tight trading connections—which led Cuba to import almost exclusively from the United States—reinforced the island's monocultural economy and deepened its economic dependency on North America. Nevertheless, the flood of U.S. capital and the rising price of sugar did much to underwrite Cuban prosperity in the first two decades of the century.[37] This prosperity was unevenly shared by the island's inhabitants but did make manifest the rewards of the new economic orientation, especially to those Cubans who were able to position themselves to profit directly from the trade connection.

The U.S. economic influence and the growth it brought to Cuba made the new relationship viable but at the same time weakened its long-run prospects. It tied the island's economy to the tempo and direction of the North American economy. It did so to such an extent that for decades all important transactions were based upon the U.S. dollar. Cuba did not create a national bank until 1948. Foreign trade and investment were almost wholly North American so that one set of foreign interests could not be played against another. The U.S. economic presence was tremendous. The value of U.S.-owned land on the modest-sized island surpassed North American holdings in any other foreign nation. By the 1920s, Cuba was the sixth largest market for U.S. goods.[38] The flood of products from large-scale enterprises in North America prevented the creation of a strong Cuban manufacturing sector. Cuban governments could not effectively protect domestic producers because the entry of U.S. goods was tied to access to the North American sugar market. As constituted, the island's economy could not function without such access.

Cuban production as well as trade fell under intense North American influence. During the first two decades of the twentieth century, North American investors bought out much of the undervalued or overmortgaged sugar properties of the old Creole elite. United States corporations also purchased large tracts of new land and built modern, high-capacity sugar mills, intensifying a process of land concentration and centralization of pro-

[36] José Martí, "The Monetary Congress of the American Republics," 1891, reprinted in Foner, ed., *Inside the Monster*, pp. 368–82.

[37] The period of prosperity is examined in Alvarez Díaz et. al., *A Study on Cuba*, ch. 21. By 1927, U.S.-owned mills accounted for about eighty-two percent of Cuban sugar production. See Jenks, *Colony*, pp. 282–84.

[38] The Cuban monetary system is examined in Henry C. Wallich, *Monetary Problems of an Export Economy: The Cuban Experience, 1914–1947* (Cambridge: Harvard University Press, 1950). Cuba did not establish state-controlled economic development institutions until the 1950s. See Jorge Domínguez, *Cuba: Order and Revolution* (Cambridge: Harvard University Press, 1978), pp. 33, 92. The trade data are from Benjamin, pp. 116–18.

duction that had begun before the war. This development reduced many sugar planters who had ground their own cane in small mills to the status of renters or small-scale growers who now sold their cane to one of the few huge industrial mills (*centrales*) that came to control sugar production.[39] Even those few Cuban mill owners who prospered were tightly bound to North American influence. For the most part, the United States supplied the technology, machinery, technicians, long-haul transportation, financing, and market for the sugar crop. As a result, Cuban sugar millers never articulated a self-interest distinct from that of their North American counterparts. Moreover, by depriving the Creole elite of an independent economic base and by turning it into a dependent of U.S. power and dollars, the United States transformed that class, whose authority and legitimacy were crucial to the social stability sought by Washington, into symbols and vehicles of North American influence.

As U.S. capital sped the consolidation of sugar milling, the huge new *centrales*, voracious in their demand for cane, expanded the acreage under their control. In doing so they pushed the surrounding farmers off the land, turning them into field hands (for the intense three-to-four-month sugar harvest) or into workers in the mill and its associated industrial and transportation facilities.[40] As it did so, U.S. capital was helping to create the insecure rural proletariat that would become fertile ground for the propagation of radical economic programs.

IV

Another victim of intense North American influence was the ideology of Cuban independence. Martí's nationalism had been anti-colonial rather than anti-Spanish. He was a child of Spanish parents and maintained that "all virtuous Spaniards are also Cuban."[41] His principal aim was the unity and dedication of the new generation of independence fighters and the framework for the new Cuba that would be built by that generation. His death, and the bitter, prolonged war of liberation that followed it, reoriented the thinking of independence leaders, focusing it on removal of the massive Spanish military presence and on gaining North American support for that daunting task. Even the PRC now came under the influence of annexationists within its ranks. When Spanish power collapsed in the wake of a direct U.S. invasion, the formidable, centuries-old colonial master

[39] Dudley Seers, ed., *Cuba: The Economic and Social Revolution* (Chapel Hill: University of North Carolina Press, 1964), pp. 74–75, 78–79.

[40] Guerra y Sánchez, *Sugar and Society in the Caribbean*, pp. xxix, xxxvii–xxxviii, 87–88, 93.

[41] Kirk, *Martí*, p. 111.

suddenly disappeared and, just as suddenly, the fruits of victory fell into North American hands. Without unity or a program for guiding an independent Cuba, the liberation movement found itself unprepared to cope with a U.S. rule that was both more powerful and more flexible than that of Spain. The independence leaders were not only without an effective ideology, they lacked an independent economic base as well. Most were men of modest means whose wealth had been confiscated or expended in the independence struggle.[42] Their only remaining assets were political, and these were now mortgaged to Washington, which until 1902 controlled access to public office on the island.

After the granting of semi-sovereignty, the impoverished independence leaders—many of whom had already made their peace with partial independence by accepting posts in the U.S. occupation government—sought public office as the only available path to social status and personal solvency. Both of these advantages normally would have been gained by the liberation leaders through the usurpation of the wealth and power of the Spaniards. But the U.S. occupation had served as guarantor of existing economic rights on the island, and Spanish property had been protected.[43] After 1902, while market forces effected important changes in the island's economy to the benefit of North American investors, Washington barred the way to any politically inspired effort by Cubans to transform the social order. As a result, the former independence leaders were unable to use political power for social ends. While their role in the struggle against Spain now made them successful candidates for office, their Hispanic heritage and U.S. injunction inclined them to use their government posts for private rather than public gain. Cuban politics did not produce powerful or popular leaders. It brought forward instead those who were successful at aggregating large numbers of votes through shrewd electoral combinations and at avoiding the wrath or gaining the blessing of Washington. This same tendency prevented the Cuban republic from producing ideologically or socially based parties of consequence.[44] Even the Liberal Party, which had led the fight against the Platt Amendment, soon turned to advocating U.S. military intervention in the hope of advancing its political fortunes.[45] Without strongly based and politically distinct parties and without leaders willing to direct the state toward important social goals, Cuban politics was personalist, corrupt and, at times, violent. Though Washington's own power over the island did much to assure this outcome, it could see in the

[42] Pérez, *Cuba Under the Platt Amendment*, pp. 56–59.
[43] Ibid.
[44] Domínguez, *Order and Revolution*, pp. 18–19, 38–40.
[45] Domínguez, *Order and Revolution*, p. 39.

THE PHILIPPINES: "What yer got?"
CUBA: "Pie."
THE PHILIPPINES: "Where'd yer git it?"
CUBA: "Mah Uncle Sam gin it to me; any maybe ef you was half way
    decent he' gin you some."
R. C. Bowman, *Minneapolis Tribune*, 1901

result only confirmation of its belief that self-government lay beyond the
ability of Cubans.

   The initial U.S. response to the weakness of Cuban politics was to assure
that only the "best" men held office. Unable to procure leadership for the
educated Spanish elite because of the popular repudiation of the colonial
era, the United States had turned to the moderate Creole landowners. But

72

UNCLE SAM TO PORTO RICO: "And to think that bad boy came near being your brother!"
Chicago Inter Ocean, 1905

the latter, as we have seen, could not compete successfully for office with the leaders of the independence struggle. In 1902, without hope of getting the "good element" to run the island, Washington turned over office to those of the independence generation who were willing to govern within the framework set by U.S. interests. Thereafter, the State Department be-

Cuba's Freedom Is Not Far Off
Thomas May, *Detroit Journal*, 1907

gan a long duel with these men over which Cuban policies were compatible with those interests.

Washington had not realized it at the time, but placing government in the hands of former independence leaders, however cooperative they might be, sealed the fate of annexationism. North American anti-imperialism—as both fact and myth—required a demonstrable Cuban willingness to join the Union. The politics of the Cuban republic, however, made a fetish of independence, a state all the more desirable because it had not been consummated. Cuban politicians could not formally remove the legal sovereignty that was the only tangible evidence of independence. The annexationist mood altered in North America as well when the flood of immigrants around the turn of the century heightened earlier fears of absorbing "nonwhite" peoples. Moreover, those who thought Cubans unworthy of citizenship were now complemented by those who saw the island's independence as a pledge redeemed and as proof that—protectorates, battleships, and punitive expeditions notwithstanding—the United States had not, indeed could not, become a colonial power. For their part, U.S. business interests in Cuba found more than sufficient protection in the right of intervention and the trade agreement. North American sugar growers added to the new consensus their preference for keeping Cuba independent and thus outside

Golly, I've Gone an' Did It Again!
J. H. Donahey, *Cleveland Plain Dealer*, 1912

the tariff wall.[46] The century-long idea that Cuba would gravitate into the Union died a quiet death in both Havana and Washington sometime during the first decade of the twentieth century.

Natural gravitation having been superseded by Cuban independence, its old corollary—that the United States would determine the island's future— had to give way to a more modest project. This new project would have to reckon with Cuban nationalism. It would also have to reflect the needs of

[46] The decline of annexationist opinion is discussed in Ramón Eduardo Ruiz, *Cuba: The Making of a Revolution* (Amherst: University of Massachusetts Press, 1968), pp. 27–31.

Another component of the decline of annexationism in the United States was the failure of large numbers of its citizens to emigrate to Cuba. It was only on the Isle of Pines, just off the southwest coast of Cuba, that significant numbers of North Americans established themselves. The U.S. Senate attempted to keep alive the possibility of retaining sovereignty over this area by continually postponing ratification of the treaty formally returning it to Cuba. Nevertheless, the U.S. Supreme Court acknowledged in 1907 that the island was Cuban territory, a status which the Senate finally formalized in 1925. See Thomas, *Pursuit*, pp. 500–3.

the new U.S. economic and cultural expansionism, as the doctrine of political gravitation had reflected those of an earlier landed expansionism. Washington only dimly perceived the conflict inherent in meeting the requirements of both Cuban nationalism and its own new, dynamic expansionism.

If Cuba herself was no longer naturally connected to the United States, her interests, it was presumed in Washington, still were. Proper political and economic behavior would be that modeled along North American lines. Moreso than anywhere else in Latin America, the Hispanic society of Cuba was expected to act out an Anglo-Saxon role. To its surprise, however, and despite its tremendous economic presence and pervasive political influence, the United States was unable to construct properly functioning Cuban institutions. In the first decades of its relationship with the new republic, Washington encountered a host of difficulties.

In the face of Cuban "instability," Washington's first instinct was to protect its economic interests. On several occasions between 1902 and the mid-1920s, the United States intervened physically in the affairs of Cuba to protect U.S. capital from attack or to assure that the violent quarrels of Cuban politicians did not interfere with (or, worse yet, raise challenges to) such investments. United States forces occupied (and governed) the island from 1906 to 1909 and were stationed in Oriente from 1917 to 1923 for the protection of U.S. property from labor unrest and political insurgency.[47]

The defense of U.S. interests by military means was only one aspect of Washington's response to Cuban instability. Since the free flow of U.S. capital and goods was held to be both a precondition for stability as well as its result, respect by Cubans for the U.S. economic presence was both prevention and cure for the ills of Cuban politics. As a result, the promotion of U.S. economic interests and the stabilization of Cuban politics were mutually reinforcing goals. In some ways, Cuba was a model for the Dollar Diplomacy era during which the State Department crafted foreign policy toward Latin America so as to protect U.S. trade and investments while at the same time calling upon North American capitalists to invest in such a way as to advance the growing geopolitical goals of the United States in the Circum-Caribbean area.[48] This intertwining of goals was particularly intimate in Cuba, where the U.S. economic stake was so large and where its political influence was legitimated by a century of gravitational pull and now by the Platt Amendment.

The defense of U.S. economic interests became enmeshed not only with

[47] Thomas, pp. 530–31, 533.

[48] Dick Steward, *Money, Marines and Mission* (Lanham, Md.: University Press of America, 1980), pp. 13–15; Arthur P. Whitaker, "From Dollar Diplomacy to the Good Neighbor," *Inter-American Economic Affairs* 4:4 (1951), pp. 13–15.

the desire to achieve political stability but with a larger desire to remake and purify Cuban society. This was so because the island was still somehow not a separate nation and because North America had entered its "Progressive Era." During the period of landed expansion, "inferior" peoples had been brushed aside. In the new age of market expansion, however, the goal was not to drive people away but to turn them into productive workers and consumers of foreign manufactured goods. North American progressives demonstrated even greater concern for backward peoples; they wished to improve them. One strain of reform was moralistic, concerned with personal vices and unorthodox behavior; another was managerial, concerned with easing the tensions of social change, while yet another was paternalistic (and sometimes egalitarian), concerned with protecting the victims of industrialization and limiting the power of magnates. Each of these streams flowed together in North American politics, and together they also informed broad policies for dealing with Cuban delinquencies.[49]

As each of the failings of Cuban politics manifested itself—armed rebellion by defeated politicians, governmental corruption, police repression, labor agitation, racial unrest, rigged elections—reformers sought to solve them with doses of North American middle-class values and behavior. Washington employed its political leverage in Cuba to bring about "honest" elections and thus prevent electoral rebellion to eliminate corruption and to draw up laws that would treat foreign capital fairly. The high point of political reformism came in 1919 when General Enoch Crowder was sent to Cuba as special representative of the U.S. president. Crowder's job was to oversee the formulation of a proper electoral code so that Cubans would come to accept the results of elections. When the contested Cuban presidential election of 1920 demonstrated that electoral rules were not effective in controlling political misbehavior that stemmed from deeper sources, Crowder returned in 1921 with plans—and demands—for the reformation of large areas of Cuban politics and government.[50]

Crowder's efforts to press political reforms were complicated when the sugar market took one of its periodic plunges at the end of 1920, thrusting the Cuban economy into a sharp recession. The economic crisis highlighted the need for economic as well as political reforms. In the midst of the financial panic, Cuban president Alfredo Zayas, having perfected techniques

[49] For an examination of North American progressivism, see Robert Wiebe, *The Search for Order*, chs. 5–7; Hofstadter, *The Age of Reform*, chs. 4–6; Daniel T. Rogers, "In Search of Progressivism," in Stanley Kutner and Stanley Katz, eds., *The Promise of American History* (Baltimore: Johns Hopkins University Press, 1982), pp. 113–32.

[50] Robert F. Smith, *The United States and Cuba: Business and Diplomacy, 1917–1960* (New York: Bookman Associates, 1960), pp. 86–98; Pérez, *Cuba Under the Platt Amendment*, pp. 195–213.

of corruption begun by his predecessors, attempted to sustain government spending so as to go on rewarding his political followers. The sugar crash had eliminated most sources of government income and Zayas turned to the expediency of a loan from J. P. Morgan and Company. Crowder saw his opening and refused to sanction a loan (under article II of the Platt Amendment) until Zayas replaced his existing Cabinet with an "honest" one of Crowder's choosing. Zayas consented and, the honest Cabinet having been installed, the loan was provided. The money arrived in time to save Zayas from fiscal and, more importantly, political and personal embarrassment. Thus fortified, Zayas soon liberated himself from his "honest" Cabinet.[51] North American reformers began to wonder whether Cubans could ever be made to act properly.

Each of Crowder's demands upon the Cuban executive had been justified in Washington by broader and broader interpretations of the Platt Amendment. At the same time, however, the State Department was moving away from actual or even threatened military intervention and toward a policy of preventive interference that would save the United States from having to pick up the pieces of the broken political system, as it had done—without much effect—under a second military government from 1906 to 1909. Indeed, Washington was beginning to figure out that its right of military intervention was itself a source of instability. Quarreling Cuban political factions attempted to bring about such intervention whenever they thought its weight would fall most heavily on their opponents.[52]

Other factors guided the United States toward less dramatic forms of intervention in Cuba as well. After World War I, the possibility of European intervention in the Caribbean area became more and more remote and thus could no longer be used by Washington to justify military landings. Another inhibiting factor was the growing anti-Yankee feeling in Latin America, on the rise since the intensification of North American economic and military activity in the late 1890s. By the 1920s, moreover, opinion in the United States, disillusioned by the political outcome of World War I, had become wary of the claim that North American armies could change the behavior of alien people. In this context, military intervention in Cuba was sure to bring forth opposition in the U.S. Congress and intensify already strained diplomatic relations with hemisphere nations. Washington had yet to understand the potential of Cuban nationalism to thwart its aims on the island, but a broader, more militant Latin American nationalism and

[51] Thomas, *Pursuit*, pp. 553–56.
[52] Louis A. Pérez, Jr., *Intervention, Revolution and Politics in Cuba* (Pittsburgh: University of Pittsburgh Press, 1978), ch. 9.

a growing North American isolationism were already narrowing its options, even in its own sphere of influence.[53]

Under these larger pressures and as each of the carefully constructed North American reforms was eluded by the normal operation of Cuban politics, State Department reformers eventually lost their progressive zeal. As time passed, Washington began to realize the counterproductive nature not simply of military intervention but of political purification as well. More difficult for Washington to discern, however, was the extent to which its own political and economic presence on the island was a source of the social tensions and political malpractice that frustrated its plans simultaneously to reform Cuba and to enhance North American interests. United States hegemony was an unrecognized source of the opportunism of Cuban politics. On a broader scale, the flood of U.S. capital in the first two and a half decades of the twentieth century had remade the island's productive system and in turn worked important changes in its social order. The tensions produced by these changes underlay the strikes, financial speculation, corruption, and racial conflict of the era as different groups of Cubans sought to secure for themselves the benefits of sugar boom or escape the dislocations that followed in its wake.

Washington's inability to "reform" Cuban society resulted not only from its own disruption of the island's social order but from the fact that Cuban society was not a backward form of North American society but rather a different culture. Four hundred years of Spanish rule and Spanish immigration had brought Catholicism, corporatism, elitism, and a concern with honor, lineage, and status that had very different social repercussions than did these traits in North America.[54] Washington's reformism presumed a commitment to individualism, party politics, and the Protestant ethic that quite naturally were uncharacteristic of Cuba. Yet so powerful was North America's influence that however unsuitable the terrain, she was able to a significant degree to override Hispanic forces—though not with the desired result. United States power, and the forced march, skewed modernization that it set in motion, weakened the old landholding pattern and social hierarchy that had sustained the *Hispanista* element of Cuban society and the non-materialist values on which the island's conservative institutions had rested. As we have seen, U.S. economic power also prevented the consolidation of a strong and independent private sector in commercial agriculture or industry. For the life of the Cuban republic, neither bourgeoisie nor ar-

---

[53] Benjamin, *Hegemony*, pp. 49–50.

[54] For studies of the Hispanic heritage in Latin America see essays by Richard M. Morse, Glen Dealy, Fredrick B. Pike, and Claudio Veliz in Howard J. Wiarda, ed., *Politics and Social Change in Latin America: The Distinct Tradition* (Amherst: University of Massachusetts Press, 1982).

istocracy could act as an effective obstacle to U.S. influence, nor, it might be added, as a barrier to radical challenges to that influence.

V

By the 1920s, Washington had moved away not only from military intervention but for the most part from preventive interference as well. It ended its close involvement in Cuban elections and accepted whomever the system brought forth. Direct U.S. interference shifted from the attempt to reform Cuban politics to an effort to guide the hand of the elected president. In the process, U.S. intervention ceased to be dramatic and episodic and became normal and ongoing.[55]

Just as Washington and Havana had begun to adjust to the new form of U.S. influence, economic collapse once again changed the rules of the game. Depression in the sugar industry after 1925 and the collapse of the world sugar market after 1929 produced a rapid and steep decline in the Cuban economy. By the early 1930s, wages on the island had fallen 50 to 75 percent and the value of Cuban exports plunged more than 80 percent.[56] This economic decline was more severe than that experienced by almost any other nation during the industrial depression. Economic collapse put into question the nature of Cuban ties to the United States and, most immediately, the informal alliance between Washington and the Creole leaders of the independence era. These leaders had accepted U.S. hegemony as unavoidable and had turned it into an opportunity to secure personal wealth through control of state revenues and by associating themselves with U.S. corporations. The collapse of the sugar market ended most of the rewards of being directly associated with North American hegemony. At the same time, Cuban politicians found themselves squeezed between Washington's desire for orthodox fiscal responses to depression and domestic pressures from the Cuban working class, the middle class, and growers, all of whom now faced intolerable living conditions.[57] These groups had expanded rapidly under the economic growth fueled by U.S. capital and rising sugar prices in the first two decades of the century. Grown numerous, if not healthy, on sugar boom, they now prepared to defend themselves from sugar collapse. As Washington settled into the comfortable pose of guiding

[55] Benjamin, *Hegemony*, pp. 26–27, 49–50, 65–68; Theodore P. Wright, Jr., "United States Electoral Intervention in Cuba," *Inter-American Economic Affairs* 13:3 (Winter 1959), pp. 50–71; Pérez *Cuba Under*, pp. 249–56.

[56] Le Riverend, *Economic History*, pp. 233–35; Alvarez Díaz, et al., *A Study on Cuba*, pp. 206, 351; José A. Duarte Oropesa, *Historiología cubana*, V (Hollywood, Calif., 1969), pp. 341, 354.

[57] Benjamin, *Hegemony*, ch. 3.

rather than purifying the island's political system, the social base on which that system rested was beginning to come apart.

The Cuban president whose fate it was to confront the new social tensions was Gerardo Machado, elected at the height of sugar prosperity in 1924. Initially, Machado's election seemed to confirm the wisdom of Washington's effort to end direct intervention in Cuban politics. Like many Cuban politicians, he had been associated with the U.S. occupation government and then with U.S. business interests. His candidacy had been supported by the large North American investors with a stake in the island. Machado associated himself with some of the aims of Cuban reformers and this, too, pleased Washington. The new low-key U.S. role in the island's affairs even allowed Machado to run a "nationalist" campaign, promising to advance Cuban interests and challenging the Platt Amendment in prudent terms. For a time, sugar boom enabled the new president to promote foreign interests while attending to domestic ones as well. As a result, Machado's initial standing with both Cubans and North Americans was high.[58]

Sugar prosperity had begun to recede in 1925 and by 1930 had become full-fledged collapse. Cuba's agricultural producers, her professionals and workers all looked to the popular president for relief. As the economic plunge steepened, Machado was forced more and more openly to choose between North American and Cuban interests. Under this pressure, his first instinct was to fortify the political ramparts around his presidency. He forestalled serious opposition from within the political arena by using his control of state funds and his backing from Washington and business interests to draw large elements of the opposition parties into a tightly controlled congressional coalition. For a time, his attentiveness to the interests of businessmen in general and his moderate nationalism protected him from all but working-class opposition—the first group to feel the effects of economic decline. Indeed, in 1927 his command of party politics was such that a compliant congress extended his term of office, and their own as well. A constituent assembly then called upon Machado to serve a second, extended term—to which he was elected (unopposed) in 1928.[59] Soon Machado had achieved full command over the rickety structure of Cuban politics. Thus fortified, he intended to ride out the trough of the sugar cycle.

No longer expecting to purify Cuban politics, Washington considered Machado an effective president. Before the depression became intense, he remained attentive to the welfare of North American investors. Moreover,

[58] Smith, *The United States and Cuba*, pp. 113–17; Jorge I. Domínguez, "Seeking Permission to Build a Nation: Cuban Nationalism and U.S. Response Under the First Machado Presidency," *Cuban Studies* 16 (1986), pp. 33–48.

[59] Benjamin, *Hegemony*, pp. 51–52; Luis E. Aguilar, *Cuba, 1933: Prologue to Revolution* (Ithaca, N.Y.: Cornell University Press, 1972), pp. 49–60.

the president's reformist rhetoric promised some of the same goals as those of the now defunct moralization program. Enoch Crowder, now serving as the first U.S. ambassador to Havana, found Machado much more cooperative than previous presidents. Machado's pseudo-constitutional extension of his mandate in the late 1920s did evoke private reservations among some within the State Department. Officially, however, Washington continued to give him its vital support.[60] Indeed, Machado's amalgamation of Cuba's party structure ended congressional bickering and seemed to provide the stability that had become the principal U.S. aim in Cuba. No one in Washington foresaw the social upheaval into which they were helping to guide the Cuban president.

VI

Machado had bought electoral monopoly at the price of political legitimacy. By raising constitutional questions about the extension of his term of office and his reelection, he assured that there would be an important political component to the economic tensions converging on the presidency. As Machado proved unwilling or unable to shift the burden of accelerating economic decline onto the North American-owned sector of the economy, the hollowness of his nationalism was exposed. The president already had a reputation for brutality in dealing with labor unrest; he now responded to growing opposition from small producer and middle-class organizations with an unprecedented police repression. Reformers, seeing that Machado had corrupted not only the day-to-day workings of government but the political system as a whole, joined the widening assault on presidential dictatorship. Many of Machado's enemies, observing that the president used his power to protect North American interests, turned naturally to the weapon of Cuban nationalism in order to secure relief from the extreme economic pressure or as a way of challenging the debased nature of the republic. The absence of U.S. criticism of the dictator reinforced his anti-nationalist image and brought Washington into the line of fire.[61]

By the early 1930s, economic collapse had brought to most Cubans a physical hardship unknown since the brutal independence war. Their pain was made sharper by the realization that semi-sovereignty denied them political institutions with which to ease their plight. By this time Machado faced a multi-faceted movement against his dictatorship. Before it spent itself, this movement produced the first radical nationalist insurgency of the post-independence era. It created a new generation of fervent nationalists

[60] Pérez, *Cuba Under*, pp. 244–48; Benjamin, *Hegemony*, p. 52.

[61] Jules R. Benjamin, "The Machadato and Cuban Nationalism, 1928–1932," *Hispanic American Historical Review* 55:1 (Feb. 1975), pp. 66–91.

who would serve as exemplars and martyrs to a later anti-dictatorial movement in the 1950s.

One component of this movement consisted of mainstream student organizations, which turned from demands for university reform to challenging the dictator and the Platt Amendment in the streets. A student left wing arose and denounced ''Yankee imperialism.''[62] Artists and intellectuals, more sensitive than most Cubans to the failure of independence-era idealism, had already clashed with the Cuban presidency when they denounced corruption under the Zayas administration. Impelled by the themes of Latinism, Indianism, and anti-Yankeeism spreading through Latin America in the 1920s, they now joined the assault on the Machado dictatorship.[63]

The Cuban middle class turned on the dictator as well. They had been augmented and distorted by the intense U.S. economic and cultural influence of the first two decades of the century. Now they reeled from the disappearance of the economic benefits that had made such influence palatable. Some continued to look to Washington for a way out of depression and dictatorship. They worked behind the scenes with the few remaining independent politicians to get Washington to force Machado to reopen the political arena. But other elements of the middle class turned to corporatist and protectionist measures to preserve their tenuous position between U.S. capital and Cuban labor. Some were even attracted to Marxism and others to Hispanic-oriented fascist or radical bourgeois organizations. Among the latter was the secret, terrorist ABC, which, at least initially, called for social discipline and state control of market forces.[64]

The intensity of the economic collapse and important changes in the Cuban working class were illustrated by the prominent role in the struggle against Machado played by the young Cuban Communist Party. While bourgeois forces were divided between allies and enemies of the dictator, and the middle class between moderate and radical challengers, working-class leadership in this period was confident and revolutionary. The party had been born only in 1925 and had shortly thereafter been banned by Machado. By 1930—after a period of intense organizing in which the party displaced the old anarcho-syndicalist leadership of the unions—dictatorship and depression had made it the almost undisputed master of a powerful

---

[62] Benjamin, ''The Machadato,'' pp. 72–74; Jaime Suchlicki, *University Students and Revolution in Cuba, 1920–1968* (Miami: University of Miami Press, 1969), pp. 24–29.

[63] Benjamin, ''The Machadato,'' pp. 76–77; Harry Swan, ''The Nineteen Twenties: A Decade of Intellectual Change in Cuba,'' *Revista Interamericana* 8:2 (Summer 1978), pp. 275–88.

[64] Benjamin, ''The Machadato,'' pp. 74–76; Pérez, *Cuba Under*, pp. 289–95; Samuel Farber, *Revolution and Reaction in Cuba, 1933–1960* (Middletown, Conn.: Wesleyan University Press, 1976), pp. 52–59.

labor federation. The party also attracted or influenced important student leaders and intellectuals.[65] As a result, the dictator and the State Department faced not only national but class-based resistance to their aims. Still, the party's mass revolutionary line, calling for the overthrow of imperialism, feudalism, "and the native bourgeoisie tied to them," isolated it from the nationalist and anti-dictatorial mainstream of the struggle against Machado.[66] Moreover, by raising the specter of revolution, it caused middle-class opposition to the dictatorship to be more conservative.

By 1933, the rift between the dictatorship and the middle class had reached the point where Machado's police and middle-class youth were engaged in urban warfare. Here and there in the countryside sugar workers were establishing "soviets" in mills that no longer needed their labor at any price. In August a wave of strikes by urban workers culminated in a general shutdown in Havana in which Communist-led unions played a prominent role. At the height of the shutdown, however, the Communist Party overreached itself and struck a deal with the dictator, trading recognition of its movement by the desperate president for an end to the strike.[67] Party leaders hoped that in doing so they were better positioning themselves for the impending proletarian revolution. The party badly misjudged the nature of the social upheaval, an error that, in subsequent decades, led it to exhibit great caution in its political actions. Moreover, the deal between the party and the hated dictator embittered relations between Communist and non-Communist radicals, a state of affairs that lasted to the end of the republic.

VII

As social tensions rose on the island, the Herbert Hoover administration sought to protect U.S. interests without invoking the Platt Amendment, despite the fact that its provisions and aims were being violated more flagrantly than ever before. Committed to stabilization through a powerful Cuban president, and with its eye on the negative response at home and abroad to the unproductive U.S. Marine campaigns against Sandino in Nicaragua, the State Department decided to stick with Machado. Initially, the United States was rewarded for its support. The Cuban president even continued to repay North American loans while government workers went un-

[65] Benjamin, "The Machadato," pp. 69–72, 81–86; James Petras, *Class, State and Power in the Third World* (London: Zed Press, 1981), pp. 195–200; Hobart Spalding, Jr., *Organized Labor in Latin America* (New York: Harper & Row, 1977), pp. 78–83.

[66] Partido Comunista de Cuba, *El Partido Comunista y los problemas de la revolución en Cuba* (La Habana: Comité Central, 1933), pp. 10–11.

[67] Benjamin, *Hegemony*, pp. 101–2.

paid and hunger spread throughout the Cuban countryside. By the early 1930s, however, Machado had no choice but to default; his government was bankrupt.[68] Hoover's ambassador to Havana, Harry F. Guggenheim, suggested to the State Department that given the U.S. inability to use its right of intervention, it would be best to revoke it, thus salvaging from the disaster some benefit to U.S. relations with Latin America.[69] Washington was in the process of putting the gunboat era firmly behind it but was slow to realize that the Platt Amendment had not become simply useless; it was actually dangerous. As the symbol—though hardly any longer the reality—of U.S. power in Cuba, the amendment had helped to inflame a renascent Cuban nationalism that now replaced corruption and instability as the principal threat to U.S. interests.

Cuban nationalism had gone into decline between 1898 and the 1920s. As noted above, many of the independence leaders, even those opposed to annexation, accepted semi-sovereignty and made a place for themselves within it. When the social and cultural tensions resulting from large U.S. investments were exacerbated by the corruption and aimlessness of Cuban politics and by the manifest failure of the idealism of the independence struggle, nationalism revived. However, just as independence sentiment in the nineteenth century had been divided between those who saw annexation and those who saw sovereignty as the goal, 1920s nationalism contained those who doubted and those who were confident about Cubans' capacity to rule themselves. Important reformers and intellectuals took up the theme of *decadencia*, the idea that Cuban culture was ill suited to sustain a republic because it had been so misshapen by colonial rule. Some members of this school were aristocratic conservatives, lamenting the end of elite rule in Cuba, but most were republicans and nationalists. The latter were often reformers who did not reject the North American view that Cuba needed close supervision. They opposed heavy-handed intervention but applauded many of the aims of the moralization program. This group of nationalist reformers was disoriented when Washington's purification program gave way to close ties to an increasingly domineering Cuban president.[70]

[68] Smith, *The United States and Cuba*, pp. 122–36; Benjamin, *Hegemony*, p. 122.

[69] Benjamin, *Hegemony*, pp. 68–69; Pérez, *Cuba Under*, pp. 295–99.

[70] The English-language literature on Cuban nationalism during this period is not extensive. See Benjamin, "The Machadato," pp. 66–91; Benjamin, *Hegemony*, pp. 26–27, 35, 38–44; Ramón Eduardo Ruiz, *Cuba: The Making of a Revolution*, ch. 2; C.A.M. Hennessy, "The Roots of Cuban Nationalism," *International Affairs* 39 (July 1963), pp. 346–58; Aguilar, *Cuba 1933*, pp. 29–32, 45–48, 60; Wyatt MacGaffey and Clifford Barnett, *Twentieth Century Cuba* (Garden City, N.Y.: Anchor Books, 1965), pp. 263–65; Antoni Kapcia, "Cuban populism and the myth of Martí," in *José Martí: Revolutionary Democrat*, Christopher Abel and Nissa Torrents, eds. (Durham, N.C.: Duke University Press, 1986), pp. 32–64.

The literature of decadencia includes Fernando Ortiz, *La decadencia cubana* (La Habana:

The other, optimistic strand of nationalist thought that appeared in the 1920s was associated with the anti-imperialism of the colonial territories and the Aprista and Leninist doctrines of the day. Borrowing more heavily from Martí than from Marx, however, it blamed the evils of Cuban politics on the denial of true independence by the United States and on the subsequent North American interventionism. Anti-hegemonic nationalists hardly noticed the declining influence of the Platt Amendment on U.S. policy, seeing its evil form in the U.S.-controlled economy and in the alliance between the State Department and the increasingly brutal Machado dictatorship.[71]

Unfortunately for U.S. interests, depression and dictatorship weakened the *decadencia* strain of Cuban nationalism and strengthened the anti-Plattist outlook. During the period of moralization, Cuban reformers who argued for the benefits of U.S. influence could describe Washington as an ally of reform. However, when the State Department began to make its peace with the Cuban political system, and when it even countenanced dictatorship, these pessimistic nationalists ran the risk of being associated with an enemy of reform. The *decadencia* perspective was also inhibited by its inability to galvanize important social forces. It could not overcome its elitism and its negative conception of *Cubanidad*. While it was outspoken in its condemnation of sugar monoculture and political opportunism, it failed to articulate solutions of which Cubans themselves might be the authors. *Decadencia* thinking survived as a literary and scholarly tradition but declined as an influential strain of Cuban nationalism.[72] This temporarily left the field to radical reformers who associated the corruption of Cuban business and politics with the absence of true independence. It was this angry nationalism, searching for a Cuban identity in opposition to the

La Universal, 1924); Carlos M. Trelles, "El proceso y el retroceso de la República de Cuba," *Revista bimestre cubana* 18 (1924), pp. 313–19, 345–64; Jorge Mañach, *La crisis de la alta cultura en Cuba* (La Habana: La Universal, 1925); Jorge Mañach, *Indagación del choteo* (La Habana: Editorial Lex., 1936); Fernando Ortiz, "Las responsabilidades de la E.E.U.U. en los males de Cuba," *Revista bimestre cubana* 33:2 (March–April 1934). Others who wrote in this vein include the important Cuban intellectuals Enrique José Varona and Cosme de la Torriente.

[71] During this period, the anti-hegemonic perspective can be found in Raúl Maestri, *El latifundismo en la economía cubana* (La Habana: Editorial Revista de Avance, 1929); Emilio Roig de Leuchsenring, *Los problemas sociales de Cuba* (La Habana: Imprenta El Ideal, 1927).

[72] Swan, *Revista Interamericana*, pp. 283–88. The classic study of sugar monoculture during this period is Ramiro Guerra y Sánchez, *Azúcar y población en las Antillas* (Madrid: Cultural S.A., 1935). Literature and the role of the intellectuals are examined in José Antonio Portuondo, *El contenido social de la literatura cubana*,- Jornadas #21 (México City: El Colegio de Mexico, 1944); Carlos Ripoll, *La generación del 23 en Cuba* (New York: Las Américas Pub. Co., 1968).

United States, that galvanized the rebellious youth of the anti-Machado struggle.

The Hoover administration, despite its lessened interference, found itself the target of the rising anti-Yankee nationalism. As the source of an overwhelming foreign presence and because of its silence on the burning issue of presidential dictatorship, Washington became an important focus of Cubans' anger at their economic and political condition. Moreover, as the struggle against Machado mobilized radical social elements—students, organized workers, and a vanguard revolutionary party—the angry anti-Plattist nationalism threatened to fuse opposition to dictatorship with the anti-bourgeois perspective rising from below. The Hoover administration, no longer willing to use its power directly and committed to a form of influence that operated through a Cuban political structure rapidly losing coherence, was unprepared to defend U.S. interests from the effects of social upheaval on the island.[73]

VIII

North American hegemony might have faced an even more formidable challenge if economic decline and political realignment in the United States had not brought the New Deal to power in 1933. The new administration brought an essential flexibility to U.S. relations with Cuba. Within a few months of his appointment, Franklin Roosevelt's ambassador to Havana, Sumner Welles, concluded that ties to Machado had to be broken. Still, Welles moved slowly, fearing that a precipitate break with the president would unravel the constitutional structure itself and thus open the gates to radical forces. Welles pressed Machado to resign and make way for a constitutionally designated successor. The dictator, naturally, resisted, but time was running out for both men. When the general strike was declared, Welles dropped his role as mediator and convinced the army to send the dictator into exile. Wholly abandoning the pretense of non-interference, Welles arranged the succession of a provisional president acceptable to Washington. He then extended U.S. influence outside the shrunken body of partisan politics and gathered a Cabinet for the new president that even included some of the middle-class radicals of the ABC.[74]

Welles's flexibility and his innovative use of U.S. hegemony seemed to have saved the day, but only momentarily. The social momentum soon

[73] Benjamin, *Hegemony*, pp. 65–71.

[74] Benjamin, *Hegemony*, ch. 6, discusses New Deal diplomacy in Cuba. The New Deal economic program for the island is examined in Jules R. Benjamin, "The New Deal, Cuba and the Rise of a Global Foreign Economic Policy," *The Business History Review* 51:1 (Spring 1977), pp. 57–78.

engulfed his provisional president in what Cubans refer to as the "Revolution of 1933." On September 5 student radicals joined a revolt by the
non-commissioned ranks of the army who were protesting their poor treatment by the officer corps. With the military temporarily headless and the
U.S.-inspired provisional president ineffectual, the students and sergeants
created their own provisional government headed by Ramón Grau San Martín. Grau surrounded himself with reformers and radicals who hoped to
make the Cuban state a tool of social reform and to change the structure of
the island's relationship with the United States, including the removal of
the hated Platt Amendment. For the first time in the history of the republic,
anti-Plattist nationalism had entered the presidential palace.[75]

Welles was greatly agitated by the undoing of his carefully orchestrated
end to the dictatorship. To revive his failed regime, he took the risk of
asking Washington to land U.S. forces, though only for a limited policing
action. He did not intend to accept Grau's government and described it to
the State Department as "frankly communistic." But the Platt Amendment
could not be disinterred. Roosevelt had too many domestic problems on his
plate, to say nothing of the persuasive arguments against military intervention that had emanated from both Republican and Democratic ranks during
the Hoover years. Moreover, F.D.R. was confronting financial interests at
home and thus was less than sympathetic to their demands for protection of
the large number of Cuban sugar properties that through default had come
into their possession. Finally, having just enunciated his Good Neighbor
policy, which seemed to promise greater respect for Latin American sovereignty and sensibility, Roosevelt was even more constrained than Hoover
from using force.[76]

While no longer prepared to intervene militarily, Washington was unwilling to let the Cuban revolt take its own course. Roosevelt sent U.S.
warships to the waters off the island for psychological effect and in case
they were needed to evacuate North Americans. Though greatly reduced in
value by the depression, the large U.S. economic stake in the island and
the old (though evolving) presumption of U.S. hegemony led the Roosevelt
administration to withhold diplomatic recognition and desperately needed
economic assistance in the expectation that the absence of U.S. blessing
would soon make Grau cooperative, or bring to power someone who was.[77]

The stick of non-recognition had a carrot tied to the end. New Deal policy toward Cuba not only accepted as unavoidable the demise of the old
independence leadership through which North American influence had

[75] Benjamin, *Hegemony*, pp. 128–39; Pérez, *Cuba Under*, pp. 301–21.
[76] Benjamin, *Hegemony*, pp. 139–48; Pérez, *Cuba Under*, pp. 324–26.
[77] Benjamin, *Hegemony*, pp. 150–60.

been conveyed, it also held out the possibility of a regulated North American sugar market (based upon quotas rather than tariffs) in which Cuban cane might reverse the drastic decline in its market share and be assured of a price above the current one, which was well below the cost of production of even the large U.S.-owned mills. The willingness of New Dealers to acknowledge the special vulnerability of the Cuban economy and to consider reform of the trade relationship came just in time to return important elements of the middle class and *decadencia* reformers to their previous North American orientation. These groups, spurred by the real fear of social revolution, readily placed their faith in New Deal agricultural marketing controls and in a Good Neighbor foreign policy that no longer paid obeisance to the god of private capital and disavowed gunboat diplomacy. Such a progressive North Americn perspective allowed liberal reformers in Cuba to adopt the popular anti-Plattist stance, as the latter no longer seemed synonymous with opposition to U.S. policy. The movement of these moderate elements back to the center dampened the polarization of Cuban politics brought on by sugar depression. Indeed, once the revolutionary period had passed, these elements formed the basis for a brand of New Deal liberalism (and later anti-fascism and anti-communism) in Cuban politics.[78] Of course, the subsequent Cuban liberalism did not carry the social weight that it did in the United States, nor was it confined to the political parameters of its North American variant.

Despite these long-term benefits to the U.S. position in Cuba, New Deal policy also sowed trouble in the future by reinvigorating the historic North American belief that Washington would solve Cuba's problems for her. In the nineteenth century, this perspective had derived from the North American belief in its racial and cultural superiority and in an inevitable destiny. In the reformist era that ran from the New Deal to the Alliance for Progress, the perspective was reinforced by the North American belief in its capacity to promote and manage social change. As in the Progressive Era, the new reformism led to an increase in the extent of U.S. interference in Cuba even as Plattist forms of intervention were finally ended.[79] Sumner Welles and his successor as ambassador, Jefferson Caffery, worked strenuously behind the scenes to convince both the former sergeants who now headed the Cuban military and the middle sectors that shunned the Grau regime to overthrow the provisional government because its radicalism blocked New Deal plans for Cuba.[80]

[78] Benjamin, *Hegemony*, pp. 171–80; Farber, *Revolution and Reaction*, ch. 3.

[79] This theme is examined in Jules R. Benjamin, "The Framework of United States Relations with Latin America in the Twentieth Century: An Interpretive Essay," *Diplomatic History* 11:2 (Spring 1987), pp. 91–112.

[80] Benjamin, *Hegemony*, pp. 160–70; Pérez, *Cuba Under*, pp. 330–32.

IX

The desire of the new Washington reformers to control the extent and direction of political and economic change in Cuba was abetted by the internal weakness of the Grau regime. Despite Welles's characterization, Grau's government was not revolutionary. It contained both moderate and radical elements and could look over one shoulder at a powerful left in which the Cuban Communist Party dominated. Over Grau's other shoulder was the Cuban army. This institution had just undergone its own revolution. The old officer corps had been removed. Former sergeant Fulgencio Batista had been named its new commander. The sergeants' revolt had been interest-oriented, reflecting tensions between the lower ranks and a corrupt officer corps. Batista had allowed himself to be carried forward by the wave of nationalism. Initially, he supported Grau, whose own seizure of power helped to justify that of the sergeants. Right- and left-wing challengers of the nationalist government were fended off by its protectors in the new military. Like most Cuban leaders, however, Batista had to come to grips with U.S. power, and the pragmatic commander soon realized the long-run disadvantages of alliance with a Cuban president who could not gain U.S. recognition.[81]

Grau's regime was chaotic. It was weak domestically because of its inability to provide economic relief. It was weak internationally because of its unwillingness to continue the traditional political and economic relationship with the United States. Though welcomed by many, active support for the government was confined to radical nationalist elements of the middle class. The regime challenged the United States rhetorically but had no economic or political base or consistent ideological perspective with which to confront U.S. power. When it became clear to Batista that Washington would never grant recognition or economic support to Grau, he began to respond to the urging of the U.S. ambassador that he install a friendlier regime. Realizing the strength of anti-Yankee nationalism among elements of the middle class and the power of the radical unions, Batista moved cautiously. Eventually, he arranged a transfer of power in January 1934 to Carlos Mendieta, whom Washington had indicated would be acceptable. By that time, Batista had consolidated his control over the army and now used it to suppress the militant Marxist and radical nationalist movements, whose resistance was not finally overcome until 1935.[82]

[81] Benjamin, *Hegemony*, ch. 9; Pérez, *Cuba Under*, pp. 321–29; Farber, *Revolution and Reaction*, ch. 3.

[82] Benjamin, *Hegemony*, pp. 167–70; Aguilar, *1933*, pp. 183–229; Farber, *Revolution and Reaction*, pp. 40–51; Pérez, *Cuba Under*, pp. 333–35.

X

By offering support to the new military and the middle class, Roosevelt's men moved just far enough to prevent the destruction of U.S. hegemony. But they did not move far enough to create the desired stability. The new administration accepted the demise of the discredited 1898 generation but worked diligently to prevent its replacement by a new generation of nationalists who might have gained the allegiance of the Cuban people.

The United States response to the revolution of 1933 was similar to its response to the earlier nationalism of the 1898-1902 period. Washington's original preference had then been annexation in alliance with conservative Creole leaders—not even excluding Spaniards. Eventually, as we have seen, Washington was forced to concede that the predominant wing of the anti-colonial rebellion was *independentista*. It then allied itself with those nationalists willing to live within the framework of the Platt Amendment.

In the 1930s, the shift of Cuban nationalism toward economic radicalism and anti-Yankeeism made another adjustment necessary. The moderates with whom the United States had been allied since 1902 became first corrupt and then dictatorial. Depression had finally wiped out what remained of the legitimacy that their role in the war with Spain had once given them. Public acclaim now moved to the anti-corruptionist, anti-militarist, and anti-imperialist nationalists who made up the non-revolutionary wing of the movement against Machado. To maintain its influence without direct rule, the United States now had to loosen its ties to the moderates of 1902 and embrace the moderates of 1933. Its alliance with Batista and middle-class reformers marked that shift. As the prize for cooperation in 1902 had been the end of the occupation and a lower sugar tariff, so the prize in 1934 was the abrogation of the despised (and anachronistic) Platt Amendment and the signing of a new trade agreement. Because the Cuban economy was devastated at both points, the relief that came from closer economic ties to North America seemed to outweigh the impact on Cuban economic independence. Nevertheless, as the need to accommodate U.S. interests had helped undermine the first generation of Cuba's leaders, so the generation of 1930 would suffer from their ties to Washington. In the end, the politicians of Batista's era would not establish themselves as legitimate rulers any more than had those of Machado's.

CHAPTER 4

THE CONTRADICTIONS OF CONSTITUTIONALISM, NATIONALISM, AND CORRUPTION

I

THE DEPRESSION of the 1930s greatly reduced the value of U.S. investments in Cuba as many of the weaker North American sugar companies went into foreclosure. These paper losses, however, did not lessen the weight of the U.S. sector of a similarly shrunken Cuban economy. The principal impact of the depression in North America was a shift of influence among the forces that determined policy toward Cuba. The capital-starved U.S. sugar companies ceded some influence at the State Department and in Congress to a host of smaller, more popularly based interest groups representing North American farmers. While the sugar men and their bankers still had privileged access to the corridors of power, New Deal policy attempted to align their interests (and those of other elements of big business) with its effort to share a smaller pie more equitably.

Washington's concern for the plight of North America's new unemployed was reinforced by Cuba's near revolution of 1933. The island was more hard-hit by the depression than almost any other Latin American country. Economic conditions there deteriorated so badly that large numbers of the population were reduced to the level of subsistence. New Dealers, impelled by fear of social revolution on the island and by their own vision of reviving the engines of capitalism, now added to the old goal of stability the new one of resuscitating the island's economy. North Americans, once certain that Cubans were unruly because of their "Latin" race and temperament, now convinced themselves that the islanders acted so because they were desperately poor. One of the results of this new policy was the earmarking of the first loans of the new Export-Import Bank to bail out the bankrupt Cuban government.

If depression modified policy toward Cuba, it also changed the politics of sugar in the United States. To resurrect its own devastated agricultural economy, the New Deal inaugurated production and market controls on important crops, including sugar. Imports of this product (predominantly Cuban) were now determined by quotas. In this system, Cuban cane lost some ground to domestic beet-sugar growers. However, it did benefit from a reduction of the sugar tariff, a more secure share of the market, and the slow progress of prices up from the ruinous levels (for both U.S. and Cuban producers) of 1930–1933. As in all agreements with Washington, the islanders paid a price. To their old dependence on market prices and tariff levels (over which Cuba had almost no control) was now added dependence on the congressional committees that periodically set the import quotas. A new trade agreement in 1934 also assured U.S. imports of their near monopoly of the Cuban market.[1] With the abrogation of the now counterproductive Platt Amendment in 1934, the marines would never come again. Still, the White House, Capitol Hill, and the dollar set firm limits to Cuban independence.

II

While the revolution of 1933 did not radically restructure Cuba's ties to North America, it did change the tone of Cuban politics. Where once campaigns had rung with evocations of the candidate's role in the war against Spain, now the great deeds were those done in the struggle against Machado. The mobilization of the urban and rural proletariat in the early 1930s and the influence of Marxism, Spanish Republicanism, and Aprismo on portions of the middle class turned political rhetoric in a populist direction. No one capitalized on this shift in the 1930s more successfully than Batista. Though he bore the burden of having removed Grau and suppressed the left-wing nationalists, he now preached a state-centered economic recovery that would address the needs of the masses. He attended to this task—and to that of assuring his own power—by employing the military both for political purposes and as a rural service agency.[2] Batista took advantage of the trust that Washington placed in him to present himself to Cubans as someone who could obtain benefits from the United States while avoiding too intimate contact with North American capitalists. The coming of the

[1] Benjamin, *Hegemony*, pp. 119–22, 174–80.

[2] Pérez, *Army Politics*, ch. 9; Thomas, *Pursuit*, ch. 59.

New Deal—itself a semi-populist episode in North American politics—enabled Batista to appear close to the popular Roosevelt and yet distant from Wall Street. Operating from his base as head of the armed forces and as the man behind a series of weak provisional presidents, Batista prepared the way for his own presidency at the end of the decade.[3]

An important step along Batista's road to the presidential palace was his alliance with the Cuban Communist Party. The Communists had taken a tortuous path to arrive at their meeting with Batista. The party had grown out of the socialist and anarchist groups established on the island around the turn of the century. In the early 1920s, when the Bolshevik revolution split these organizations, the first Communist groups arose. In 1925, with the aid of the Comintern, the Cuban Communist Party was formed. Almost immediately, the party became involved in the opposition to Machado and attracted to its ranks several of the most active student radicals at the University of Havana. Machado declared the party illegal in 1927, but it continued to expand, especially into labor organizations originally established by anarchosyndicalists.[4] The deep sugar depression assisted the work of the party. By 1930, it controlled the largest worker organization on the island, the National Confederation of Cuban Workers. The powerful Communists now left behind their left-wing rivals as well as the moderate unions organized by the AFL-affiliated Pan American Federation of Labor (PAFL). Despite U.S. support, the PAFL never gained importance on the island because its unions were often led by Machado supporters.[5]

In its struggle against Machado, the party took a highly militant stand. It attacked both the dictatorship and the "bourgeois" opposition as well as U.S. "imperialism." The party led a series of major strikes in Havana in the early 1930s and began to organize among the sugar workers, on whose labor much of the economy rested. Late in 1932, having defined the situation as a revolutionary one, the leadership described its task as one of establishing "the revolutionary democratic dictatorship of the workers and peasants based upon soviets." The party acknowledged the role of nationalism and of the middle class in the anti-Machado movement but, confident of the historic destiny of the worker-peasant bloc, believed that the bourgeois revolution, if successful, could be rapidly succeeded by a socialist one.[6]

---

[3] Irwin F. Gellman, *Roosevelt and Batista: Good Neighbor Diplomacy in Cuba, 1933–1945* (Albuquerque: University of New Mexico Press, 1973), chs. 8 and 9.

[4] The early history of the party is traced in Jorge García Montes and Antonio Alonso Avila, *Historia del Partido Comunista de Cuba* (Miami, Fla.: Ed. Universal, 1970); Thomas, ch. 60 and pp. 733–34.

[5] The role of the American Federation of Labor is examined in Sinclair Snow, *The Pan American Federation of Labor* (Durham, N.C.: Duke University Press, 1964).

[6] The party's position during the Third Period of the Comintern is found in Partido Comu-

The revolutionary hope of the party and the militant sectarianism to which it led collapsed in the mid-1930s when Batista, as head of the army, was able to divide the nationalist forces and destroy their radical wing. Batista also suppressed the Communists and left their organization in a greatly weakened state. A sadder but wiser Communist leadership eagerly embraced the arrival on the island of the Comintern's Popular Front period.

By 1936, the party assumed a reformist orientation and began looking around for allies for the long haul. At that point, they discovered Batista, who was eagerly seeking a popular base for his own new career as reformer. Haltingly, over the next few years, the reluctant courtship reached the stage of informal agreement. For his part, Batista allowed the party first to operate openly, then legally, and finally with government support. In return, the party placed its revived propaganda and organizational resources behind Batista's populist and (later) anti-fascist programs. As Communists returned to power in the reorganized unions—now gathered under the Cuban Confederation of Workers (CTC)—they channeled the strength of organized labor into Batista's successful candidacy in the 1940 presidential election.[7]

During World War II, the Communists renamed their organization the Popular Socialist Party (PSP) and enjoyed a season as the overseer of a semi-official trade union movement. The strength of the PSP now depended on its close relationship to the Cuban president, yet its organization, though buttressed by official favor, would survive its patron's departure. Moreover, the party leadership still steered by the changing Comintern definition of the "world situation," even as it learned to grasp the opportunities provided by shifts in Cuban politics.

III

The United States, even during the New Deal period, was not always happy with the new Cuban populism. It was even less enamored of the rising profile of the PSP. Nevertheless, Batista was clearly the most powerful figure, and Washington had learned to have confidence in him. He had eliminated the radical nationalist and revolutionary socialist threats of the early 1930s and had restored coveted stability to the island.

With calm reestablished, the United States returned to its long-range goal

---

nista de Cuba, *El Partido Comunista y los problemas de la revolución en Cuba*. The quotation in the text is from p. 11.

[7] The party's Popular Front period is examined in Farber, *Revolution and Reaction*, pp. 66–70, 84–91; Harold D. Sims, "Cuban Labor and the Communist Party, 1937–1958: An Interpretation," *Cuban Studies* 15:1 (Winter 1985), pp. 43–58. Also see U.S. National Archives (hereafter N.A.), Record Group 59 (hereafter R.G. 59), 810.00B/165, "Comment of Soviet and Comintern Publications on the Activities of the Communist Parties in Latin American Countries," Wiley (Riga) to Secretary of State, 8/29/39.

of permanently stabilizing Cuban politics. By mid-decade, Washington began to press Batista for a return to the constitutional legitimacy that had been broken with the overthrow of Machado. Retaining the goals if not the methods of its earlier reformism, Washington held that long-term stability required fundamental statutes and an honest electoral system. With what remained of the nationalist Left in exile and with the Communist Party still weak, an effort was made in 1936 to end the provisional character of Cuban government. A presidential election was held, but the victor, Miguel Mariano Gómez, soon encroached on the expanding power of army chief Batista and was impeached after only seven months in office.[8]

True constitutional legitimacy was not finally reached until 1940 when all political tendencies—gathered behind a moderately corporatist and populist Batista on the one hand and a now mildly reformist and nationalist Grau on the other—hammered out a new constitution. The two coalitions—both composed of radical, conservative, opportunist, and personalist factions—then contested a relatively honest election in which Batista gained the presidency.

The United States now had the stable and legitimate rule in Cuba it had long sought. The process, however, had required writing the goals of the 1933 revolution—nationalism, egalitarianism, anti-authoritarianism, and corporatism—into the new constitution. The 1940 constitution made clear that the center of political gravity had shifted during the 1930s. As a result, the legitimate presidents of the constitutional period were pledged to respect the radical-nationalist mandate of the new document, which now replaced the U.S.-influenced constitution of 1901. Unlike the North American model, the 1940 constitution provided for popular sovereignty and the outlawing of discrimination ''by reason of sex, race, color, or class.'' It established worker rights to employment, housing, unions, strikes, minimum wages, social security, and paid vacations. Native Cubans were granted preference in employment. Organizations of employers were allowed and those of professionals made mandatory. Large landholdings were prohibited and provision was made for ''measures tending to restore the land to Cuban ownership.'' Ownership of land and enterprise by foreigners had to be ''adjusted to the socio-economic interests of the nation.'' The state was given responsibility for the direction of the national economy.[9]

Privately, Washington was very unhappy with the new constitution but

[8] Gellman, *Roosevelt and Batista*, pp. 146–54.

[9] The full English text can be found in Russell H. Fitzgibbon, *The Constitutions of the Americas* (Chicago: University of Chicago Press, 1948), pp. 226–96. The articles of the constitution referred to in the text are, respectively, numbers 2, 20, 60–68, 71, 72, 73, 69, 70, 90, 272, 271.

found it difficult to criticize openly a document that Cubans heralded as the fulfillment of long-standing goals. The U.S. ambassador, George Messersmith, reported to the State Department that he had warned Cuban leaders not to support the creation of a "radical" consitution but that the resulting document was nonetheless "utterly hopeless and most of it dangerous."[10] Despite its unhappiness, the State Department contented itself with the belief that much of the document was merely rhetoric. It hoped that emphasis would be placed upon the more moderate provisons concerning the rights of property, due process, and compensation for expropriated property.

Given the illiberal provisions embedded in the statute that was to stabilize political rule in Cuba, the United States found it difficult to require both constitutional orthodoxy on the one hand and moderate politics and market-oriented economic development on the other. Thus legitimacy now worked to some extent against the stability and moderate change preferred by Washington. The Cuban constitution defined fundamental powers, rights, and obligations differently from those prevailing in North America. Moreover, it was not simply an organization of authority but a statement of social goals. As a result, Havana officials who conformed to U.S. wishes could be charged by their compatriots with ignoring fundamental Cuban principles and the public aspirations that lay beneath them. Ironically, the cooperative behavior that the United States desired from Cuban leaders could reduce rather than enhance their legitimacy. Though officials on both sides preferred not to face the fact, Cuban governments could not in many instances fulfill their constitutional mandate, certainly not if they also wished to retain Washington's support.

Being measured against a fundamental law that they could not or would not fulfill was not the only difficulty faced by the governments that held office during the period of constitutional rule between 1940 and 1952. Cuban presidents in this period were leaders not of formal, bureaucratic, constituency-based political parties but rather of constantly shifting coalitions of factions, groups, and splinter parties that had no political program as North Americans would have defined that term.[11] These coalitions often bound together groups with particularistic and even antagonistic interests and philosophies. Hispanic, nationalist, populist, Marxist, and personalist "parties" went in and out of coalition every few years as each endeavored to position itself best to obtain the power, wealth, or status that came with political office. The result was not the stable, effective, modernizing bu-

---

[10] George Messersmith Papers, University of Delaware, Diplomatic Papers, Box II, 1940, Folder A, letter to Lawrence Duggan, 4/10/40; letter to Sumner Welles, 4/19/40; Folder C, letter to Welles, 10/22/40.

[11] Mario Riera Hernández, *Cuba republicana, 1899–1958* (Miami: Editorial AIP, 1974), pp. 26–29.

reaucracy with which the United States preferred to deal. Instead, Cuban politics was authoritarian, rhetorically nationalist, corporatist, populist, corrupt, and inefficient. This form of politics satisfied neither the aims of the United States nor the higher aspirations of most Cubans.

Despite their many deficiencies, Washington learned to live with these Cuban governments. As long as such regimes did not embrace ideologies and programs that exceeded the boundaries prescribed by U.S. economic and strategic interests, they were allowed access to the North American resources on which the Cuban economy and their supporters depended. In doing so, however, the United States acquired a stake in the Cuban political system. Despite the hopes for reduced visibility with which it had given up direct intervention, Washington continued to present itself as an essential prop of the reigning regime. In the end, both the U.S. desire for republican stability and its opposition to radicalism would be frustrated. The long Spanish era of Cuban history as well as the episodic eruption of an angry Cuban nationalism stood in the way, as did, ironically, the U.S. economic and political presence on the island. As it turned out, the constitutional period was one in which left-wing groups gained in public stature in part by leading the anti-fascist cause and in part by availing themselves of the opportunity to accuse the incumbent regime of succumbimg to the Yankees. It was during this period as well that the Cuban Communist Party became one of the largest and most influential of such bodies in Latin America.[12]

IV

The stabilized political system of the post-1940 period with which the United States identified itself was set in an altered Cuban economic structure. There had been a decline in U.S. economic influence in Cuba during the 1930s because of the cessation of the flow of new North American capital. During that same period Cuban unions became powerful, and Cuban entrepreneurs increased their presence in the business sector, though less so than in some other Latin American nations. The depression left in its wake larger and more politically potent interest groups on the island. The state also became more responsible for maintaining economic life and came to reflect to some degree the desires of these interest groups. By the time U.S. investments and products returned after 1945, Cuban presidents were expected to enforce the nationalist legislation meant to shield native producers and professionals from North American competition and native labor from exploitation. United States firms in public utilities, services, and

[12] Montes and Avila, *Historia del Partido*, chs. 11–13.

real estate or in competitive imports were now hemmed in by a tangle of regulations. Sugar-grinding quotas were set by the government to assure the survival of the smaller Cuban-owned sugar mills. Labor regulations made it difficult for U.S. companies to employ non-Cuban skilled workers. North American employers also confronted a classic barrier, erected during the 1933 revolution, requiring that one-half of the total payroll of an enterprise be paid to Cubans.[13]

Whatever the mix of costs and benefits in its increasingly close economic ties to North America, the process of economic integration itself—so natural and desirable from the U.S. point of view—constantly reminded Cubans of the dependent nature of the relationship. Though the trait was recessive in this period, Cuban nationalism remained potentially anti-Yankee. On occasion, it poked its head above the surface. In 1947 the Cuban congress officially changed the name of the independence war from "Spanish-American War" to "Spanish-Cuban-American War." In 1948, when three drunken U.S. sailors cavorted on (and, it was said, urinated upon) the famous statue of José Martí in central Havana, it caused a serious incident in U.S.-Cuban relations and kept U.S. navy men from shore leave for many months. Open obedience to U.S. desires on the part of a Cuban government was usually unpopular. When President Prío Socarrás (1948–1952) offered to send a battalion of troops to aid the United States in the Korean War, the public reaction was negative. As a result, when Cuban leaders came under intense pressure from Washington, they often chose the stance of defender of Cuban sovereignty—in public at least.[14]

V

Washington never fully understood Cuban nationalism. It was treated as an atavistic phenomenon that would abate as accumulating U.S. influence led to a mature society. The State Department did realize that opposition to U.S. policy often served as an outlet for an emotional Cuban patriotism. It did not, however, consider the possibility that the U.S. presence in Cuba was the principal source of such nationalism. By inextricably mixing its rewards and punishments and by continually requiring Cuban society to recast itself, the United States assured that the question of Cuban independence—both in its practical and ideal forms—would never stray far from its original focus on North American power over the island's affairs.

[13] For Cuba's nationalist legislation see U.S. Department of Commerce, *Investment in Cuba* (Washington, D.C.: U.S.G.P.O., 1957), pp. 4–5, 18–19, 138, 163–69.

[14] Ruby Hart Phillips, *Cuba: Island of Paradox* (New York: McDowell, Obelensky, 1959), pp. 250–51, 253, 255; Tad Szulc, *Fidel: A Critical Portrait* (New York: Morrow, 1986), pp. 199, 240; Thomas, pp. 709–10, 763.

One of the reasons why the United States, despite the end of direct intervention, never ceased to be a center of controversy in Cuba was that its pressure—both structural and political—was unrelenting. This constant pressure derived from the open-ended nature of U.S. goals. The United States required of the island not only stability but *both* stability and change. Stability, as we have seen, was to be achieved by political peace and the regular administration of law. Change was to be produced by creating a political and economic order flexible enough to adjust to alterations in the extent or direction of U.S. interests. In 1898 stability had meant an end to the war against Spain and a guided transition to semi-sovereign statehood. Change at that time meant the removal of the old Spanish mercantilism and land laws. These blocked the development of large sugar complexes that could employ advanced technology and a modern work force and also prevented the integration of such complexes into the capital-intensive and highly concentrated sugar-refining industry in the United States. This change was accomplished by the early 1920s. By that time, however, change had produced instability. The massive U.S. sugar investment disrupted the island's existing economic and social arrangements. Moreover, when sugar boom turned to depression in the early 1930s, the need for stability once again became predominant. Responding to the revolution of 1933, the New Deal administration set up a sugar program that dampened the swings of the market and informally accepted the rise of a moderate nationalism and of Batista's populism.

By the time restoration of constitutional rule and the election of Batista in 1940 brought the needed stability, U.S. interests—and hence the mix of stability and change needed to promote them—were changing again. As the United States entered World War II, the island's sugar industry had to shift from enforced underproduction to all-out production for war. Cuban politics, meanwhile, now had to embrace hemispheric security, the Atlantic Charter, and the ideological crusade against the Axis.

As the North American perspective became internationalist, anti-fascist, and anti-totalitarian, Washington became concerned with what it called "anti-democratic" forces in Cuba. As if suddenly discovering the Catholic and Hispanic elements of Cuban society, the State Department began to worry about right-wing groups on the island. While it was common for the department's studies of the island's politics to make the self-flattering observation that "the Cuban people are warmly pro-democratic," these now cautioned that "many conservative leaders have pro-Axis sympathies" and that Cuba was the "headquarters of one of the largest and most effective Axis spy rings in Latin America."[15] During this period the United States was forced to consider not only the problem of Axis espionage in Cuba but

[15] R.G. 59, Office of Intelligence Research (OIR), Research Analysis (R & A) Report #294, "Present Anti-Democratic Forces in Cuba," 6/5/42, p. 1.

also the *Hispanidad* program of the well-organized Spanish Falange on the island, among whose purposes was the promotion of traditional Iberian values and the undermining of Anglo-Saxon influence.[16] As with all deviations from the North American norm, the State Department's tendency was to understand these illiberal forces in Cuba not as signs of cultural difference whose trajectory could not easily be aligned with U.S. requirements but rather as sinister, alien elements that, once removed, would reopen the path to the fulfillment of U.S. goals.

Hispanic and Falangist forces in Cuba, while not as strong as in some other Latin American societies, were not surface phenomena. Important elements of the island's power structure were of conservative or pro-Franco persuasion. These included influential individuals in the business community, the media, the military, and government. One of the most important Havana newspapers, *Diario de la Marina*, was outspokenly Francoist.[17] Moreover, Batista had personal and political ties to elements of the right-wing community. Because of this situation, it took strong pressure from the United States to get the newly elected president to crack down on the substantial pro-Axis activity in Cuba. As a result of U.S. pressure—reinforced at this point by the great upsurge in war-derived U.S. sugar purchases—Batista slowly moved to counteract and eventually outlaw overt support for the Axis.[18] Washington was pleased at this outcome, which reaffirmed its

[16] For background on Spain's efforts to reestablish its influence in Latin America see Fredrick B. Pike, *Hispanismo: 1898–1936* (South Bend, Ind.: University of Notre Dame Press, 1971).

[17] R.G. 59, OIR, R & A Report #294, "Present Anti-Democratic Forces," judged Falangist strength to have arisen principally from within the large Spanish community of about 500,000 on the island. The report named many prominent Cubans as active pro-Franco supporters. *Diario de la Marina* editor José Ignacio Rivera was described as "Franco's leading apologist" (p. 4), while Minister of State José Manuel Cortina was "known to be an Axis sympathizer" (p. 7). Others described as Falangists were Minister of the Interior Victor Ceballos Vega and Batista's personal secretary, Jaime Marine y Montes (p. 8). A more detailed study of this subject is found in "The Spanish Falange in Cuba," (Dec., 1942) OIR, Division of Research for American Republics, Box 13. Also see R.G. 59 "German Penetration in Cuba during the War" (Jan. 30, 1946), Records of the Office of American Republics Affairs, Division of Analysis and Liaison, Memoranda, Box 16.

[18] For examples of pressure on Batista to remove Falangists from office see the efforts of U.S. Ambassador George Messersmith in Messersmith Papers, Diplomatic Papers, Box II, 1940, Folder C, letter to Undersecretary Welles, 1/31/41. The efforts of Messersmith's successor, Spruille Braden, appear in Franklin D. Roosevelt Library (FDRL), Harry Hopkins Papers, FBI Reports: Cuba, "Political Situation in Cuba—Strained Relations between the U.S. and Cuba," 8/2/43, Box 142.

Batista's decision to cut his ties to right-wing elements completed the alienation of Cuban conservatives from his regime—a process that had begun with his destruction of the old officer corps in 1933 and then with his pact with the Communists in the late thirties. This break was never healed and meant that Batista could not appeal to such forces when he began a desperate search for allies in the late 1950s.

convictions about the ideological affinity of the two nations. In its view, Cuba's Hispanic heritage was eclipsed after 1898 by a union of liberal forces in the two societies. Hence, Washington missed another chance to understand the tendencies toward political centralism, charismatic leadership, and economic corporatism that bedeviled its desire to reform and "open" Cuba. It also failed to detect a preference for formal social hierarchy among elements of the middle and upper classes, to whom it would turn in 1959 for the defense of liberal institutions.

Though U.S. ideological priorities were now principally anti-fascist, Washington also worried about the other illiberal allies of the Cuban president—the Communists. In this instance, pressure on Batista was less successful. While conformity to U.S. ideological perspectives had cost Batista personal and business friends on the right, he was less willing to pay the price when it meant loss of political support from the left. Such support had significantly determined his success in the electoral arena against the heirs of the radical nationalist movement of the early 1930s. In the civilian phase of his career, the lifeblood of Batista's power was the political coalition that won him the presidency. He was not very effective as either a charismatic or an ideological leader. During the period of constitutional order, he was at his best as a power broker among the political forces that hoped to benefit from his rule. Batista's electoral alliance with the Cuban Communist Party had not only widened the gulf separating the Communists and radical nationalists, it had been a key to his success at the polls.[19] While both the assured purchase of the entire sugar crop by the U.S. government and the military projects on the island financed by the War Department more than compensated Batista for alienating his pro-Franco friends, U.S. requests that he end his affair with the Cuban Communists met greater resistance.

Once the Soviet Union and the United States became partners in the struggle against totalitarianism in 1941, Batista could place United Nations' rhetoric and Allied solidarity in the service of defending his important alliance with the Cuban Communists. Now that Soviet foreign policy coincided with U.S. wartime goals, the PSP became one of the most vociferous and effective supporters of close cooperation between the United States and Cuba. Under these circumstances, Batista was able to ignore U.S. complaints about the growing strength of the party. Indeed, he rewarded his influential allies with Cabinet posts—though without portfolio.[20]

[19] Sims, "Cuban Labor," pp. 43–59.

[20] For the wartime program of the Cuban Communist Party see R.G. 59, Office of Intelligence Research for American Republics, "Current Communist Tactics in the Other American Republics," 12/8/42, Box 13, and N.A., Lot Files, Records of Harley Notter, "The Objectives of Soviet Policy with Respect to Cuba," 10/14/44, Box 136.

The same wartime alliance that enabled Batista to protect his left-wing allies from North American disapproval also lessened U.S. concern over communism in Latin America. The same Popular Front atmosphere that made left-wingers more acceptable in New Deal and wartime Washington also brought Latin American communists greater acceptance in the eyes of some in the State Department. Communist parties in Latin America had several advantages over the United States in the task of mobilizing the hemisphere for war. Unlike the U.S. embassies, whose staffs conducted their business with Latin elites, the Communist parties had extensive contacts among the working class. Moreover, their work was not inhibited by the popular Latin prejudices against North American Protestantism, liberalism, and interventionism. As a result, they turned out to be some of the most effective anti-fascist organizers at the grass-roots level. Since Rooseveltian rhetoric painted World War II as a struggle by and for the "common man," the ability of Latin American Communists to enlist such people in the struggle did not go unnoticed in Washington, though the ideological contradictions made some people there uneasy.[21]

In any event, Washington's concern over Batista's dalliance with the Communists eased as the Cuban president won high marks for his cooperation with U.S. strategic and economic goals during the war—something that it might otherwise have had to compel. He had suppressed fascism in Cuba, provided numerous air bases and training facilities for U.S. forces, and managed a large increase in sugar production for the war effort. By the end of Batista's presidential term in 1944, the U.S. government felt very comfortable with him. Washington had by now worked closely with Batista since 1933 when it encouraged him to remove the radical nationalist Grau regime. By the late 1930s, as head of the Cuban army, Batista was already treated by the United States as the de facto ruler of Cuba.[22] His cooperation (well rewarded) during World War II thus capped a decade of good relations. Despite the fact that he was hardly a democrat—he ignored the Cuban congress, retained suspect ideological alliances, and used the state treasury and the army for personal and political purposes—Washington found him reliable. Relations were better with him than with any preceding Cuban president.[23]

[21] R.G. 59, OIR, Div. of Research for American Republics, "United States Policy with Respect to Soviet Actions in Latin America," 11/17/44, Box 10.

[22] For U.S. relations with Batista before his presidency see FDRL, PSF, Welles to FDR, 11/7/38, Box 95. Also see R.G. 59, 711.37/289, memorandum by Lawrence Duggan, 11/9/38; 711.37/299, U.S. Ambassador (Butler) to Welles, 12/29/38, and Welles to Butler, 1/4/39.

[23] For an assessment of Batista's relationship with the Cuban congress see William S. Stokes, "The Cuban Parliamentary System in Action, 1940–1947," *Journal of Politics* 11 (1949), pp. 344–50. For U.S. relations with Batista during this period see U.S. Department of State, *Foreign Relations of the United States*, (Washington, D.C.: U.S.G.P.O., 1962–

In the final analysis, U.S. relations with Batista had been good principally because the war had reduced some of the contradictions in the demands made by Washington on Havana. Getting Cuba to conform to U.S. requirements for hemispheric security and economic mobilization for war was relatively easy for Washington since both brought substantial economic rewards to Cuba. Lend-Lease funds helped to assure the cooperation of the Cuban army and of the president, who was thus able to act in his preferred role as its benefactor. Guaranteed purchase of the entire sugar crop by the Allies—coming after many years of overproduction and low prices—eliminated the notoriously dangerous market risk to sugar producers and created a rising (though uneven) prosperity on the island. Some contradictions remained, however. The increasing stream of dollars from Washington made Cuban officials more cooperative, but it also nourished a system of corruption that violated elements of the North American reform program. Such corruption was a logical outcome of the meshing of the colonial heritage of Cuban politics with the massive public funds that war placed in the service of U.S. foreign policy. Batista—the former cane cutter, railroad worker, and stenographer—was able to retire to his Florida mansion at the end of his term a very wealthy man.

United States aims in Cuba were advanced not only by the wartime expenditures that secured Batista's cooperation but by a general legitimation on the island of democratic ideology that the crusade against the Axis engendered. This development never erased the contradiction between the monistic and charismatic politics and radical nationalism of Cuba on the one hand and the U.S. desire for moderate, market-oriented rulers in Havana on the other. Nevertheless, this period saw a decline in anti-Yankee rhetoric and an improved image of the United States as a result of North American leadership in the anti-fascist struggle. The social programs of the New Deal, the anti-interventionism of the Good Neighbor policy, and the egalitarian rhetoric of the war helped many Cubans, especially those in the middle class, to set aside old fears of U.S. political and economic domination.[24] By the time the war ended, Cuban nationalism was less hostile to the United States than at any time since 1898. This did not mean, however, that it had disappeared or that it could not revive.

VI

Washington was gratified when the new constitutional system seemed to pass its first major test in 1944, as Batista made no effort to overturn the

---

1965), 1941, vol. 7, pp. 97–252; 1942, vol. 6, pp. 253–359; 1943, vol. 6, pp. 136–279. (This collection hereafter referred to as FRUS.)

[24] Farber, *Revolution and Reaction*, pp. 106, 115–16.

presidential election victory of his old political enemy Grau San Martín. While the maintenance of constitutional norms pleased Washington, it was nonetheless uneasy about exchanging the familiar and reasonably dependable Batista for the possibly unpredictable and radical Grau. The State Department worried that Grau might revive the radical nationalism of the 1933 revolution, elements of which were now enshrined in the 1940 constitution.[25] For a time after Grau's overthrow and exile in the mid-1930s, his movement—the Partido Revolucionario Cubano (PRC)—had espoused armed insurrection against the Batista "dictatorship." It had denounced the domination of foreign capital, the sacrifice of native labor at its hands, the "continental hegemony of financial imperialism," and had described its own doctrine as "nationalizing, socialistic and anti-imperialistic."[26] By the late 1930s, however, the Auténticos, as the PRC had by then become known, had accepted the electoral path to power and had become a reform party with only tenuous connections to its radical past. As a result, U.S. fears concerning the new president's party were quickly put to rest.

Though Grau made no effort to challenge the nature of Cuban ties to the United States, like all Cuban presidents under the new populism he had to avoid the appearance of collaborating with Washington. A pattern set in whereby in private conversations with U.S. officials Grau would agree to meet U.S. requests such as those concerning overdue debts, control of inflation and government expenditures, a commercial treaty that would have assured the favored position of U.S. imports, and the removal of legislation harmful to U.S. interests.[27] However, when such matters entered the realm of public debate and electoral campaigning (forums provided in part by U.S. pressure for political reform), the private assurances evaporated. Interest groups on the island that suffered disadvantage in the competition with U.S. goods, capital, technology, or work skills had over the years built up pressure for protective legislation. In each case, particularistic demands would be underwritten by the strength and electoral appeal of nationalism. Grau was required by political expediency to acknowledge these claims and, indeed, to proclaim them as his own. Paradoxically, from the U.S. point of view, a more open political arena worked against Washington's goal of an open Cuban economy.[28]

Even more than Batista, Grau needed to placate Cuban nationalism so as

[25] For U.S. worries about Grau see FRUS, 1944, vol. 7, pp. 900–2, 918; 1945, vol. 9, pp. 896–98, 907–9, 912, 915—16, 939, 972.

[26] FDRL, OF, 195a, Cuba: Misc., 1934–1935, Cuban Revolutionary Party, Bureau of Foreign Propaganda, Bulletin No. 2, 9/1/35.

[27] These requests are described in FRUS, 1944, vol. 7, p. 914; 1945, vol. 9, pp. 959, 963–65; 1948, vol. 9, pp. 543, 560, 570.

[28] FRUS, 1947, vol. 8, pp. 616–17, 620; 1948, vol. 9, pp. 554, 564.

to preserve his party's *Cubanidad* credentials and thereby its electoral potential. As a result, he would not allow the United States to retain use of the air bases it had built on the island during the war; he dragged his feet on the payment of claims and debts and would not agree to the expansion of the U.S. naval base at Guantánamo. In general, he defended well-organized consituencies—native sugar-mill owners, producers, professionals, and skilled workers—against the competing interests of U.S. mill owners, exporters, and investors.[29]

Fortunately for Washington, these tensions were reduced by the sugar boom that had begun during the war and continued into the Grau presidency (1944–1948). After the war's end, the U.S. government continued to purchase the entire sugar crop, this time for the European Recovery Program. These purchases assured government revenues in Cuba sufficient to satisfy Grau's supporters. At times they enabled him to finesse the issue of collaboration by compensating local interests for advantages granted to U.S. interests. Of course, sugar boom also preserved the imbalance in the island's productive base and freed the Cuban president from pressure to restructure the economy.

WHILE GRAU dragged his feet on certain economic questions important to Washington, he did respond to its ideological preferences. Though hardly for the preferred reasons, his regime fulfilled the North American desire for ideological rectitude. As Batista had accepted the role of anti-fascist, so Grau donned the mantle of anti-communist. In the end, Grau moved against the Cuban Communist Party for the same reason that Batista defended it. As the political allies of Batista, the Communists had been the Auténtico's political opponents. Grau's party also held in its political memory the Communist Party's opposition to his brief rule in 1933 and its alliance with the Auténtico's old enemy Batista after 1938.

For a time in 1945, the Auténticos and Communists eyed each other warily. The PSP, looking around for a "progressive" ally to replace Batista, made overtures to the new president, who, lacking a majority in congress, needed their votes. By 1946, however, a cold-war mentality took hold in the United States, and Washington began to make all bilateral relations turn on the issue of anti-communism. Grau came under increasing pressure to recognize the evils of communism and the need to control its activities.[30]

---

[29] FRUS, 1944, vol. 7, pp. 898, 901–2; 1945, vol. 9, pp. 896–98, 907–11, 915–16; 1946, vol. 11, pp. 702–6, 708–9, 713, 717; 1947, vol. 8, pp. 609–10; 1948, vol. 9, pp. 551, 553, 564, 573, 577.

[30] FRUS, 1945, vol. 9, p. 973; 1947, vol. 8, pp. 608–9, 621; 1948, vol. 9, p. 565; R.G. 59, Records of the Office of American Republics Affairs, Division of Analysis and Liaison, ARA Memoranda: "United States Policy Toward Cuba: Supplement, 9/1/44 to 12/1/44, and Cuba

To U.S. pressure was added the needs of Grau's constituency. Under Batista's aegis and as a result of effective organizing, PSP members had attained many of the highest leadership positions in the constituent labor unions as well as the leadership of the Cuban Confederation of Workers (CTC). This was by far the largest labor organization on the island and one of the most powerful union confederations in Latin America.[31] Within the confederation leadership, Auténtico labor officials competed with Communists, though rarely on the basis of ideology. The removal of Batista, the Communists' patron, coinciding as it did with increased anti-communist pressure from Washington, strengthened the desire of Auténtico labor officials to take control of the CTC. Grau now had an opportunity to solidify the labor base of his party. At the height of the ensuing leadership conflict within the confederation, Grau's labor minister sanctioned the withdrawal of the Auténtico and independent elements of the CTC. The government then aided this group in forming a separate labor body and granted it official recognition. In succeeding years, Auténtico administrations employed both legal and illegal actions to break up Communist-run labor groups and mass-media outlets. Loss of governmental preferment and growing repression led to a significant decline in Communist strength in both the labor movement and the political arena. The party, however, still retained its legal status.[32]

The United States was pleased with the declining fortunes of Cuban communism. As the idea of communist subversion became more influential in Washington, communism in Cuba came to be seen as the principal source of anti-U.S. nationalism and radicalism. For its part, the party had responded to the growing cold-war atmosphere by returning to its pre-Popular Front attacks on U.S. intervention in Cuban affairs. The State Department became concerned that party pressure on the Cuban government was a principal reason for lack of cooperation from Havana. U.S. Ambassador R. Henry Norweb reported to Washington in 1946 that Communist Party

---

(Box 41) Memoranda of 3/24/47 and 8/14/47. Harry S. Truman Library (HSTL), President's Secretary's File (PSF), Box 254, Intelligence File, ORE: 1947 (15–39), "Soviet Objectives in Latin America," ORE #16 (4/10/47) and ORE #16/1 (11/1/47).

This period of Communist-Auténtico relations is examined in Montes and Avila, *Historia del Partido*, pp. 327, 351, 355, 360, 364–65, 373; Farber, pp. 137–38; and Thomas, pp. 752–53.

[31] N.A., OSS., OIR, R & A Report No. 3076.1, 9/18/45.

[32] HSTL, PSF, Box 261, Intelligence Reports, Situation Reports (29–31), CIA Report "Cuba" (SR–29), pp. 5–7. At the height of its influence in 1946, the Communist Party had elected three senators and nine representatives. MacGaffey and Barnett, *Twentieth Century Cuba*, p. 156. The vote-getting capacity of the CCP, a rough estimate of its political strength, was as follows: 1939–90,398; 1943–122,283; 1945–151,923; 1947–157,225; 1949–126,524; 1951–59,900. For election results during this period see Riera Hernández, *Cuba republicana*, pp. 26–29.

use of the nationalist issue had "the effect of encouraging high government officials to delay or avoid concessions to the United States."[33] Since U.S. officials now attributed much of the virulence of Cuban nationalism to Communist agitation, the successful effort to undermine the party in the late 1940s left them unprepared for the revival of nationalism in the 1950s. Moreover, by failing to note the connection between government patronage and the fortunes of the Communists, the party's resurrection after 1959 was misunderstood as the result of "subversion."

VII

Despite Grau's anti-communism, the United States was unhappy with the results of his administration. He had failed to remedy old U.S. grievances concerning debts, Cuban trade taxes, unequal treatment of U.S. and Cuban nationals, and misuse of government funds, among others. More disturbing yet was the declining likelihood of attaining U.S. goals under the rule of a party whose popular appeal derived from its past radicalism. Though U.S. leaders were slow to understand the full impact of the development, the victory of the Auténticos in 1944 had reinforced the influence in Cuban politics of the high-flown nationalist rhetoric that derived its motive force from the 1895 and 1933 revolutions, gained legitimacy in the 1940 constitution, and now spread its way into almost every aspect of Cuban governance—as emotionally captivating as it was programmatically shallow.[34]

While not understanding the true depth of Cuban nationalism and generally deemphasizing its important anti-Yankee component, the U.S. embassy and U.S. citizens in Cuba were continually reminded of its presence.

---

[33] FRUS, 1946, vol. 11, pp. 719–38. Norweb's memorandum also states that Communist "whittling away at the character and motives of the United States, combined with ardent encouragement of nationalism, has already created an atmosphere in which the Cuban Government hesitates to respond to important requests from our government because a response might receive adverse publicity in Cuba and unfavorably influence voters" (ibid., p. 728).

The CIA viewed the party as even more dangerous. To them it was an important asset in what was assumed to be the Soviet policy of preparing for "inevitable conflict with the capitalist world." In this regard, it warned in 1947 that "Communist non-political organization in Latin America has already proceeded so far and so effectively that in the event of war with the United States, the U.S.S.R. can, by merely giving the necessary orders, paralyse the economies of Chile and Cuba." HSTL, PSF, Box 254, Intelligence File, ORE: 1947 (15–39), ORE #16/1, 11/1/47, "Soviet Objectives in Latin America," pp. 1–3.

[34] Grau created additional headaches for the United States when he took his party's nationalistic and anti-dictatorial rhetoric to international forums. His foreign minister denounced "economic aggression" at the Inter-American Conference held in Quitandinha, Brazil, in 1947 (FRUS, 1948, vol. 9, p. 553). Members of his administration gave verbal support to the Nationalist Party in Puerto Rico, which was demanding independence (FRUS, 1950, vol. 2, p. 848). Grau's involvement with the Caribbean Legion is noted elsewhere in the text.

After the war, U.S. businessmen and policymakers increasingly complained that any public efforts on their part to influence Cuban affairs or even to defend rights granted them by Cuban law were usually counterproductive. Inevitably, these efforts became bogged down in the swamp of *Cubanidad*.[35] At times, cynical Cubans used the nationalism issue not so much to oppose U.S. influence as to gain some benefit for themselves from the Cuban government or from the rich Yankees. This annoyed Washington and only reinforced its belief that Cubans did not have valid grievances. More damaging to U.S. interests in the long run, however, was the assumption that all Cuban nationalism was opportunistic. The response of much of Cuba's younger generation to its appeal was of a very different nature. They were motivated less by cynicism than by idealism and by the sense that North America lay like an oppressive weight on the idealized body of Cuban society. The actions of the young, however, were dismissed in Washington as overly emotional, ephemeral, and inconsequential. In the end, anti-Yankeeism was seen only as an irritant, not as a danger signal.

After the war, the tension between the two societies was further obscured by the increasingly close structural ties of the two economies. The war-inspired sugar boom brought Cuba an increasing supply of U.S. goods and dollars. Important economic groups on the island were becoming, if anything, even more dependent on continued close ties to the North American market and on favorable treatment by the State Department and the U.S. Congress in order to sustain their prosperity. That cultural issues might rupture economic ties seemed as unlikely to Washington as that the economic ties themselves might exacerbate cultural tensions.

The cultural issue was complicated, and Washington had, it seemed, good reason to presume it an asset rather than a liablilty. This was easy when so much of island society evidenced North American cultural influence. By the 1950s, Cuban media were filled with advertisements for U.S. products, and store shelves were filled with them. Cuban products—where competitors existed at all—were considered far inferior. On every street, especially in Havana, one passed theaters playing Hollywood movies and well-to-do Cubans wearing North American-style clothes and driving big Detroit-made cars. In the home there was radio and—exhibiting even greater U.S. influence—television. English words popped up regularly in conversation. Then there was the Cuban national pastime: baseball. Downtown was crowded with U.S. tourists who arrived without visas and did not even have to convert their dollars into pesos. (Indeed, many Cubans pre-

[35] For complaints concerning Cuban unwillingness to accommodate U.S. interests see FRUS, 1945, vol. 9, pp. 939, 960; 1946, vol. 11, pp. 708–9, 719–36; 1947, vol. 8, pp. 616–17, 620; 1948, vol. 9, pp. 551, 553–54, 564, 573, 576–77.

ferred and used U.S. money in their local transactions.) The tourists then shared the short flight back to Miami with middle- and upper-class Cubans on their own vacations.[36]

Even poor Cubans, correctly identifying the U.S. life-style with success, bought the cigarettes, appliances, and household products that were within their reach. But if North American culture was attractive, it was also resented. Those unhappy with the state of Cuban society, like the poor and the young, could easily blame the omnipresent Yankees. When the grievance was combined with nationalism, North American goods and ways could turn into monsters that were destroying Cuban culture. Even conservative Cubans were susceptible to this view.[37]

Washington found itself on something of a treadmill. Pursuit of its economic interests on the island led to an increased North American cultural presence which, instead of drawing Cuba more securely within her sphere, seemed somehow to create a resentment that, under the right circumstances, might endanger the relationship at a fundamental level. Some of the most resented enterprises on the island were the U.S.-owned utilities (all monopolies)—electricity and telephone. Rate raises were vociferously—sometimes violently—resisted. Utility bills were treated more like an unfair tax than a payment for service. And complaints about service were a mainstay of daily conversation.[38]

IN CERTAIN ways, the prosperity that resulted from closer ties to the U.S. economy had helped to produce the political stability desired by Washington. At the same time, however, the growing U.S. influence strengthened the barriers to radical solutions to many of the economic and social problems only partly hidden by sugar prosperity and constitutional rule. Because the United States opposed the illiberal measures that might have dealt with problems such as monoculture, lack of legitimate authority, and partial sovereignty, it stood in the way of the stable social order it desired. Moreover, given the volatility of Cuban nationalism and its anti-Yankee

[36] Nita R. Manitzas, "The Setting of the Cuban Revolution," in David B. Barkin and Manitzas, *Cuba: The Logic of the Revolution* (Andover, Mass.: Warner Modular Publishers, 1973), p. 12; MacGaffey and Barnett, *Twentieth Century Cuba*, pp. 44, 55, 64–65. There was a large North American community in Cuba, especially in Havana. Its extent and activities can be seen in *Anglo-American Directory of Cuba* (Marianao: A.A.D.O.C., 1954–1955).

[37] MacGaffey and Barnett, *Twentieth Century Cuba*, pp. 45, 123, 263–64; Thomas, *Pursuit*, pp. 1062–64; Oscar Lewis, Ruth M. Lewis, Susan Rigdon, *Four Men: Living the Revolution* (Urbana: University of Illinois Press, 1977), pp. 178–81, 211–12, 222, 243–55, 258–59.

[38] Alfred Padula, Jr., "The Fall of the Bourgeoisie: Cuba, 1959–1961" (Ph.D. diss., University of New Mexico, 1974), pp. 368–389.

bias, Cuban executives could never play the role in the liberal reform of the island designed for them by the United States.

Unknowingly, the U.S. government was playing a dangerous game. By demonstrating once again the connection between prosperity (uneven as always) and economic dependence, it was invigorating both the acquisitiveness and resentfulness of the Cubans. It only compounded the problem by funneling U.S. economic influence more and more through the White House and Capitol Hill rather than Wall Street. In this manner it substituted executive authority in Washington and Havana for market forces and thus helped assure that any revival of anti-imperialism on the island would focus on the "treason" of the Cuban president and the "domination" of the U.S. government. As always, the goals of U.S. policy and the actual effects of U.S. influence assured continued tensions in the relationship.

VIII

The rule of the Auténtico Party was continued by the victory in the 1948 elections of its candidate, Carlos Prío Socarrás. Once again, as under Grau, official relations with the United States were characterized by private assurances of cooperation paralleled by public resistance to U.S. influence. Prío continued his predecessor's policy of protecting important Cuban constituencies from North American competitors. The Cuban president even failed to implement decisions of the Cuban supreme court that went in favor of U.S. plaintiffs.[39]

The tactic of anti-communism was continued as well. In fact, a form of McCarthyism was adopted by Auténticos (and other non-communist politicians) who used the black cold-war image of the Soviet Union beamed from the United States to intensify existing assaults on the PSP. Prío came down more forcefully on the Cuban Communists than had his predecessor. He closed down the party's radio station and newspaper and arrested party leaders for various violations. Prío even went so far as to threaten the Soviet Union with a break in diplomatic relations.[40]

Prío's anti-communism, like Grau's, was pragmatic. In fact, like much else in U.S.-Cuban relations, the anti-communism of the Auténtico presidents actually worked against U.S. goals. In its campaign to weaken the Communists' hold over the unions, the Auténtico leadership had to demonstrate that it was an effective defender of the wartime wage increases

---

[39] FRUS, 1948, vol. 9, pp. 546–48, 551, 553–56, 564, 573, 577; 1949, vol. 2, pp. 627, 637–38, 643–44; 1950, vol. 2, pp. 844–45, 848, 851–52; 1951, vol. 2, 1334–50, 1356–62, 1364–65.

[40] FRUS, 1948, vol. 9, p. 565; 1950, vol. 2, 850–51. Lionel Martin, *The Early Fidel* (Secaucus, N.J.: Lyle Stuart, 1978), pp. 37, 46, 61, 90.

obtained by Cuban workers. This meant that it had to take a firm stand in favor of those workers during negotiations with their North American employers. As a result, U.S. firms regularly complained that labor relations was their most difficult problem. This issue continually spilled over onto the political side of U.S.-Cuban relations. Since the Communist Party—now part of the political opposition—took every opportunity to denounce any failure to defend the rights of workers, the government had to be careful to avoid any appearance of capitulation to North American "exploiters." In private discussions with their U.S. counterparts, Cuban representatives often used the U.S. desire to weaken the Communists as a reason for allowing the Cuban government to obtain concessions for organized Cuban labor. Thus the U.S. goal of stability on the island, because it required a legitimate Cuban executive, ran counter in some measure to the defense of U.S. economic interests.[41]

Since wage levels, like much else, depended on the value of the sugar crop, Havana's defense of Cuban workers entailed active pursuit of higher prices for sugar sales to the United States. During this period U.S. government agencies still bought a large percentage of the Cuban crop and thus effectively set the price. As a result, intergovernmental negotiations over the sale were crucial in determining the amount of sugar income that flowed into the hands of millers and planters and, indirectly, into the pockets of those large numbers of Cubans tied to the sugar economy. The desire to protect their nationalist flank led Cuban officials (as in the case of Cuban labor) to employ the U.S. opposition to communism in their support of Cuban sugar. As the Cuban ambassador to the United States explained to Secretary of State Dean Acheson in August 1949, the Cuban government could not agree to a reduction in the price of sugar "because of the grave political considerations involved." He argued that "the Communists were openly accusing the government of 'selling out' to the United States on this question and that other political opponents of the Government would play up the theme to dangerous proportions."[42]

Political stability and the containment of communism in Cuba were so important to U.S. policymakers that they were highly susceptible to arguments like those of the Cuban ambassador. Indeed, in an earlier round of sugar negotiations, the director of the Office of American Republic Affairs at the State Department warned his colleagues that "unless Cuba gets an equitable share of our market the present 'flash flood' prosperity [there] can rapidly be converted into economic distress which can in turn plunge the

[41] FRUS, 1949, vol. 2, pp. 627, 629, 632–33, 637–38.

[42] HSTL, Acheson Papers, Box 64, Memoranda of Conversations, Aug. 1, 1949. Because the Cubans were almost always bargaining from an inferior position, they were naturally attracted to the possibility of exploiting the conflicts in U.S. goals to gain leverage.

island into political chaos.'' He concluded that ''a proposal unfair to Cuba (or even one generally regarded as unfair) would be a bonanza for the communists.''[43]

The director's warning had to be taken seriously in Washington, but it had to contend, of course, with the fact that the State Department was also charged with protecting the almost one billion dollars of U.S. investments in the island. After all, Cuban stability was to serve not merely as the basis for dependable rule but also as the guarantor and framework for the enhancement of U.S. capital as well.

At times, the State Department tried to escape from its dilemma by reversing the pressure, threatening Havana with decreased sugar sales unless it acted more effectively to advance the interests of U.S. capital on the island. Such efforts, however, had to remain secret. As we have seen, once they entered the public realm, they became counterproductive. To deal with this problem, the State Department had been pressing the Cubans since the late 1930s to sign a trade treaty whose provisions would have transferred the treatment of U.S. capital from the political and administrative level in Cuba—with its mass pressures and pecuniary temptations—to the juridical level. The trouble was that the same Cuban nationalism that caused the ''unfair'' treatment of U.S. interests that the treaty was meant to end also stood in the way of any Cuban government agreeing to sign it.[44]

What the State Department needed was some additional lever with which to pry Cuban officials away from their patriotic duties. When the logic of cold war convinced the U.S. Congress to agree to foreign-aid spending as a way of demonstrating Washington's commitment to help poor nations that might otherwise fall prey to communism, the State Department was handed a new weapon in its campaign for better treatment of U.S. interests. The reform side of U.S. policy had always included the modernization of the Cuban economy. A development loan to the Cuban government could thus fit several agendas. In 1948 and 1949, as sugar purchases for European recovery wound down, the Cuban economy greatly needed alternative sources of capital to take up the slack. Moreover, the U.S. Congress— influenced by domestic sugar producers desirous of keeping inexpensive Cuban sugar off the U.S. market—tightened the noose by tying sugar purchases to fair treatment for U.S. investments. President Prío, for his part,

---

[43] FRUS, 1947, vol. 8, p. 614. For a full statement of U.S. policy during this period see ''Current U.S. Policy Toward Cuba,'' in FRUS, 1948, vol. 9, pp. 562–66.

[44] FRUS, 1947, vol. 8, pp. 608–11; 1948, vol. 9, pp. 553, 564; 1949, vol. 2, pp. 637, 646. Secretary of State George Marshall reported to Truman that ''conclusion of a commercial treaty . . . is of paramount importance to American business interests because of discriminating practices against U.S. firms and the rising tide of nationalism'' (FRUS, 1947, vol. 8, p. 617).

eyed a U.S. loan hungrily, as it would fund the public works with which he hoped to make up for the government's inability to spread sugar money to favorites here and there in the island's economy. In 1949 the State Department thought it had maneuvered Prío into a position where the offer of a development loan would gain his signature on the long-awaited trade treaty with its promise of depoliticizing protection of U.S. interests once and for all.[45]

Treaty and loan negotiations—slowed by Cuban nationalism and the push-pull of conflicting North American interests—dragged on into 1950. Then, just as it looked as if the State Department had finally found its way around one of the major contradictions in U.S.-Cuban relations, the world sugar market turned up sharply due to the outbreak of war in Korea. Sugar carried so much weight in the Cuban economy that even small increases in world demand rewarded politicians there far more than loans or even investments. Cuban presidents, reflecting a national psychology, could not resist playing the sugar lottery as a painless way of obtaining the funds they needed to promote their political fortunes. Moreover, given their role as dispensers of sugar income, and in the absence of any coherent vision of state-directed economic growth, Cuban leaders had not become serious about programmatic economic development. For its part, Washington was not ready to dispense aid on a level sufficient to attract the Cuban leadership away from its sugar orientation. Until the 1960s, economic policy in the U.S. Congress remained by and large under the old dispensation in which capitalism was understood to grow by the investment of private rather than public funds. As it turned out, with the tempting sugar option, Cuban leaders could not be enticed by a modest loan, especially one tied to improved treatment of U.S. interests. When war pushed up the price of sugar in 1950 and 1951, the State Department lost its leverage and Cuban leaders were relieved of the necessity to make concessions to the Yankees.[46]

The resurfacing of the sugar contradiction came just as the State Department was faced with another. With the trade treaty slipping from its grasp, the department had to turn its attention to Congress, where the regular at-

[45] FRUS, 1947, vol. 8, pp. 608–9, 615–17; 1948, vol. 9, pp. 562–66; 1949, vol. 2, pp. 623–36. Concerning Truman's attitude toward foreign aid see his *Memoirs* (New York: Signet, 1965), II, pp. 267–76. Truman boasted of his Point Four program of technical assistance that it would aid in "disarming hostile propagandists and in discouraging the advances of both communism and extreme nationalism" (p. 274).

[46] For the attitude of U.S. policymakers toward economic aid during this period see FRUS, 1948, vol. 9, pp. 5–9; 1949, vol. 2, pp. 623–25; 1951, vol. 2, pp. 1342–43. For unpublished documents see N.A., R.G. 353, Records of Intra- and Interdepartmental Committees, Box 78, "Suggested Plans for Economic Aid to Latin America," Jan. 1948, and HSTL, Office Files of the Assistant Secretary of State for Economic Affairs, 1946–1947, Box 15, Memoranda of Conversations, 1948–Folder 1, "Economic Program for Latin America," 1/19/48.

tempt to amend the Sugar Act was in process. As domestic sugar interests applied their usual squeeze to what they considered a bloated Cuban quota, the State Department was forced to drop its pressure on Havana and swing into its role as lobbyist in Congress for "fair" treatment of Cuban sugar— and of the significant percentage of it that was grown and milled by Cuban-based U.S. sugar companies.[47] Faced with the need to rescue the Cuban economy as a whole (and the prized stability that went with it), the department had to forego the effort to secure improved protection of the U.S. portion of that economy. Stability and change once again pulled in differing directions.

IX

Despite hopes in Washington, the gap between the U.S. desire for political and economic cooperation and the electoral needs of the Cuban president widened during the term of Prío Socarrás. The growing anti-Soviet orientation of Auténtico foreign policy turned out to be mostly an expedient of Cuban politics. Cuba took her turn in international forums like the United Nations denouncing Soviet aggression and testifying to her loyalty to the free-world alliance. Her cold-war initiatives were on the whole, however, mostly verbal. When Prío was asked by the United States to follow through with his offer to send Cuban troops to Korea, the president vacillated. In a demonstration that even cold-war issues could run afoul of Cuban nationalism, students and opposition politicians opposed the president's offer. Prío let the idea die.[48]

Even when the Auténticos were free of foreign-policy pressures coming from the Communists or the nationalist opposition, they occasionally acted on their own brand of internationalism. While holding the U.S. coat in the global contest with the Soviet Union, the Auténticos pursued an energetic foreign policy in the Caribbean area—indeed, too energetic for Washington. While the party had dispensed with the domestic side of its 1930s radicalism, it retained a vehement opposition to dictatorship. However tawdry their own rule at home, they saw themselves as defenders of democracy and enemies in particular of Caribbean strongmen. Moreover, an aggres-

---

[47] In the 1950s about 40 percent of the Cuban crop was ground by U.S.-owned mills. See Benjamin, *Hegemony*, p. 242n8.

[48] The issue of Cuban troops for Korea is discussed in FRUS, 1951, vol. 2, pp. 1347–49, 1356–57, 1361–63. Gonzalo Guell, special consultant to the Cuban Ministry of State, explained to the counselor of the U.S. embassy that "for political reasons stemming principally from next year's elections it has been decided that it would not be politic to send Cuban troops to Korea" (p. 1356). The Korean batallion issue is also mentioned in Szulc, *Fidel*, pp. 199, 240, and Phillips, *Island of Paradox*, p. 255.

sive regional foreign policy helped to demonstrate Cuba's sovereignty and thus acted as a psychological counterweight to the great U.S. influence on the island.

Since the time of Simón Bolívar, the struggle against tyranny in Latin America has often been cast in a continental dimension. José Martí had continued this theme, envisioning that an independent Cuba would be an example to all of Latin America. In similar fashion the Auténticos interpreted the history of their party and its electoral victories as part of a larger process of democratization that would, with their help, remove the remaining dictatorships of the area—particularly Nicaragua's Somoza and the Dominican Republic's Trujillo. Anti-dictatorial crusading became a plank of Auténtico foreign policy in the late 1940s, and Cuba became a haven for political exiles from the surrounding dictatorships.

Numerous plots and abortive raids against entrenched regimes in the Circum-Caribbean area punctuated the decade following the end of the war. Contingents of political exiles, supplemented by soldiers of fortune and anti-fascist fighters left over from the Spanish Civil War, set forth to unseat local tyrants. Armed with war-surplus equipment bought at bargain-basement prices, they came to refer to themselves as the "Caribbean Legion." Despite its imposing name, however, the Legion had no formal organization and its military punch often depended on the possibility that its aging equipment would get off the ground or out to sea without mishap.

The most serious expedition mounted by these forces was sponsored by the Auténticos against Trujillo in 1947. With the unofficial backing of the Grau administration, Cubans organized an invasion force of over a thousand men (including the university student Fidel Castro) complete with vintage bombers and landing craft. Funds for the invasion were channeled through the Cuban Ministry of Education—which regularly acted as a sieve through which Cuban government funds poured into deserving hands. However, when the Havana press took notice of the ill-concealed training camps, Trujillo raised a loud protest with the Organization of American States. When Washington got wind of the expedition, it put pressure on Grau, who first moved the expeditionaries to a deserted key fifty miles off the Cuban coast and, finally, sent the Cuban navy to break them up. Washington viewed the Caribbean Legion as not much more than comic opera but strongly opposed its activities as upsetting to the stability it preferred in the area.[49]

[49] The aborted invasion of the Dominican Republic is discussed in Charles D. Ameringer, *The Democratic Left in Exile: The Antidictatorial Struggle in the Caribbean* (Coral Gables, Fla.: University of Miami Press, 1974), pp. 64–71. For Fidel's participation see Rolando

Washington held itself forward as the leader of the world's democratic forces, but it insisted on defining the quest for democracy in its own terms. In its own sphere of influence, agitation against tyranny that was emotional, violent, and unpredictable and that was likely to lead to radical, unstable, or non-traditional authoritarian regimes was not what the United States had in mind. Since it associated constitutionality with stability and U.S. influence, Washington was pleased that the Auténtico presidents were duly elected heads of state. It did not wish them, however, to invest that status with a political content of their own making.

ONE OF the problems inherent in constitutional regimes was that they held regular elections. Electoral contests in Cuba were particularly sensitive to nationalist agitation and thus inauspicious times for the advancement of U.S. goals. As the island's 1952 election approached, Prío led a party sunk in corruption and unsure of its ability to perpetuate its hold on the presidency. This made him all the more troublesome to Washington.

The same Korean War boom that had boosted sugar prices had also brought sharp inflation to Cuba, and President Prío was determined to keep down the rapidly rising price of food in an election year. This was not easy to do because the tight bonds between the U.S. and Cuban economies made it more difficult for the Cuban executive to manage price levels than for his counterparts in other primary-producing countries.[50] Strong state action was needed, and Prío had to insulate himself from the traditional U.S. opposition to such tactics. U.S. Ambassador Willard Beaulac warned Prío against government intervention in the marketplace. Invoking the reigning North American belief in the inextricable connection between capitalism and democracy, Beaulac told the president that "it was disappointing to see that Cuba, with its precious freedoms still intact, was thinking of limiting those freedoms." Prío responded obediently that his "government was on the side of liberalism in economic as well as political matters."[51] This colloquy notwithstanding, Prío continued his attempt to subsidize food prices.

Despite the fertility of the island's soil and its favorable climate, much

---

Bonachea and Nelson Valdés, *Revolutionary Struggle: Selected Works of Fidel Castro* (Cambridge: MIT Press, 1972), I, pp. 22–23.

Washington's analysis of Cuban foreign policy during this period is indicated in HSTL, PSF, Intelligence File, Situation Reports: SR–29 (12/23/48), "Cuba," pp. 25–28. Analysis of the Caribbean Legion is in Intelligence File, ORE 11–49 (3/17/49), "The Caribbean Legion."

[50] FRUS, 1951, vol. 2, pp. 1363–65. For Cuba's monetary system see Henry C. Wallich, *Monetary Problems of an Export Economy*. Also see Padula diss., pp. 333–39, and Domínguez, *Order and Revolution*, pp. 33, 35. Cuba did not have a national bank until 1950. The U.S. dollar ceased to be legal exchange only in 1951. See Phillips, *Island of Paradox*, p. 249.

[51] FRUS, 1951, vol. 2, pp. 1363–65.

of Cuba's food came from the United States. Its price, therefore, was highly sensitive to price levels in North America. This simple fact—like the roller-coaster price of sugar—was a clear sign that market forces, set in motion by the powerful North American economy, continually got in the way of Washington's efforts to align the promotion of U.S. economic interests with its larger foreign-policy aims. Like many other contradictions in its relations with Cuba, Washington did not find it easy to recognize the implications of this one.

X

After the interventionist period in U.S.-Cuban relations ended in the early 1930s, Washington came to rely more and more on the Cuban president to mediate tensions between nationalism and the promotion of U.S. interests. Thus it should have been an ominous sign that Cuban presidents, measured against a social ideal that they could not fulfill, experienced declining popularity in the 1940s. The political and economic dependence that was built into the relationship between the two states continued to disturb the island's politics. To this burden was now added the pressure of Cuban interest groups organized along corporate lines and demanding protection from the tremendous shifts to which the sugar economy subjected the island. By the early 1950s, the gap between the U.S. desire for political and economic cooperation and the electoral needs of the Cuban president had reached serious proportions.

As if to mock the theories of development coming into vogue in North America, the growth of the island's economy and the stabilization of its politics after 1940 led not to a rational bureaucratic order but rather to a system in which economic decisions were made to defend political factions, while political office was sought as a means to economic advantage. If public corruption originated in the centuries of Spanish colonial administration, the lack of real political power in semi-sovereign Cuba reinforced the tradition of using office for political and personal gain. The Auténtico administrations, brought to office as heirs of the long heritage of social idealism, wasted their assets in ineffectual nationalist rhetoric and left an inheritance of unprecedented corruption. Grau went so far as to steal the evidence of his misappropriation of funds from the very court hearing the charges against him. When Batista broke the constitutional order by overthrowing Prío just prior to the 1952 elections, few Cubans mourned his passing. For its part, Washington maintained a discreet silence.

CHAPTER 5

EMBRACING DICTATORSHIP:
THE UNITED STATES
AND BATISTA

I

B ATISTA's regime was to last for almost seven years, many of them reasonably prosperous one. But its unconstitutional origin deprived it of even the symbols of authority possessed by previous presidents. Batista spent most of his time in office attempting to make the same transition from military dictator to popularly elected president that he had accomplished in the years between 1934 and 1940. But this time his populist rhetoric had a hollow ring, and it was soon replaced by the vocabulary of economic development that the small group of North American-trained technocrats had introduced during the Auténtico years. The language of growth economics and the bureaucracy it entailed were attractive to the new Cuban leader because it made Washington happy and expanded state budgets and his access to them. Real economic development—should that actually occur— was also advantageous because it would quiet opposition from unionized workers and small producers down to whom some of the wealth would trickle.[1]

Batista's real leadership skills, however, were those of the non-charismatic caudillo. He rewarded his friends with government office, state pre-

---

[1] Batista's claim to responsibility for the island's economic development after 1952 is made in his *The Growth and Decline of the Cuban Republic* (New York: Devin-Adair, 1964), chs. 7–28. Batista as a political opportunist is described in Carlos Alberto Montaner, *Secret Report on the Cuban Revolution* (New Brunswick, N.J.: Transaction, 1981), pp. 5–7. Batista's populist period is discussed in Robin Blackburn, "Prologue to the Cuban Revolution," *New Left Review* 21 (Oct. 1963), pp. 71–73.

ferment, and outright graft. He lured his most vocal opponents with these same inducements. If they were unresponsive, he employed the legal and police power of the state against them. His was an unexceptional authoritarian regime. He repressed those who actively resisted his power, caring little about the ideological or cultural claims they or others made. Batista did not understand expansionist economics nor did he identify it as crucial to his survival. As a non-ideological head of state, he did not wish to propel Cuban society in any particular direction. He wished merely to preside comfortably over it. Indeed, corruption and opulent life-styles became so predominant among his supporters that the institutions of autocratic power lost their effectiveness as time wore on.

On a deeper level, the developmentalism of the 1950s was a veneer laid over autocratic institutions and rigid interest groups, just as the populism of the 1930s had only barely obscured that era's class tensions and violence. Symbolically, Batista was even more naked than before. One of the palpable results of developmentalism—the resurgence of North American capital—created its own problem. It raised the old charge of *vendepatria*: the crime of selling the honor and resources of the nation to foreigners. At least the social-welfare rhetoric of the 1930s had had a certain mass appeal. Developmentalism, with its urban, trickle-down emphasis, on the other hand, was attractive only to that portion of the relatively small middle class employed in government jobs and to those businesses and unions that were first in line at the trough of state spending. In actual practice, growth took the form of government "contracts" with favored clans and interests. In any event, state-oriented economic growth was not something that Batista took seriously, except in his memoirs.[2]

WHAT did come naturally to Batista was the process of purchasing political allegiance—a far more established tradition in the politics of the Cuban republic. Political favoritism served a social as well as political function for him. Despite his humble origins, he was now more interested in buying his way into the upper class than in earning the love of the masses. His earnest efforts to have himself admitted to the aristocratic Havana Yacht Club indicate that his gaze was fixed on the top rather than the middle or the bottom of the social pyramid. Except for his fading egalitarian image as the man who opened the officer corps to poor Cubans, Batista's relation to the mass of Cubans was an undefended flank.[3]

[2] Corruption under Batista in the 1950s is discussed in Padula, diss., pp. 66, 101, 255–57, 327, 338; Ruby Hart Phillips, *The Cuban Dilemma* (New York: Ivan Obolensky, 1962) p. 55; Warren Hinckle and William Turner, *The Fish Is Red* (New York: Harper & Row, 1981), pp. 7, 25.

[3] Batista's social climbing and the related social aspirations of the business class in general are discussed in Padula, diss., ch. 1.

Believing that the themes and tensions of the 1930s had played themselves out in the World War II sugar boom, Batista expected that control of government revenues and the loyalty of the upper ranks of military officers were more than sufficient to secure power and the wealth that went with it. As a result, he was completely unprepared (practically as well as intellectually) for the renaissance of the radical and utopian nationalism that had lain dormant since the struggle against Machado. This sentiment, events would make clear, had been made more uncompromising due to the debasement of the creed under the Auténtico presidents. The resurgence of radical nationalism coincided—as it had in the Machado era—with U.S. support for the dictator. Once again, opposition to presidential authoritarianism and foreign domination would reinforce one another.

II

The United States did not long grieve over the Batista coup. Constitutional rule had not turned out to be the royal road to stability. Though less racist in their view of Cubans by this time, State Department officers were still cynical about Cubans' ability to produce stable government. Ironically, the North Americans—despite their long advocacy of constitutional rule—turned out to be less disturbed by the assault on republican order than the Cubans.

Batista immediately gave Washington private assurances that U.S. interests would be respected. After a week of meetings with his emissaries, the U.S. embassy in Havana became convinced that Batista would eventually hold elections, that he had the backing of the military and the important business and labor organizations on the island, and that he would protect foreign capital. What is more, it was convinced that he would not renew his old ties to the Communists. As a result, Secretary of State Dean Acheson advised President Truman that diplomatic recognition should not be withdrawn because of the coup. State Department officials also turned away requests by Prío's adherents that the United States declare its support for constitutional rule in Cuba. With few regrets, Washington accepted the coup of March, 1952.[4]

United States relations with Batista turned out to be more amicable than those it had had with the Auténtico presidents. Batista met a long-standing U.S. desire by breaking relations with the Soviet Union—which he himself had established in 1942. He went further and outlawed the Cuban Com-

---

[4] The U.S. reaction to the coup is in: FRUS, 1952–54, vol. 4, pp. 867–72; R.G. 59, 737.00/3-1152, Embtel #599; 737.00/3-1352, Memorandum of Conversation between Wellman and Espinosa; 737.00/3-1752, Deptel #542; 737.00/3-1852, Wellman to Miller; and 737.00/3-2252, Tel.#673.

Batista (*left*) and General Malin Craig, Chief of Staff of the U.S. Army, arriving in Washington, D.C., November 1938. *U.S. Information Agency photo*

Batista (*left*) and U.S. Secretary of State Cordell Hull lunching at the Pan-American Union, December 1942. *U.S. Office of War Information photo*

munist Party. He created more favorable conditions for foreign capital and oversaw a significant increase in U.S. investments and tourism. He established a close relationship with the new U.S. Ambassador, Arthur Gardner. They became so friendly, in fact, that some in the State Department began to wonder whose views of Cuba they were receiving.[5]

[5] U.S. relations with Batista are in FRUS, 1952–54, vol. 4, pp. 881–82, 916–18, 921–26, and 1955–1957, vol. 6. p. 797. Also see Dwight D. Eisenhower Library (DDEL), Whitman File, Dulles-Herter Series, June 1954 (3) Memorandum from Cuban Embassy, 6/8/54.

The growth and changing character of U.S. investments during the Batista period are discussed in Thomas, pp. 1057–59 and 1182–88; Germán Sánchez Otero, "La Crisis del Sistema Neocolonial en Cuba: 1934–1952," in *Los partidos políticos burgueses en Cuba neocolonial, 1899–1952* (La Habana: Editorial de Ciencias Sociales, 1985), pp. 172–78; Morris H. Mor-

U.S. Ambassador Earl E. T. Smith (*left*) after presenting his credentials to President Batista, July 1957. *Wide World Photos*

Ties between the United States and Cuban militaries were also strengthened in this period as the Pentagon began to concern itself with the question of "hemisphere defense" and returned to the generosity in supplying arms that had characterized the World War II period. Batista wholly adopted this perspective and attempted to draw from the Pentagon not only military hardware but a close relationship with the group of U.S. military advisers whose job it was to help train Cubans in use of the weapons with which they would take up their share of the cold-war burden. That relationship served Batista as an important demonstration of Washington's blessing. As time went on, it also helped to convince some of Batista's enemies that the United States was a principal prop of his regime.[6] Other Batista opponents, however, would continue to see Washington as a power that might be turned against the dictator if only it could be persuaded to live up to its professed ideals. The old tension within Cuban nationalism between those who saw North America as a resource and those who saw it as a danger was still alive—though in a few years it would be resolved decisively in favor of the anti-imperialist position.

Batista's cooperative attitude led the State Department to oppose with unusual vigor the attempt by North American beet-sugar interests in 1954 and 1956 to lower Cuba's quota. Washington's efforts to defend the Cuban sugar quota brought it even closer to the still illegitimate Cuban president.[7]

---

ley, *Imperial State and Revolution: The United States and Cuba, 1952–1986* (London: Cambridge University Press, 1987), pp. 48–54; Padula, diss., 61–62, 81; Edward Gonzalez, *Cuba Under Castro: The Limits of Charisma* (Boston: Houghton Mifflin, 1974), p. 63.

  [6] FRUS, 1952–1954, vol. 4, pp. 116–85; 1955–57, vol. 6, pp. 213–99.

  [7] FRUS, 1952–1954, vol. 4, pp. 910–12, 924–26; 1955–57, vol. 6, pp. 777–830.

Washington's appraisal of the first years of Batista's rule was positive. After a trip to Cuba in 1953, Secretary of State for Inter-American Affairs John M. Cabot testified to a committee of the House of Representatives that "we have no serious problems in Cuba. Anti-Americanism is not too difficult there." Vice President Nixon, after visiting the island in 1955, reported to the Cabinet that Batista was "a remarkable man" who "seems desirous of doing a job more for Cuba than a job of [*sic*] Batista and is also concerned about the social progress of his country."[8]

Social progress, of a kind, did characterize the first part of Batista's rule. He continued the public-works projects of the Auténticos and expanded the developmental role of the state. The fledgling national bank grew and a development bank was established.[9] Some of the funds in these institutions, of course, were directed by political rather than market forces. Statism in Cuba was not headed in a technocratic direction, despite the small band of economists trained at U.S. universities.

Batista also cracked down on the university-centered, violent gangs that were a sterile residue of the once-radical student organizations of the 1930s. He allowed the U.S. Mafia to operate in Havana, and their new hotels and casinos contributed to the tourist boom that for a while nourished the economy. Like all Cuban presidents since the rise of a powerful union movement in the 1930s, Batista defended the wage levels of the organized working class, though he did so less vigorously as working-class economic demands increased in the late 1950s. He formed an alliance with the head of the Cuban Confederation of Labor, the Auténtico Eusebio Mujal, which provided for the welfare of the confederation's leadership, if not always for its rank and file.[10]

Despite his good standing with Washington and with business and labor leaders on the island, Batista had no political base, nor, as it turned out, would he be able to create one. He ruled with the aid of the growing state bureaucracy, the police, and the military as his "party." With so much power, there was little need to accommodate his political enemies. But

[8] Cabot's remarks are in U.S. House of Representatives, Committee on Foreign Affairs, Historical Series, *Selected Executive Session Hearings, 1951–1956*, vol. 16, *The Middle East, Africa and Inter-American Affairs* (Washington, D.C.: U.S.G.P.O., 1980), pp. 409–10. Nixon's remarks are in DDEL, James C. Hagerty Papers, Diary, March 1955, Cabinet Meeting of 3/11/55.

[9] Jaime Suchlicki, *Cuba, From Columbus to Castro* (New York: Scribner's, 1974), pp. 151–53; Batista, *Growth and Decline*, pp. 138–41, 146–47.

[10] Batista's relationship to labor is discussed in Domínguez, *Order and Revolution*, pp. 89–92; Farber, *Revolution and Reaction*, pp. 145, 153–61; and Petras, *Class, State and Power*, pp. 210–15. The role of the Mafia in Cuba is discussed in Nicolas Gage, "The Little Big Man Who Laughs at the Law," *Atlantic*, (July 1970), pp. 67–68; Penny Lernoux, "The Miami Connection," *The Nation*, February 18, 1984, pp. 186–87.

without the strength to survive reasonably honest elections, he was forced to use that power openly to maintain himself. Though Cuban politics had been a tawdry affair under the Auténticos, the end of party competition only increased tensions. Grau and Prío had dashed the hopes of the electorate; in time, Batista was to enrage it.[11]

III

Batista might have made his rule more acceptable to Cubans or at least have passed his office on to a trusted successor if he had been able to lure the established political parties into the electoral arena. Though they wavered at times, on most occasions they refused to meet him at the polls until he had relinquished the reigns of power. Batista's failure to co-opt other parties was surprising in light of the opportunist character of most of them. The parties from the pre-Machado era were now nothing more than political clubs in which personal ambition wrestled with personal animosities to produce a wilderness of changing alliances and aims. The principal post-Machado party, the Auténticos, was torn between its need to stand as the passionate defender of sovereignty and social justice and the fact that political advantage and personal gain had replaced these earlier goals. The youngest party, the reform-minded Ortodoxos, went into decline after the suicide of their charismatic leader, Eduardo Chibás, in 1951 and spent the Batista years in fruitless debate over tactics while spinning off small activist elements that went underground and prepared for warfare with the regime. The Communists, too, spun off sects, most of which turned out labor bureaucrats or fascists of the Caribbean sort. The Communist Party itself kept as many of its options open as possible and survived this period of illegality and moderate repression fairly well. It avoided active opposition to the regime and used the time to build up its small force of loyalists in the student and union movements. For whatever reason, it was less affected by the general corruption of politics from which all other parties suffered.[12]

Unable to become president except by his own hand, Batista withstood the rising demand that he step down and slowly hardened his rule into a dictatorship. Even without elections, Batista might simply have worn down the opportunistic, partisan elements of the opposition. But in a turn of events that he hardly understood, he became the focus of the hostility of a new generation of alienated youth. They revived the old antipathy toward

[11] Thomas, *Pursuit*, chs. 66 and 70.

[12] Cuban political parties during this period are discussed in Thomas, *Pursuit*, pp. 852–53, 857–62, 869–75, and in Charles D. Ameringer, "The Auténtico Party and Political Opposition in Cuba, 1952–1957," *Hispanic American Historical Review*, 65:2 (May 1985), pp. 327–51. Election results are recorded in Mario Riera Hernández, *Cuba republicana, 1899–1958*.

Batista from the 1930s. In radical circles, he already stood accused as the murderer of charismatic young leftists of that era and as the man who brought the praetorian military into control of the state. To these crimes he now added the destruction of the constitutionalism of the 1940s. Moreover, he was opening the fragile Cuban economy to a new wave of North American investment and was openly deferential to Washington. Batista's dictatorship unwittingly presented itself as the barrier against which could be flung the disparate, deep-seated grievances of republican Cuba: tyranny, militarism, corruption, and imperialism.[13]

Facing a renascent nationalism, Bastista discovered that there was no class to whom he could turn for support. The army was a personal organization, not an independent or class-based institution; Batista himself had assured this when he destroyed the old officer corps in 1933. The Church and the Hispanicized upper class were weak and stigmatized by their one-time support of colonialism and their more recent dalliance with Falangism. Moreover, some wealthy Cubans, attracted by the North American belief in the virtues of an open marketplace, resented the fact that Batista had moved from personal enrichment to the more corporate role of dispenser of state contracts to friends and allies—a practice that closed off larger and larger parts of the Cuban-owned economy to native competitors. Like many who entered the bourgeoisie through the perquisites of office, Batista could never assure the business class that he was one of them. When he openly courted wealthy Cubans, moreover, he encountered deep-seated personal hostility. His populist stance in the 1930s served as a constant reminder to them that he was a potential demagogue, while the support he had elicited earlier from darker-skinned Cubans (Batista himself was of mixed Chinese-Cuban parentage) raised the upper class's historical fear of race conflict. Finally, Batista had sacrificed his pro-Franco friends in the 1940s and had become the ally of the Communists. Conservative forces in Cuba, themselves weak due to the absence of an independent, landed upper class, would not manifest loyalty to such a dictatorship.[14]

IV

By the 1950s, the Cuban presidency had become a very powerful office. It now stood at the center of interest mediation and had authority over many

[13] Szulc, *Fidel*, pp. 144, 160–62, 186, 238; Suchlicki, *Columbus to Castro*, pp. 58–81; Kapcia, "Cuban populism," in Abel and Torrents, *José Martí: Revolutionary Democrat*, pp. 55–64. Hostility to imperialism was still a theme even of moderate opponents of Batista. See Teresa Casuso, *Cuba and Castro* (New York: Random House, 1961), chs. 2 and 3.

[14] Blackburn, "Prologue", pp. 52–91. For the role of the army see Pérez, Jr., *Army Politics*, chs. 9–14.

aspects of the sugar industry, which had come under increasing state regulation since the 1930s. In Batista's case, the powers of office were complemented by the loyalty of the Cuban military and the backing of the United States. This combination seemed more than enough to compensate for his lack of popular or class-based support. Yet Batista's power was flawed at its economic core. He could speak in the increasingly attractive terms of economic diversification and could dispense a growing array of favors, but he could not control the price of sugar or the terms on which it entered the vital North American market. Since these conditions, in turn, determined the health of the Cuban economy, Batista could not avoid being caught between this essential dependence and the Cuban nationalism that was energized by it.[15]

In the early years of his rule, business and organized labor stood by Batista, seeing him as an essential source of favors. To some businessmen the Cuban president was also indispensable as an advocate of more favorable treatment of Cuban exports to the United States. Other businessmen, however, looked to him for a different kind of relief. For them, he was the only counterweight to decisions in Washington directly harmful to their interests. As always, the Cuban president had to walk a fine line between attracting U.S. capital and protecting Cuban interests. The Cuban bourgeoisie was torn in its attitude toward the United States between its exposure to the influence and intense competition of North American investments and products on the one hand and its eagerness to take advantage of the innumerable business and professional opportunities that followed in the dollar's wake on the other. As Batista came to rely more and more on U.S. support, he began to lose his balance. He made greater efforts to meet the conditions desired by Washington for better treatment of U.S. capital. In doing so, he necessarily strained his relations with segments of Cuban business.[16]

As time wore on, even businessmen who benefited from the regime or from ties to the U.S. economy had to worry about too close an association with Batista or Washington. The same North American influence that protected wealthy Cubans from radical solutions to the structural weaknesses of the Cuban economy potentially exposed them, as partners of that influ-

---

[15] The nature of sugar bargaining between the Cuban and U.S. executive branches makes this dependency clear. See FRUS, 1952–54, vol. 4, pp. 901–14, 921–26, and 1955–57, vol. 6, pp. 777–820, 822–30. Also see DDEL, Whitman File, Dulles-Herter Series, June 1954 (3), Embassy of Cuba Memorandum, 6/8/54.

[16] The Cuban economy during the Batista years is examined in James O'Connor, *The Origins of Socialism in Cuba* (Ithaca, N.Y.: Cornell University Press, 1970), chs. 2 and 5; Alvarez Díaz et al., *Un estudio sobre Cuba*, chs. 31ff.; Domínguez, *Order and Revolution*, pp. 54–57, 66–76, 85–94, 97–98, 121–23.

ence, to the crosscurrents of Cuban nationalism. The bourgeoisie's ambivalence toward North America was registered by the great pride it took in gaining ownership (for the first time since the 1890s) of the majority of sugar production and, at the same time, in having its sons earn North American bachelor's degrees. They were partisans of order, but when the winds of nationalism and of class tensions began to buffet the dictator in 1957 and 1958, some moved to distance themselves from the regime. If their sons or daughters joined the underground resistance (not an unusual occurrence) and became victims of brutal police methods, ties of interest were sundered. Not a few wealthy families contributed funds to the militants, including the 26th of July Movement led by Fidel Castro. The lure of a purified republic tugged even at those who lived well amidst its corruption.[17]

The alienation of the organized working class from the dictatorship was also partial and gradual. Class consciousness still oriented the perspective of many workers from the generation of the 1930s.[18] Even younger workers, some of whose unions were led by Communists, took a militant stance toward their employers. Many others resented the corrupt bargain between the president and the union leadership that set limits on the gains they might make even as it assured the political clout of their organizations. The relative decline in purchasing power experienced even by organized labor in the late 1950s left them more jealous than ever of the conspicuous consumption of the wealthy politician-businessmen.[19]

Unorganized, unemployed, and underemployed workers made up the core of the Cuban proletariat. It was their fate to be for the most part superfluous to the needs of the existing economy and to suffer periodic want during the "dead season," which lasted for as long as nine months between the spasm of work and income that attended the sugar (and less so the coffee) harvest. This group of laborers was alternately intimidated and angered by its inability to secure steady work and even a modest standard of living. They were not impotent, however. They lived on a small island with a homogeneous population and few geographical and communications barriers. They were not members of minority ethnic communities nor tied to paternal relationships with landholders. There was no Cuban peasantry to speak of. There *was* a racial barrier—between white and black workers—but blacks had been too important a source of labor to be kept out of employment either in rural or urban areas and they were by now well mixed

---

[17] Alfred Padula, "Financing Castro's Revolution, 1956–1958," *Revista Interamericana* 8:2 (Summer 1978), pp. 234–46.

[18] Maurice Zeitlin, "Political Generations in the Cuban Working Class," *American Journal of Sociology* 71:5 (3/66), pp. 493–508.

[19] The declining position of the organized proletariat is discussed in Domínguez, *Order and Revolution*, pp. 72, 89–92, 97, and Farber, *Revolution and Reaction*, pp. 156–61.

with whites among the employed and unemployed. Blacks, moreover, had preferred the path of integration since emancipation from slavery in the late nineteenth century, and no organized violence against blacks had occurred since 1912 when whites had suppressed the organization of a black political party. Batista was unsuccessful in attracting poor or black support to his regime. Except for service in the military—fast turning from a privileged to a dangerous occupation—he offered them little. He made no use of his own humble origins, which in this period he did nothing to emphasize. The superfluous labor force, then, was not tied to the dictatorship. They could, however, be easily attracted to any movement that spoke in the name of the "humble" masses.[20]

Batista's most immediate problem with labor, however, was not that the lumpen proletariat took to the streets but that the organized working class became restive and demanded favors of the dictator that he could no longer provide. There were militant strikes by bank and sugar workers early in his rule, and both the Communist Party and the nationalist opposition began to win adherents among union members who resented their declining welfare or who were beginning to see the dictatorship in patriotic terms. As Batista sensed that work stoppages and union demands were now catching him in the midst of a struggle between workers and owners, he began to use his police to suppress strikes. Eventually, he was forced to ban them altogether, depending more and more on his labor-leader allies to control their rank and file—something that by 1958 they were less and less able to do. At that point some unions began to break away from the control of Batista's ally Eusebio Mujal, while more and more individual workers joined the underground opposition. In Oriente, the center of the major guerrilla insurgency, labor began to move away from the dictator by the spring of 1958. As the war-ravaged economy spiraled downward in that year, workers by and large lost both their hopes and their fears of the dictator. During this period, the 26th of July Movement began to have some success in recruiting second-level labor leaders.[21]

The group that served as the fulcrum for the large lever that finally toppled the dictator was Cuba's young people. These were for the most part

[20] Race and society in Cuba is examined in Rafael Fermoselle, *Política y color en Cuba: la guerrita de 1912* (Montevideo: Ediciones Geminis, 1974); Knight, *Slave Society in Cuba*; Leslie B. Rout, Jr., *The African Experience in Spanish America* (London: Cambridge University Press, 1976), pp. 288–312; Rebecca Scott, *Slave Emancipation in Cuba*; and Geoffrey E. Fox, "Race and Class in Contemporary Cuba," in Irving Louis Horowitz, ed., *Cuban Communism*, 4th ed. (New Brunswick, N.J.: Transaction, 1982), pp. 309–30.

[21] Petras, "The Working Class and the Cuban Revolution," pp. 210–15; Maurice Zeitlin. *Revolutionary Politics and the Cuban Working Class* (New York: Harper & Row, 1970), pp. 226–27.

students, workers, and professionals in their twenties and thirties. From the start of Batista's rule, the University of Havana had been a principal center of militant opposition. Hundreds of its students were funneled into the urban underground. Their movement into violent opposition to Batista reverberated with the memory of student opposition to Machado and of students martyred (as they saw it) by Batista's army in 1935. Many young workers and professionals, eager to renew the long struggle against authoritarian rule and find a place for their talents in a less jaded society, joined with students and former students in a new crusade. They, in turn, were assisted—and in some instances led—by members of an older generation now in its forties and fifties who had participated in the political and social struggles of the 1930s.[22]

The movement against the dictatorship gathered intensity because it arrived at the culmination of a decade-long struggle against corruption. Cuban youth, inspired by a series of charismatic puritans, had for many years attacked the venality of the Auténtico regimes. They had been joined in that effort by a portion of the middle class alienated by the rigging of almost all competition for jobs and offices under the Grau and Prió administrations.[23]

In 1947 the anti-corruption movement had spawned a new and vibrant political party, the Ortodoxos, led by Eduardo Chibás. Chibás broke from the Auténticos and took with him much of the youth wing of that party as well as important elements of the middle class. Employing the radio media that had spread widely throughout the island, Chibás relentlessly exposed and ridiculed the personal venality and partisan opportunism that had become the essence of Cuban politics. The Ortodoxo movement attracted young (and some not so young) Cubans who responded to Chibás's call for social justice, honest government, and political freedoms. Ortodoxos, as had every radical and reform movement in modern Cuban history, embraced the banner of Cuban nationalism and its corollary, economic independence. Except for this latter point, however, Ortodoxos directed their fire against the presidential palace rather than the White House. One young adherent to the Ortodoxos in the early 1950s was the twenty-five-year-old lawyer Fidel Castro.[24]

[22] Suchlicki, *University Students and Revolution*, ch. 4; Bonachea and Valdés, eds., *Revolutionary Struggle*, pp. 16–27; Ramón Bonachea and Marta San Martín, *The Cuban Insurrection: 1952–1959* (New Brunswick, N.J.: Transaction, 1974), ch. 3.

[23] E. Vignier and G. Alonso, *La corrupción política y administrativa en Cuba: 1944–1952* (La Habana: Editorial de Ciencias Sociales, 1973).

[24] The Ortodoxo program is described in Partido Ortodoxo, *Doctrina del Partido Ortodoxo* (La Habana: Editorial Fernández, 1951); Chibás's use of the radio media is examined in Belkis Cuza Malé, "Reflections on Radio Martí," in Stephen Schwartz, ed., *The Transition from*

Cuban youth were particularly susceptible to the call of nationalism. The independence movement of 1895–1898 had lost its most vital, younger leaders in the struggle, leaving older men and a weary liberation army to acccept the compromise of independence demanded by the United States. The goals of the second heroic era—the struggle against Machado—were likewise unfulfilled, although in this instance blame for the failure was placed on Cubans as well as North Americans. The idea of a new generation redeeming the *patria* runs through modern Spanish-American history and is accentuated by the importance of personal honor and heroism in Hispanic idealism. As each new generation of Cuban intellectuals reassessed the one undiminished creed—the thought of José Martí—they passed on to their students the ideal of a true independence and a purified social order. With these emotional resources, the young people of Castro's generation reinvigorated the old anti-imperialist and anti-dictatorial tradition and turned them against Batista. As this commitment to destroy the dictatorhsip and redeem the failed revolutions of 1895 and 1933 engaged the energies of more and more young Cubans, it gave direction to the anomic violence and inflated rhetoric that had come to characterize student politics since the suppression of the insurgent movement in the mid-1930s.[25]

With these powerful psychological and social forces at work, it was not long before urban underground and rural guerrilla movements of significant strength were built. Nevertheless, because the armed elements of these movements were small—the largest body, led by Fidel Castro, numbered fewer than three or four hundred in all but the last months of the conflict—and because their more impressive urban support structures were necessarily hidden from view, Batista and Washington consistently underestimated them. The power of the old idealism to sustain the active enemies of Batista and to undermine the will of his supporters operated almost invisibly, hollowing out the buttresses of the dictatorship until it was an easily broken shell.

V

Washington was ill prepared to understand what was happening in Cuba, let alone to foretell that the opposition to Batista might one day grow into

Authoritarianism to Democracy in the Hispanic World (San Francisco: Institute for Contemporary Studies, 1986), pp. 131–34.

[25] Miguel Jorrin and John D. Martz, *Latin American Political Thought and Ideology* (Chapel Hill: University of North Carolina Press, 1970), pp. 70–78, 113–19, 159–64, 388–89; C. Fred Judson, *Cuba and the Revolutionary Myth: The Political Education of the Cuban Rebel Army, 1953–1963* (Boulder, Colo.: Westview Press, 1984), pp. 23–35.

a threat to the close relationship between the two nations that North Americans assumed to be natural. It had long ago given up any serious attempt to purify Cuban politics because these efforts had produced such meager results and required a form of intervention that had become unacceptable to most Americans, north as well as south of the Rio Grande. The United States had learned to be content with affairs in Cuba as long as its president was cooperative, its economy reasonably open to U.S. capital and goods, and its Communist Party weak. By these criteria, Batista was more than acceptable. He expanded economic ties to North America to unprecedented levels, ended the shabby political dealings that had frustrated Washington's desire for rationalized administration, and had forced the Cuban Communists underground. Finally, he was clearly in control of Cuba. It was assumed that he would eventually strike a bargain with the older generation of political leaders and become, at some point, the legal and accepted, if not beloved, chief executive. This, no doubt, was Batista's expectation as well.[26]

The break in constitutional succession troubled some in the State Department, but more because it seemed to testify to the continuing failure of Cubans to live up to North American standards of governance than because it might ignite a dangerous, deeply held sense of political betrayal among the Cuban people. In any event, the rhetoric of Cuban politics had been moving away from social radicalism and anti-Plattism since the 1930s and had adopted anti-communism. This latter fact attested both to the opportunistic practice of the Cuban Communist Party since the mid-1930s and to the influence of the strong anti-Soviet direction of U.S. foreign policy after World War II. Washington had little reason to believe that it might be taking a fatal step in supporting Batista.

THE RISE and fall of the Batista dictatorship coincided with the Eisenhower years in Washington and also with slow changes in U.S. policy toward Latin America that eventually affected relations with Havana. Eisenhower and his advisers retained the cold-war perspective on foreign policy that they had inherited from the Truman era, though some members of the new administration claimed allegiance (rhetorically at least) to the more vigorous notion that communism should be rolled back rather than merely contained. Well into the second Eisenhower term, the principal theaters of the cold war were in Europe and, more recently, in Asia. Latin America was considered a reasonably secure area of what Washington referred to as the

---

[26] The State Department's relations with Batista during this period are in FRUS, 1952–54, vol. 4, pp. 867–72, 881–82, 892–93, 899–901. Also see John F. Kennedy Library (JFKL), Arthur Schlesinger, Jr. Papers, Subject Files, Cuba-Background Materials (Box 5), "Considerations Affecting United States Policy Toward President Batista's Regime," pp. 20–23.

free world. In fact, Washington did not worry much about communism in the hemisphere until it discovered the "subversion" of the government of Guatemala in the early 1950s. This episode caused only brief alarm because the infected regime of Jacobo Arbenz was easily dispatched in 1954 with the aid of a new weapon in the U.S. cold-war arsenal—covert warfare undertaken by the Central Intelligence Agency. With little effort and with only minor embarrassment to the U.S. image as defender of freedom, the tainted regime was overthrown and the country's Communist Party broken. Moreover, Washington was able to utilize the episode to wring from the Organization of American States (OAS) a resolution declaring

> That the domination or control of the political institutions of any American state by the international communist movement . . . would constitute a threat to the sovereignty and political independence of the American states.

In this way, the United States hoped to satisfy its long-standing desire to have the hemisphere organization legitimize efforts to keep the New World free of what North Americans considered alien ideologies. OAS support of U.S. intervention was necessary because Washington had forsworn unilateral military intervention in the 1930s in order to draw the Latin American nations into an effective U.S.-led. hemisphere organization.[27]

With the exception of the Guatemalan episode, the research and intelligence reports of the State Department and the CIA during this period emphasized that communists—while always potentially dangerous—had no prospect of gaining power in a Latin American country through election or even through coalition with other parties.[28] In 1957 the National Security Council saw "no critical problems or difficulties which are major threats to the U.S. security" in the area. Even as late as 1958, Allen Dulles, director of the CIA, testified to Congress in executive session that direct Soviet penetration of any Latin American nation was unlikely.[29] Any direct threat to

[27] Gordon Connell-Smith, *The Inter-American System* (London: Oxford University Press, 1966), ch. 5. Also see Benjamin, "The Framework," pp. 91–112.

[28] *Declassified Documents Index* (DDI) 1977, #272A; U.S., N.A., State Department Lot Files, Office of Intelligence Research, Report 7116, "Latin America: Recent Developments and Future Prospects," January 10, 1956; FRUS, 1955–57, vol. 6, pp. 17, 25, 31.

[29] DDEL, WHO, OSANSA, U.S. Policy Toward Latin America (3), "Progress Report . . . on NSC 5613/1," 10/1/57; U.S. Senate, Committee on Foreign Relations, *Executive Sessions* (Historical Series), vol. 10, pp. 110–11. A general discussion of U.S. policy toward Latin America during this period is in Arthur M. Schlesinger, Jr., ed., *A Documentary History of United States Foreign Policy, 1945–1973* (New York: Chelsea House, 1983), vol. 3, pt. 1, Latin America, pp. xxxv–xl. Also see Dwight D. Eisenhower, *Waging Peace* (New York: Doubleday, 1965), ch. 22.

U.S. interests by the government of a nation well within the U.S. sphere of influence was deemed remote.

If Washington was able to ease its mind about communist control of a Western Hemisphere state, the problems of communism as a strategic and social threat still remained. Ever since the late 1940s, the CIA had warned the White House of two special dangers from communism in Latin America. The first was that in a war with the Soviet Union, Latin American communists would attempt to sabotage the flow of strategic materials moving north to the United States. This scenario greatly occupied the minds of the Joint Chiefs of Staff, whose reference point was the role played by local fascist organizations in aiding German submarine warfare against hemisphere shipping in 1942 and 1943. This reprise of World War II took up much of the Pentagon's brain power and was reinforced by the 1950s belief that the United States was exhausting its domestic supply of strategic minerals.[30]

The real conundrum, however, was the second theme of the intelligence reports: that communist movements would take advantage of the social tensions and political instability in Latin America to threaten U.S. interests. State Department analyses emphasized this latter danger and added that a residual anti-Americanism and a rising economic nationalism provided openings for communist agitation.[31] The problem here was that an effective antidote to anti-Americanism and economic nationalism required major changes in U.S. policy: on the political side, lessened intervention; on the economic side, several things, including reduced protection for U.S. overseas investors and U.S. domestic markets, higher prices for Latin American raw materials, and more economic assistance on more lenient terms.

As the overthrow of Arbenz indicated, the Eisenhower administration was prepared to make the shift from military to covert intervention so as to dampen anti-Americanism. However, it stood firm, as had the Truman administration, in its opposition to economic nationalism. The paternalism with which the United States had always viewed Latin American states convinced successive administrations that violation of marketplace laws would lead Latin America to economic disaster and toward an economic

[30] See HSTL, Papers of Harry S. Truman, President's Secretary's File, Intelligence File, ORE: #16/1 (11/1/47); FRUS, 1955–57, vol. 6, pp. 28, 32. On the concern with raw-materials exhaustion see Gabriel Kolko, *The Limits of Power* (New York: Harper & Row, 1972), pp. 624–27.

[31] DDEL, WHO, OSANSA, NSC Series, Political Papers, Subjects, NSC 144/1 - Latin America (2), "United States Objectives and Course of Action with Respect to Latin America," 3/18/53. The NSC series demonstrates the rising concern with Latin American nationalism at the very outset of the Eisenhower administration and can be followed in the various drafts and revisions of NSC 144, NSC 5432, and NSC 5613 in NSC Series, DDEL. Portions of this documentation appear in FRUS, 1952–1954, vol. 4, pp. 1–115.

structure resembling that of the cold war enemy. Statist economic programs in Latin America were also opposed, of course, because they would threaten the profitability of U.S. investments or even the investments themselves.

Beginning with the Export-Import Bank in the 1930s, however, policymakers in Washington had demonstrated a willingness to underwrite U.S. trade with Latin America by means of government-backed loans. This particular tampering with the marketplace was popular in Congress and with U.S. exporters. Beginning in the Good Neighbor era, a hardy band of liberals, mostly in the State Department, had begun to call for generous aid to Latin American economies as a way of spreading U.S. influence.[32] The Truman and Eisenhower administrations, however, were unwilling to fund a broad program of government grants or loans for Latin American development. When Latin American leaders, anxious to respond to the growing demand for economic growth among rising middle- and working-class sectors in their nations, pointed to the vast Marshall Plan aid going to Europe, Washington replied that those funds were to rebuild war-torn economies and that Western Europe was on the front line of defense against communist aggression.[33] The thought may have occurred to Latin American leaders that a communist threat in the hemisphere might likewise loosen North American purse strings.

VI

Opposition to economic orthodoxy was becoming a powerful current in Latin American thinking after World War II. Sustained by liberal economists at the United Nations Economic Commission on Latin America (ECLA), many spokesmen for these countries had for many years been criticizing the structure of hemisphere economic relationships. The depression and World War II had severely restricted Latin American access to foreign capital and goods and led many governments to support local industrialization as an alternative. After the war, prices of raw materials went into a long decline (except for a short-lived Korean War boom), depriving these governments of the revenues with which they had supported young indus-

---

[32] The role of the liberals is discussed in Jordan Schwartz, *Liberal: Adolf A. Berle and the Vision of an American Era* (New York: Free Press, 1987), pp. 130–33, 152, 256–76, 282; Claude C. Erb, "Prelude to Point Four: The Institute of Inter-American Affairs," *Diplomatic History* 9:3 (Summer 1985), pp. 249–69. Also see Jules R. Benjamin, "Scholars and the Good Neighbor Policy," paper presented at the convention of the Organization of American Historians, Minneapolis, Apr., 1985.

[33] Washington's economic policy toward Latin America in this period is discussed in Stephen G. Rabe, "The Elusive Conference: United States Economic Relations with Latin America, 1945–1952," *Diplomatic History* 2:3 (Summer 1978), pp. 279–94.

trial enterprises, including state-owned corporations. This problem arose just as the return of foreign-made goods threatened the market for local products. Latin American states attempted to move out of this difficulty in two ways: gaining higher prices for their exports and obtaining loans and grants from the United States to continue state financing of economic development. By the 1950s, these efforts led to insistent economic requests that the Eisenhower administration found difficult to dismiss. The new Latin American economic proposals competed on the agenda of inter-American conferences with the U.S. idea that Latin America solve its economic problems by making itself more attractive to foreign private capital. Most frustrating to Washington was the fact that Latin American economic demands distracted attention from the U.S. emphasis on a hemisphere-wide front against communism. As the decade progressed, even a Republican administration began to see the connection between the success of its cold-war agenda and its willingness to change its economic foreign policy.[34]

THE ASSAULT on Washington's Latin American policy also came from within. The Republicans had been attacked in the 1956 presidential campaign by Democratic candidate Adlai Stevenson, who charged that their policy had worsened U.S.-Latin American relations because it failed to address economic grievances and because it maintained too friendly relations with dictatorial regimes. The Democrats regained control of Congress in 1956 and increased their strength in 1958. Liberal Democrats took control of the Senate Committee on Foreign Relations, whose chairmanship soon passed to William Fulbright. The committee contained such rising liberal stars as Hubert Humphrey, Mike Mansfield, John Kennedy, Wayne Morse, and Frank Church. Slowly the committee began to challenge Eisenhower administration policies in the Third World. It questioned the landing of troops in Lebanon in 1958 and the larger policy of opposing Nasser in

[34] Changing policy on economic aid to Latin America can be traced in FRUS, 1952–1954, vol. 4, pp. 186–263,and especially pp. 345–51, as well as in FRUS, 1955–1957, vol. 6, pp. 101–4, 198–99, 300–436. Also see HSTL, PSF, Intelligence File, CIA, NIE-70 (12/12/52), "Conditions and Trends in Latin America Affecting U.S. Security," and PSF, Subject File: Latin America, Thomas Mann to Charles Murphy, "Latin America and U.S. Policy," 12/11/52; DDEL, Papers of The President's Citizen Advisers on the Mutual Security Program and Papers of the U.S. Council on Foreign Economic Policy. Documents illustrating the position of economic conservatives toward economic aid to Latin America are in Nathaniel R. Howard, ed., *The Basic Papers of George M. Humphrey as Secretary of the Treasury, 1953–1957* (Cleveland: Western Reserve Historical Society, 1965), pp. 464–77. Also see DDI, 1981, #611C; 1982, #2224; 1984, #1318, #1319. A good summary of this period is in Thomas Zoumaras, "Eisenhower, Dulles, and the Preservation of Pan Americanism, 1957–58," paper presented at the convention of the American Historical Association, Washington, D.C., Dec. 28, 1987.

the Middle East. Committee liberals also pressed for greater understanding of the problems of Latin American nations and criticized U.S. support for right-wing dictators there as well as the emphasis on military rather than economic aid.[35]

IN TIME, internal political pressure and the contradictions of hemisphere diplomacy worked away at the fiscal conservatism and close ties to big business of the Eisenhower administration. By 1957, two important economic conservatives had retired from the administration: Secretary of the Treasury George Humphrey and Assistant Secretary of State for Inter-American Affairs Henry Holland. Secretary of State John Foster Dulles resented the pressure for aid coming from Latin America but was willing to be flexible in the tools used to maintain the proper cold-war orientation of the hemisphere. In any event, by 1958, Dulles was becoming incapacitated as a result of his losing battle with colon cancer and was replaced by the even more pragmatic Christian Herter. During this same period, the president's brother, Milton Eisenhower, who served as an adviser on Latin American affairs, had come to accept aspects of the Latin American and liberal critique of U.S. economic policy. He used his influence to urge a more flexible approach to economic issues. Despite the firm belief in capitalism that made the administration innately suspicious of the growing statism of the Latin American economies, its concomitant anti-communism forced a consideration of ways to assure that Latin America stayed on the free-world side of the cold war. This growing ambivalence gave Latin American governments new leverage when presenting economic-aid proposals.[36]

Another blow to economic orthodoxy in Washington was the initiation in the mid- and late 1950s of what U.S. government officials referred to as

[35] The critique by the Senate Foreign Relations Committee can be found in Senate, Committee on Foreign Relations, Historical Series, *Executive Sessions*, vol. 10, pp. 242, 249, 252–54, 258–59, 262–66, 274–78, 293, 410–11, 464–66, 474, 606; vol. 11, pp. 423–35, 521–32, 605–10, 613–18. Relations with dictators was at issue within the administration as well. See FRUS, 1955–1957, vol. 6, pp. 4–5, 23, 30, 140, 195. Also see Michael Foley, *The New Senate: Liberal Influence on a Conservative Institution* (New Haven: Yale University Press, 1980), pp. 1–12, 17–33.

[36] An insider's account of this change is discussed in HSTL, Merwin L. Bohan Papers, Subject File: Cuba, Bohan to C. O. Cobb, 9/22/71, pp. 5–6. The best scholarly account is in Thomas Zoumaras, "Eisenhower's Foreign Economic Policy: The Case of Latin America," in Richard Melanson and David Mayers, *Reevaluating Eisenhower: American Foreign Policy in the 1950's* (Urbana: University of Illinois Press, 1987), pp. 155–91. See also Robert A. Pollard and Samuel F. Wells, Jr., "1945–1960: The Era of American Economic Hegemony," in William R. Becker and Samuel F. Wells, *Economics and World Power* (New York: Columbia University Press, 1984), pp. 371–78.

the Soviet "economic offensive." This menacing phenomenon was nothing more, in fact, than an attempt by Premier Nikita Khrushchev to employ some of the resources of a growing Soviet economy to gain friends for Moscow in its competition with the United States in the Third World. Growing Soviet trade, loans, and aid to countries like Egypt and Iraq—both ready to grab at the opportunity to counterbalance U.S. or Western European economic pressure—were somehow seen by President Eisenhower as "the gravest threat to our way of life." The apocalyptic rhetoric reflected not only Eisenhower's profound anti-communism but also his need to weaken the opposition of protectionists and fiscal conservatives in the U.S. Congress who regularly whittled away at his modest but growing requests for economic and military aid to Third World states. These aid requests indicated the administration's increasing resolve to meet the Soviet "economic offensive" head-on. Fearful of the Soviet ability to play on Latin American dissatisfaction with U.S. economic policy, Washington began to show greater flexibility in the employment of U.S. public capital for loans and grants to hemisphere nations.[37]

The full weight of the contradiction between the need to defend vested U.S. interests in the hemisphere and the need to outbid Moscow and appease Latin America was brought home forcefully in May 1958, when Vice President Nixon's good-will tour of Latin America was met at several points with violent anti-U.S. demonstrations, supported in part by local communists. Demonstrators were able to embarrass and even physically threaten Nixon because the Vice President had been assigned the job of meeting with student groups and making himself accessible to the people— an unusual posture for visiting North American dignitaries, who usually spent most of their time huddled with chief executives and in elite conclaves. Nixon's visibility was an effort to counter the voyages of Third World glad-handing on which Premier Khrushchev had recently embarked. Instead of demonstrating that the United States had friends across the spectrum of Latin American society, however, the trip resulted in Nixon's being insulted, spat upon, and almost killed.

It was a chastened and thoughtful Nixon who returned to Washington.

[37] Burton I Kaufman, *Trade and Aid: Eisenhower's Foreign Economic Policy, 1953–1961* (Baltimore: Johns Hopkins University Press, 1982), pp. 122–24, 133–37, 161–66. The more liberal members of the administration and Congress began in this period to look beyond the appeasement of Latin American demands to an economic program broad enough to promote healthy economic growth in Latin America and thereby—it was presumed—reduce the dryness of the tinder that the Soviets seemed always trying to ignite. See Zoumaras, "Eisenhower, Dulles, and the Preservation of Pan Americanism, 1957–58." The most solidly documented study of U.S. policy toward Latin America in this period is Stephen G. Rabe, *Eisenhower and Latin America: The Foreign Policy of Anticommunism* (Chapel Hill: University of North Carolina Press, 1988).

There he presented his prescription for dealing with the hemisphere dilemma to a meeting of the National Security Council. He told them that "the threat of communism in Latin America is greater today than ever before." He said that the new generation of Latin American leaders were "drawn from the middle class and the intelligentsia," and "are oriented toward Marxism in their thinking and are frighteningly naive about communism." The Vice President was not so much worried about the rise of a communist government in Latin America as he was about the ineffectiveness of U.S.-inspired anti-communist propaganda there. Nixon recommended that the United States direct its attack against communism as a "political dictatorship" rather than as a socialist economic system, as this would "take advantage of two violent hatreds among the emerging power groups in Latin America, namely, hatred of dictatorship and hatred of foreign intervention and control."[38] In the Cuban context—to which we now return—Nixon had correctly identified the "violent hatreds." His thought that they could be turned more easily against the communists than against the United States was to prove, however, quite wide of the mark.

[38] Nixon's remarks are in DDEL, WHO, OSANSA, Memorandum for the Honorable Robert Cutler from Deputy Executive Secretary, NSC, 5/26/58. On the motives behind Nixon's trip see U.S. Senate, Committee on Foreign Relations, *Executive Sessions*, vol. 10, 1958, pp. 217–55 (esp. pp. 239–40).

CHAPTER 6

SHUNNING DICTATORSHIP:
THE UNITED STATES
AND BATISTA

I

By THE LATE 1950s, the rising tide of hemisphere economic nationalism and anti-Yankee sentiment, the Soviet "economic offensive," and the domestic critique of coziness with dictators all combined to place the United States in an uncharacteristically defensive posture concerning developments in Latin America. As a result, when threats mounted against the regime of Fulgencio Batista, the State Department worked to solve its Cuban dilemma in ways that would not increase existing difficulties in hemisphere relations. This was not easily done. The task was further complicated by the fact that U.S. policymakers did not realize how volatile the situation in Cuba had become.

Washington had not understood the angry university-based nationalism that underlay the demonstrations against Batista's coup in 1952. It had not even taken seriously the earlier warning signal: the repeated outbreaks of student discontent over the corruption of the Auténtico governments. That discontent moved up the generational ladder and by the late 1940s had spawned a new middle-class reform party, the Ortodoxos, which took the issue of malfeasance into the political arena.[1] Under the charismatic leadership of Eduardo Chibás, the Ortodoxos held together in growing tension the forces of moderate political reform and those of political purification. The aims of the purification forces were social, often structural, and im-

---

[1] Suchlicki, *University Students and Revolution*, pp. 47–57; Farber, *Revolution and Reaction*, pp. 122–30. Sporadic anti-Yankee outbreaks among students occurred during this period. Angry protests followed an incident in which drunken U.S. sailors caroused on the statue of José Martí. See Szulc, *Fidel*, p. 186.

pelled by the national myths of Cuban history. By forcing the reform element of the movement out of the political arena and by adding the highly explosive issue of dictatorship, Batista had squeezed purification into an explosive charge. Rather than understanding these developments as manifestations of a long-simmering, fundamental dissatisfaction with the means and ends of Cuban politics, Washington treated them as deviant products of that politics itself: bombastic, violent, irresponsible.[2]

By 1957, however, the United States was forced to pay attention to the situation in Cuba. By that year, a small guerrilla force in the rugged Sierra Maestra Mountains of Oriente Province at the eastern end of the island began to attack the nearby army garrisons. Soon it gained respect from the impoverished local farmers and attracted the allegiance of a growing urban underground movement that fed it with fighters, arms, and supplies. The guerrillas, led by Fidel Castro, clothed themselves in the venerable mantle of rural rebellion against misrule and oppression based in Havana. Castro's heroic actions and defiant challenges, broadcast across the island from the rebel radio station based in the mountains, struck a responsive chord in many Cubans, one that Washington could not appreciate but with which it would soon have to reckon.

II

Fidel Castro had been a member of one of the political gangs at the University of Havana in the late 1940s but became attracted to the politics of purification and joined the Ortodoxo movement when it was formed in 1947. He obtained a law degree, practiced briefly, and was an Ortodoxo candidate for congress when Batista's coup closed off the electoral road to reform. With a small group of young Ortodoxos and a few ex-students and workers attracted by his forceful personality and his talent for leadership, Castro abandoned politics for the tradition of armed rebellion. On July 26, 1953, in the first major assault against the power of the state since the mid-1930s, Castro led an attack by about 123 men (and two women) against the Moncada barracks, a large military installation in Santiago, the capital of Oriente Province. It was hoped that the assault would spark a popular rebellion against the dictator. The attack failed, however, and no other uprising occurred. But Batista, frightened by such a direct threat to his power, gave orders for the torture and murder of the large number of rebels who had been captured. When the slaughter became known, it thereafter marked the dictator as a butcher and helped to excuse the violence of the opposi-

---

[2] The U.S. reaction to Cuban nationalism during this period can be found in HSTL, Truman Papers, President's Secretary's File, Intelligence File: ORE 9–48 and Situation Reports SR-29, pp. 4–6, 42, and in FRUS, 1950, vol. 2, p. 852; 1951, vol. 2, pp. 1360–65.

tion. The charm that would surround the life of Fidel prevented his captors from executing him—an honorable officer intervened at the last moment.[3]

At his closed trial Fidel spoke in his own defense and delivered the oration that was later redrafted and published as a pamphlet under the title *History Will Absolve Me*. The thesis of the pamphlet followed the moral reformism of Eduardo Chibás and drew inspiration from the utopian egalitarianism of José Martí. Basing his action on the right of rebellion against tyranny, Castro condemned the illegality and militarism of the Batista regime as well as the weakness of the civilian presidents and politicians that had made the coup possible. Evoking the populist conception of "the vast, unredeemed masses" against "the conservative elements of the nation," he declared that had his movement succeeded

> The first revolutionary law would have returned power to the people and proclaimed the Constitution of 1940 the supreme Law of the land, until such time as the people should decide to modify or change it. And in order to effect its implementation . . . the revolutionary movement . . . would have to assume the legislative, executive and judicial powers.

Castro then outlined the judicial, agrarian, edueational, housing, and other reforms that the revolutionary government would have carried out, including confiscation of the holdings of the corrupt generation of politicians. These reforms were defended in the name of social justice and the (radical) provisions of the 1940 constitution, emphasizing the communitarian and egalitarian features of that document rather than its individualistic ones. The pamphlet expressed about as much disdain for the empty reformism of the Auténticos as for the constitutional usurper Batista. The problem with the economic structure of the island, Castro contended, was not its backwardness but its distortion by a public corruption and private cupidity that robbed the people of its benefits. The radicalism of the document lay in its emphasis on expanding political rights into the realms of property rights, job rights, and income rights that would be enjoyed by each citizen. It contained no direct indictment of the United States, finding the source of Cuba's problems within the island itself.[4]

[3] The early history of Castro's movement is discussed in Bonachea and San Martín, *The Cuban Insurrection*, chs. 1–5, and Bonachea and Valdés, *Revolutionary Struggle*, pp. 31–87. Also see Judson, *Revolutionary Myth*, chs. 1–3.

[4] There are several translations of Castro's "speech" at his trial. The quotations here are from *History Will Absolve Me* (New York: Lyle Stuart, 1961), pp. 33–44. Though Castro's speech did not attack the U.S. presence in Cuba, anti-Yankee sentiment had always been just below the surface of the Ortodoxo critique of Cuban politics from which he had drawn inspiration. See the anti-U.S. statements of Ortodoxo spokemen quoted by Sánchez Otero, "La Crisis del Sistema Neocolonial en Cuba," in Otero's *Los partidos*, pp. 253–56.

Fidel was sentenced to fifteen years in prison but was released in 1955 in a general amnesty for political prisoners (not unusual in Latin America) and soon thereafter went to Mexico, where he established the 26th of July Movement (M-26-7), which was, as he described it, "not a political party but a revolutionary movement." Its goals were "political democracy" and "social justice," and it was "formed by new men of strong will who are not accomplices of the past." In Mexico, Castro gathered a force dedicated to armed struggle against the dictatorship and the evils of Cuban society that it represented. On December 2, 1956, with eighty-two men, Castro landed in Oriente. The invasion had been delayed by bad weather and thus failed to coordinate as planned with an underground uprising in the province. Still, Castro had fulfilled his public promise to begin warfare against the dictatorship in 1956. Slowly he gained the reputation of being a man whose rhetoric—unlike that of Cuban politicians—was not empty.[5]

As at Moncada, however, disaster befell the expedition. In an episode that became another element of the leader's heroic image, all but Fidel and a handful of his companions were killed or captured by the army. The survivors (including Fidel's brother Raúl and the Argentine physician Ernesto Guevara) retreated into the rugged Sierra Maestra Mountains. Rather than despairing that the Oriente uprising and the guerrilla landing had been defeated, in characteristic fashion, Fidel declared to his exhausted comrades that Batista's days were numbered. A developing master at the art of psychological warfare, Fidel invited reporters up to his mountain outpost even before his handful of men had engaged the forces of the dictatorship in more than skirmishes. When his interview with *New York Times* reporter Herbert Matthews appeared, it humiliated Batista, who had maintained that Fidel and all of the other rebels had been captured or killed. Matthews's exaggeration of the strength of the rebel force (of which Fidel had convinced him) and his sympathy for their anti-tyrannical goal helped establish a positive public image of the rebels in the United States—one that lasted throughout the war against Batista.[6]

---

[5] This phase in the development of the tactics and ideology of Fidel's movement is examined in Bonachea and San Martín, *The Cuban Insurrection*, pp. 34–40, 65–92. The quotation from Fidel in Mexico is from Bonachea and Valdés, *Revolutionary Struggle*, p. 68. Fidel's writings during this period are in Bonachea and Valdés, *Revolutionary Struggle*, pp. 221–340; some of his private correspondence is in Carlos Franqui, *Diary of the Cuban Revolution* (New York: Viking, 1980), pp. 9–19, 65–98. Studies of Fidel and his followers before 1957 which attempt to assess the nature of his radicalism include Szulc, *Fidel*, pp. 118–368; Lionel Martín, *The Early Fidel*, chs. 1–3; Sheldon Liss, *Roots of Revolution: Radical Thought in Cuba* (Lincoln: University of Nebraska Press, 1987), pp. 171–74.

[6] Szulc, *Fidel*, pp. 272–73, 407; Thomas, *Pursuit*, pp. 838–41, 843, 917–21. The attitude of the U.S. press toward the 26th of July Movement is discussed in Mario Llerena, *The Unsuspected Revolution* (Ithaca, N.Y.: Cornell University Press, 1978), pp. 93–95, 167–73;

Castro and the 26th of July Movement were not the only armed opponents of the regime; there were dozens of small insurrectionary groups, mostly in Havana. There were also fighting arms of the Auténticos, Ortodoxos, and splinter parties, all of which engaged in assaults on the symbols and agents of the dictatorship. One such group, the Revolutionary Directorate, attacked the presidential palace in 1957 and came close to assassinating Batista. There were even rebellions within the armed forces by officers opposed to the dictatorship. None of these forces grew, however, while the M-26-7 organization gathered adherents and became the major center of resistance in the urban areas. Castro's armed force likewise grew in strength and scored a series of small military victories against local garrisons. Moreover, Fidel's willfulness, his singleness of purpose and tight organization, and his skillful use of propaganda soon made his guerrilla force the best-known and most successful opponent of the regime.[7]

III

The Eisenhower administration pondered the deteriorating situation in Cuba not only in the context of rising discontent with its Latin American policy but also in the historic context of the island's being considered part of the North American system. If the former made some in Washington ambivalent about close ties to Batista, the latter reassured others that the stakes were not high. Whatever transpired on the island, the result would not seriously affect the close economic ties between the two nations or the cultural and ideological affinity between Cubans and North Americans. As a result of this sense of security, instead of sending a troubleshooter as ambassador after Batista's coup, the State Department chose Arthur Gardner, a wealthy businessman with no diplomatic experience, from the list of major Republican Party contributors. Even as the dictatorship ran into trouble in 1957, Gardner was replaced not by an experienced Foreign Service officer but by another Republican businessman, Earl E. T. Smith, who knew no Spanish and could not even properly pronounce the names of Cuban government officials.[8] Because of the assumption that Cuba was safely in the orbit of North American society, Washington did not become

---

Richard Welch, Jr., *Response to Revolution* (Chapel Hill: University of North Carolina Press, 1985), p. 161; Mario Lazo, *Dagger in the Heart* (New York: Funk & Wagnalls, 1968), pp. 122–29, 132, 164.

[7] The other opposition movements are discussed in Suchlicki, *University Students and Revolution*, pp. 50–81; and Bonachea and San Martín, *The Cuban Insurrection*, pp. 41–60. It is interesting to note that the statements of José Antonio Echeverría, leader of the Federation of University Students, had a more anti-imperialist focus than those of Fidel. See Bonachea and San Martín, pp. 51–52, 59–60, 180.

[8] Wayne Smith, *The Closest of Enemies* (New York: Norton, 1987), pp. 18, 33.

alarmed even at the prospect of Batista's demise. It could not imagine a successor regime breaking the relationship. In any event, unable to calculate the depth of the opposition, Washington assumed, at least until the latter part of 1957, that Batista or his chosen successor would be able to retain control of Cuban politics.[9]

Well into 1957, the statistics by which U.S. agencies monitored the Cuban economy (and the U.S. elements of it) were encouraging. The U.S. Department of Commerce pamphlet *Investment in Cuba: Basic Information for United States Businessmen* saw no danger on the horizon. It noted the "generally favorable attitudes toward private initiative" and stated that the middle class was "unusually large and influential."[10] At the end of 1956, the ever-optimistic U.S. ambassador, Arthur Gardner, told the State Department that Cubans were "enjoying high-level prosperity" and that there was "no evidence [that] insurrectionary groups have a large following."[11]

Those few in Washington who began to ponder the possibility of a post-Batista era did not worry about social revolution but rather chaos. They feared that a successor might be too weak to maintain order or be no more than another illegitimate ruler with whom other political leaders would refuse to bargain. The belief of the intelligence community in 1957 was that Batista's most likely replacement would be "a military-dominated junta."[12] Little attention was paid to the militant opposition, whose pronouncements were treated as quixotic and whose violence was seen as a sadly familiar product of traditional Cuban politics. The ideology of the militants did not worry State Department officials because they did not take it seriously. Should the militants ever rule, the expectation from them was not social revolution but anarchy. Indeed, Washington's willingness to stick with Batista derived in part from the belief that, whatever his difficulties, he represented greater stability than would exist in his absence.[13]

Even the danger that made Washington most uneasy did not seem imminent. The Central Intelligence Agency's National Intelligence Estimate of April 1957 stated that "the communists do not now constitute a serious threat to the stability of any regime in [Central America or the Caribbean]."[14] The Cuban Communist Party (known in this period as the Partido Socialista Popular) was much weaker than it had been a decade before and was not even an active foe of Batista. Moreover, since the dictator sought

---

[9] FRUS, 1955–1957, vol. 6, pp. 831–32, 835–37, 838–40.

[10] *Investment in Cuba*, pp. 3–4.

[11] FRUS, 1955–1957, vol. 6, p. 836. Also see p. 422. Not all views of Batista's position were so sanguine. See p. 633–34.

[12] FRUS, 1955–1957, vol. 6, p. 629.

[13] FRUS, 1955–1957, vol. 6, pp. 865–76.

[14] CIA, NIE 80–57, p. 7.

to retain U.S. support by branding all of his enemies communists, Washington's normal receptivity to the issue of subversion was weakened. In fact, the Cuban government's Bureau for the Repression of Communist Activities, set up with CIA support in 1954 as part of a program to get Latin American countries to show increased awareness of the threat of communism, was itself criticized as ineffective by Washington because it was concentrating on Batista's political opponents rather than on *real* communists.[15]

The principal source of information from Cuba was the U.S. embassy in Havana, which continued to report, well into 1958, that Batista's forces were prevailing against the violent opposition and that continuing prosperity kept both business and labor in his corner. The growing list of favors to U.S. businessmen by Batista and the close ties between the new U.S. ambassador, Earl E. T. Smith, and the Cuban president ensured that reports from the U.S. embassy would be optimistic.[16]

The first U.S. officials to raise danger signals about Cuba were on the staff of the U.S. consulate in Santiago. This city was the provincial capital of Oriente and very near the zone of operations of Castro's growing guerrilla force. Santiago was also a center of M-26-7 urban strength and had been the scene of a general strike in August 1957 in protest of the murder by the police of Frank País, the head of the movement there. The major landowners in Oriente were beginning to have to pay "taxes" to Castro's forces to save their cattle and sugar from confiscation. Cables from the consulate noted the rebels' strength and the popular sympathy for them. Consulate personnel were also the first to note an anti-Yankee element in the guerrilla mentality. It was apparent in their anger at the United States for supplying the bombs and napalm that Batista's forces rained down on them and the local civilian population, and which they were helpless to combat.[17] Such cables, however, had to compete with the more high-level and optimistic messages from Ambassador Smith in Havana. There, generalizing from the strong position of the president in the capital city and the personal assurances of his friend Batista, Smith rejected such reports and kept telling Washington that opposition to Batista came only from fringe elements and communists.

---

[15] Lyman Kirkpatrick, Jr., *The Real CIA* (New York: Macmillan, 1968), ch. 7.

[16] See reports from the Havana embassy in R.G. 59, 611.37/2–1858 and 611.37/2-1958, Emb. Disp. #660 and #661, Braddock to Department of State.

[17] DDI, 1975, #92I, #93A, and #93C; JFKL, Schlesinger Papers, Subject Files, Background Materials, "Considerations Affecting United States Policy," pp. 83, 85. The effect of the guerrilla war on landowners in Oriente is noted in Padula, "Financing Castro's Revolution," pp. 234–45.

In September 1957 a crack appeared in Batista's control of the military when the naval base in Cienfuegos mutinied and joined with the local M-26-7 underground to take over control of the city. Though loyal elements of the army and air force suppressed the revolt, second-level staff in the Havana embassy and in its CIA station began to conclude that Batista's position was much weaker than Ambassador Smith was contending. At that point they did not expect Batista to be forced from power but suggested that he should be advised to broaden his base of support and that the United States should show greater discretion in supporting the dictator and should seek out trusted members of the opposition for consultations. Smith refused to do this because he feared it would be taken as a sign of lessening U.S. support for the president.[18]

At the end of the year, William Wieland, director of the Office of Middle American Affairs, visited Cuba and later informed Assistant Secretary of State Roy Rubottom that "the political situation in Cuba has deteriorated to such an extent in recent months that the safety of our citizens and our substantial investments in that country (about $1 billion) is [sic] seriously threatened. If the government were to fall," he continued, the "opposition is so short-sighted and disjointed that a period of chaos and anarchy would follow." Wieland then formulated a project for finding a middle way between the instability of oppressive rule and the instability of violent opposition. As in many such instances where the U.S. goal was the return of stability, Wieland thought he saw a large middle group of Cubans committed to ending dictatorship gradually and peacefully without roiling the waters. He suggested convincing Batista to come to agreement with the "responsible opposition parties" on holding free elections. However, if there proved to be no middle way out—and here Wieland was breaking new ground—the United States should use its influence to remove Batista, but not in a way that benefited "extreme radicals" and "terrorists" like Castro.[19]

Forces were building in Washington that also called for a less friendly attitude toward Batista. As noted above, the Democrats had regained control of Congress by 1956, and a growing band of liberals in that body, influenced by the effective propaganda of the anti-Batista organizations, became openly critical of a Cuban policy that arrested the legally elected Prío for violating U.S. neutrality laws and sent arms to the man who overthrew him.[20] They also attacked the Eisenhower administration's penchant

[18] Morris Morley, "The U.S. Imperial State in Cuba, 1952–1958: Policy Making and Capitalist Interests," *Journal of Latin American Studies* (May 1982), pp. 156–57, 167–68.

[19] FRUS, 1955–1957, vol. 6, pp. 870–76.

[20] Examples of anti-Batista propaganda can be found in U.S. Congress, 85th Congress, 2nd Session, Senate, Committee on Foreign Relations, "Study Mission in the Caribbean Area,"

for honoring Latin American dictators. The liberal Democrats said that such actions tarnished U.S. principles. Moreover, as many of these dictators were unseated in the late 1950s by what liberals saw as a democratic wave sweeping Latin America, they claimed that U.S. interests had been harmed as well.[21] Thus liberals were able to present the State Department with a critique that was both moralistic and realistic—a potent combination in American politics. Finally, liberals were able to reinforce their point by citing the widespread criticism of U.S. "imperialism" that characterized the demonstrations against Vice President Nixon in May 1958.

Critiques of U.S. policy in Cuba lent fuel to those few within the administration who were becoming aware of the growing strength of the opposition to Batista. Wieland and Rubottom and, to a lesser extent, Deputy Under Secretary of State for Political Affairs Robert Murphy were aware of Batista's weakening position and more sensitive than their colleagues to the issue of Cuban nationalism. When Raúl Castro kidnapped a large group of Americans, including marines and naval personnel who were traveling in Oriente in July 1958, Rubottom had blocked an effort by the Joint Chiefs of Staff to use force to free them.[22]

The Joint Chiefs, and especially Arleigh Burke, chief of naval operations, were disturbed by the ambivalence toward Batista that seemed to be gaining influence at the State Department. They had hoped that an intervention by U.S. forces would not only rescue the military personnel and teach radicals that they could not grab U.S. citizens with impunity but that

---

Jan. 20, 1958 (U.S.G.P.O., 1958), pp. 4–5; also "Mutual Security Act of 1958," Mar. 1958, pp. 443–51, 474–77, 746–50; JFKL, Pre-Presidential Papers, Senate Files, Legislation, Foreign Policy, Latin America, Committee on Foreign Relations, Press Release for Oct. 27, 1958, pp. 1–3, and Foreign Policy, Latin America, 8/22/58–12/3/58, Letters, Movimiento 26 de Julio, Comite del Exilio, Aug.–Sept. 1958. An official report to the National Security Council on May 21, 1958, noted: "The tense situation in Cuba was used as the principal example by anti-Batista and liberal groups in the U.S. Congress, press and general public to attempt to prove the charge of U.S. support for dictatorships." See OCB Report (5/18/58) on NSC 5613/1, p. 2.

[21] The general mood in Congress is revealed in Senate Committee on Foreign Relations, *Executive Sessions*, 1958, pp. 201–83; "Mutual Security Act of 1958," pp. 443–51; *Congressional Record*, House of Representatives, 85th Congress, 2nd Session, vol. 104, pt.4 (3/20/58), p. 4948, and R.G. 59, 611.37/3–558, Dulles to Am. Emb., Havana. A good summary is in Cole Blasier, "The Elimination of United States Influence," in Carmelo Mesa-Lago, ed., *Revolutionary Change in Cuba* (Pittsburgh: University of Pittsburgh Press, 1971), pp. 44–49.

The "wave" of democratization in Latin America in the late 1950s swept away two dictators awarded the Legion of Merit by Eisenhower: Manuel Odría (Peru) and Marcos Pérez Jiménez (Venezuela). Other strongmen who fell in this period were Paul Magliore (Haiti), Juan Perón (Argentina), and Gustavo Rojas Pinilla (Colombia).

[22] DDI, 1981, #170B, #171B, #171C.

it would also signal strong, open support for Batista and prevent any future threat to use of the naval base at Guantánamo Bay.[23] The State Department, more sensitive to the likely reaction in Cuba and Latin America to the use of U.S. troops, obtained release of the American servicemen through negotiations between members of the Santiago consulate and the rebels. Castro, who always assumed the worst about U.S. intentions toward him, ordered the release to avoid a pretext for U.S. intervention. As usual, he also turned the episode into a propaganda victory of sorts by publicizing the good treatment afforded the Americans while held by his brother's forces.[24]

This open challenge to the Pentagon position was another sign of the State Department's growing distrust of the comforting news from the U.S. Ambassador in Havana. Ambassador Smith—and the American businessmen who were his regular luncheon companions—now seemed to some dangerously out of touch with the mood of the Cuban people. State Department officials who disparaged his reporting now attempted to gain a hearing in Washington for the idea that the United States should distance itself from the dictatorship.

A policy of lessening the U.S. association with Batista was also reinforced by the general mood in the North American press. Stories about the torture and murder of young opponents of the regime ran side by side with generally (but not glowingly) favorable descriptions of the opposition and especially of the M-26-7, which had the best public relations arm. The public statements made to North American reporters by Batista's opponents were usually ambiguous or silent about the issue of economic reform. Instead, these spokespersons emphasized a hatred of dictatorship and love of freedom that, in the absence of anti-imperialist rhetoric, North Americans took to be an espousal of their own ideals.[25] Since for Cuba to follow in the footsteps of the great democracy to the north was deemed natural, the opposition gained a crucial legitimacy in North America.

IV

The growing dislike for Batista in the United States led to the first important change in Washington's dealings with the Cuban president. Batista's op-

[23] Robert Murphy, *Diplomat Among Warriors* (New York: Doubleday, 1964), pp. 369–70; DDI, 1981, #143D, #150A.

[24] Franqui, *Diary of the Cuban Revolution*, p. 354–65; JFKL, Schlesinger Papers, "Considerations Affecting United States Policy," pp. 70–72.

[25] The major programmatic statement by the 26th of July Movement during this period was its Manifiesto-Programa "Nuestra Razón." For its origins see Llerena, *The Unsuspected Revolution*, ch. 7. The text is in Llerena, pp. 275–304. Other statements by 26th of July leaders can be found in *The Nation*, Nov. 30, 1957, pp. 399–401. Statements by Fidel appear in *Coronet*, Feb. 1958 and *Look*, Feb. 4, 1958.

ponents had long been calling for an end to U.S. support for the dictator, but without much success. One part of their critique of U.S. policy did, however, strike home: their demand for an end to the supplying of U.S. weapons to Batista's army. These weapons were being used to attack Castro's forces, in the course of which many civilians were killed. Without realizing it, exile propagandists had hit upon a central contradiction of U.S. cold-war policy in the Third World. Washington supported the military in Latin America as a partner in the defense of the hemisphere against aggression and (more uneasily) as a source of internal stability. However, the Latin American military was a corporate body that often saw its role as the center or overseer of political authority. Thus it tended to act in ways that could not easily be rationalized in terms of North American cold-war morality, in which armies acted to defend liberty at the behest of legitimate civilian executives. What made the argument against arming Batista even more potent in the United States was that doing so was not only immoral but illegal. In 1951, when a penny-pinching Congress had finally agreed to a program of military aid to Latin America, it had done so only under the weight of the argument that such aid was necessary to deter invasion by the Soviet Union. Thus the ensuing legislation stated that arms provided by the United States could be used only for "hemisphere defense." Units of a Latin American military armed under this program could not be employed in civil conflicts without the agreement of the United States.[26] Cuban and North American opponents of Batista could now argue that they were merely requiring that Washington ensure that his regime abided by U.S. law.

Since there was no communist threat to Cuba, neither external nor internal, Batista could not argue convincingly that Castro was part of an international communist conspiracy. Indeed, he was not even having much luck with his argument that *Cuban* communists were behind his enemies. To much of the North American public, the issue was clear. The United States should not be arming an unpopular dictator who was using the weapons against his own people. Those in the State Department who were seeking a change in U.S. policy now had their issue. A cutoff of military sales might be the very thing needed to demonstrate that the United States was not wedded to the dictator and to convince Batista that he should find a graceful way of stepping down.

The issue of arms for Batista had originally surfaced within the Washington bureaucracy in September 1957 when he clearly misused U.S.-supplied aircraft to subdue the Cienfuegos rebellion. Moreover, the U.S.-equipped

---

[26] FRUS, 1955–1957, vol. 6, p. 867, and JFKL, Schlesinger Papers, "Considerations Affecting United States Policy," pp. 35–40, 51–53.

battalion specifically created for the hemisphere defense program was being used against Castro's forces in the Sierra Maestra. Soon each delivery of weapons to the island became a tug of war between the State Department on the one hand, which wanted to keep the issue low-key, and both the Cuban opposition and Batista on the other, which for very different purposes, of course, wanted to publicize the event.[27]

Debate over an arms embargo within the administration reached its climax early in 1958 and was, in effect, the first serious discussion of U.S.-Cuban relations since the fall of Prío. The Pentagon vigorously opposed an embargo, citing Batista's many contributions to the anti-communist cause, the strategic position of the island, and the importance of close ties between the Cuban and U.S. militaries. Military officials warned that such an act would strengthen the opposition and weaken Batista's ability to defeat the insurgency.[28] The State Department was divided over the issue, but those in Washington concerned with Cuban affairs felt that in the long run U.S. interests would be better protected by a sign of displeasure with the dictatorship. They wished to proceed cautiously, however, because they were uneasy about any act that might redound to Castro's benefit. Even Batista's detractors were suspicious of the guerrilla leader. Some of them, however, considered certain elements of the M-26-7 and of the other opposition groups to be responsible. Their hope was that the embargo might open a path between Batista and Castro.[29]

In March 1958 the United States placed an embargo on further arms shipments to the Cuban government. The U.S. military missions remained in Cuba (another source of opposition ire), and Batista obtained enough arms elsewhere to retain his vast superiority in firepower. Nevertheless, the psychological effect of the embargo, though impossible to measure, was probably significant. The dominant position held in Cuban affairs by the United States was a fact that many in Washington preferred to ignore (or treat as benign) because it conflicted with their cold-war image of their country as upholder of self-determination against communist aggression and domination. Cubans, however, could not afford to ignore U.S. influence, and many took the embargo to mean the waning of active U.S. support and hence the beginning of the end of Batista's power. Batista himself recog-

[27] FRUS, 1955–1957, vol. 6, pp. 852–58; JFKL, Schlesinger Papers, "Considerations Affecting United States Policy," pp. 35–40; Szulc, *Fidel*, pp. 377, 394, 412.

[28] DDI, 1981, #149C.

[29] By this time the Havana embassy was deeply divided over what to do about the decline of Batista and the rise of Castro. See Thomas, *Pursuit*, pp. 964–65; Earl Smith, *The Fourth Floor* (New York: Random House, 1962), pp. 30–34, 58–60; Lazo, *Dagger*, pp. 147–49, 151–53; Morley, "The U.S. Imperial State," p. 168. The best discussion is in John Dorschner and Roberto Fabricio, *The Winds of December* (New York: Coward, McCann and Geoghegan, 1980), pp. 51–58, 144–49.

nized it as such and spent the remainder of his tenure attempting to gain restoration of military supplies, first by offering to lessen his repression and then, in the last months, by declaring his willingness to step down if his chosen successor would be assured of U.S. arms. Ambassador Smith, however, was one of the few U.S. officials to take these offers seriously. As it turned out, Batista's power declined rapidly in 1958, and he would not voluntarily weaken his regime further by granting real concessions to the opposition without first assuring himself that such weakening would be compensated by a renewal of U.S. support. Thus the State Department became more committed to the policy of aloofness and began to look more closely at the opposition to see on whom it might be willing to bestow its blessing.[30]

V

The position held by the United States in Cuba in the twentieth century was very different from that held by Spain in the nineteenth, especially after the element of direct control was removed with the abrogation of the Platt Amendment in 1934. Spain had been a conservative force on the island— indeed, so much so that, as we have seen, by the second half of the century she had alienated the more modernist element of the Cuban elite. The U.S. role in Cuba by contrast was both conservative and progressive; that is, it wished to stabilize the Cuban economy and polity while at the same time opening the island to the modernizing force of its capital and its rational-bureaucratic political system. This is why U.S. officials were able to see opportunities as well as dangers in Batista's decline. The restoration of constitutional law and civil liberties and the end of a political warfare that by the fall of 1958 was having a devastating effect on U.S. economic interests were promising prospects. Still, the practical questions of how Batista might be removed and how the United States could influence the choice of his successor were not simple ones.

By 1958, the opposition to Batista on the island was very broad. It stretched from traditional politicians like former president Prío Socarrás who wanted simply to restore electoral politics to those like the leaders of the Revolutionary Directorate who spoke of social revolution. Spanning this spectrum but with much of its base toward its center was the 26th of

[30] For Batista's requests for the continuation of arms from the United States see Smith, *The Fourth Floor*, pp. 90–93, 96–100, and R.G. 59, State Department, 611.37/8-158, Memorandum, "Cuban Government Requests for U.S. Support." M-26-7 opposition to U.S. arms shipments to Batista (which they felt were never effectively terminated) is documented in Carlos Franqui, *Diary*, pp. 299, 317, 325, 338, 361, 438. Rabe, *Eisenhower and Latin America*, pp. 96–98 and 104–6, discusses the question of Washington's ties to Latin American dictators.

July Movement, headed by Castro. Of the opposition organizations, M-26-7 was now the largest, best-organized, and strongest in military terms. It was also rapidly outdistancing its rivals and allies as the year wore on. Of subsequent importance was the fact that the movement was developing two more or less distinct elements. Out of sight, the guerrilla fighters, who came in the main from the least-advantaged segments of society, were undergoing an experience in the mountains that exposed them to the lives and problems of the poorest population on the island. The camaraderie of battle also deepened their loyalty to Fidel and to his hostility to anyone or anything that seemed to block the "revolution." Closer to the surface was the M-26-7 urban organization, characterized by the affiliation or cooperation of moderates, including middle-class professionals and technocrats—some of the very people to whom the United States had looked in recent decades in its residual desire to clean up Cuban political behavior and rationalize its economic order. Many of these well-connected opponents of Batista were in exile in the United States and enjoyed access to those officials in Washington who were casting about for a reliable successor to the dictator.[31]

While certain elements of the M-26-7 seemed attractive—with their command of English, their familiarity with North American culture, and their affection for democracy—there was little sympathy in Washington for the movement as a whole. This reserve arose despite the fact that Castro endeavored to avoid antagonizing Washington. He was cautious in his statements, never going beyond the Moncada program and at times stopping well short of it. In general, he avoided structural issues, hammering away at the brutality and illegitimacy of the regime on the one hand and the forceful (yet general) vision of a purified polity on the other. Occasionally, his anger at the United States—apparent though hardly extensive in his private correspondence—showed through in his public statements. On a few occasions in his speeches over the rebel radio station, Castro chastised the United States for the arms it was giving to Batista and toward the end of the war accused Ambassador Smith and other U.S. officials of looking for a pretext for military intervention. Still, he never vented his suspicions of the United States without at the same time affirming that he sought no confrontation with the country.[32]

---

[31] The 26th of July Movement is discussed in Judson, *Revolutionary Myth*, chs. 3–7; Martín, *The Early Fidel*, chs. 8–10; Llerena, *The Unsuspected Revolution*, pp. 119–28, 143–53, 185–204, Appendix A; Bonachea and San Martín, *The Cuban Insurrection*, ch. 8; Bonachea and Valdés, *Revolutionary Struggle*, parts 5 and 6. The class composition of the movement is discussed in Judson, *Revolutionary Myth*, pp. 146, 168–70; Gonzalez, *Cuba Under Castro*, pp. 97–99.

[32] *Fidel en Radio Rebelde* (La Habana: Editorial Gente Nueva, 1979), pp. 35, 66–71; Bonachea and Valdés, *Revolutionary Struggle*, pp. 364–67, 383–84, 429–32.

Despite Castro's caution, the movement's published program—which included land reform, some controls over foreign investments (especially public utilities), and a hemisphere-wide commitment to struggle against dictatorship—made Washington nervous. Modest as it was, such a program opened the prospect that the economic modernization and political purification for which it called might harm U.S. interests. Moreover, the tactics of the movement—guerrilla warfare, economic sabotage, assassination—spoke to U.S. policymakers in a voice very different from the one employed by the neatly dressed, U.S.-educated representatives of M-26-7 as they were ushered into appointments with lower echelon State Department personnel or sympathetic members of Congress. Finally, there was Castro himself, acknowledged by now as the most powerful and popular opposition leader but almost always described in official documents as impractical, power-hungry, irrational, politically naive, radical, unpredictable, and with a tendency toward anti-Americanism. The inevitable cold-war question "Is Castro a communist?" was pondered in Washington in its myriad forms and with a variety of answers. Most thought not, but nonetheless there were few in Washington who trusted him or wished to see him in power.[33]

The most extensive study of Castro and his movement was the one prepared by the State Department's Bureau of Intelligence and Research in August 1958. The document noted the growing strength of the movement, its "high morale and discipline," and its effective use of propaganda. The study stated that such propaganda was occasionally directed against the United States, but almost always for its support of Batista. The bureau found no basis for the Cuban government's charge that the movement "is penetrated or influenced by communism," although it did note the Marxist orientation of Fidel's brother Raúl. Ironically, it found the movement "to lack any significant ideology" and stated that "their vaguely defined terms seem to be more reformist than revolutionary." It characterized most Cubans as opposed to Batista but apathetic rather than militant. Concerned, as were all U.S. officials, with stability on the island, it concluded:

> Should the revolutionists displace the present Cuban Government, their ability to operate a successor government would depend upon the cooperation and unity of the various revolutionary groups and their success in dealing with the military and organized labor. If the diverse factions were to cooperate, a comparatively stable left-of-center government can be envisaged. However, the dominant role achieved by

[33] FDRL, Adolf A. Berle Papers, Diary: 11/25/57, 3/26/59, 4/2/58, 4/7/58, 7/9/58, 10/16/58, 10/24/58; CIA, NIE 80-57, "Political Stability in Central America and the Caribbean," (4/23/57), pp. 4–5.

the 26th of July Movement and the irresponsibility and youthful ambition of its leadership lend serious doubt to the prospect of its continued cooperation with these groups. Should the 26th of July Movement try to "go it alone," without the restraining influence of the more moderate members from other opposition groups, continued civil strife and violence would be expected.[34]

While judgments of Castro in Washington ranged from moderately to decidedly negative, there was a growing consensus that he would be the most likely successor to Batista unless the United States could arrange for the dictator to be replaced by a more trustworthy opponent. The attempt to create such an alternative and to prepare the way for it by convincing Batista to step down was the task that preoccupied the State Department in the last months of the year. But it was a delicate operation, and the maneuvering room was rapidly diminishing.

VI

Washington was slow to implement its search for an alternative to both Batista and Castro. This was because there was opposition in some segments of the U.S. government to a policy that withdrew U.S. support from the Cuban president. The opposition sprang in part from those in the Commerce and Treasury Departments who thought principally in terms of protection of the large U.S. investments in land and productive enterprises, which Batista had defended, that were beginning to be the focus of the guerrillas' program of economic sabotage. These departments were also recipients of warnings from U.S. property owners that the proposed reforms of the 26th of July Movement, however inchoate, threatened their interests.[35] As we have seen, the Pentagon for its part was convinced that Batista was an effective and loyal cold warrior. The military also resisted a change in policy because they saw it as part of a growing retreat from the willingness to use power to defend U.S. interests in the Third World. Indeed, there *was* a growing concern in the State Department that overt interventionism would harm the U.S. position in a Third World experiencing a growth of nationalism and ambivalent about the moral distinctions of cold-war bipolarity. From their perspective, however, the Joint Chiefs of Staff

---

[34] R.G. 59, State Department Records, Bureau of Intelligence and Research, R & A Rept. #7780, "The 26th of July Movement Since the Abortive General Strike of April 9, 1958," 8/15/58, p. iii.

[35] Morley, "The U.S. Imperial State," pp. 156, 161n67; Padula, "Financing Castro's Revolution," pp. 234–46; *Wall Street Journal*, Sept. 6, 1957, p. 3, "U.S. Businessmen Eye Castro's Policies as Cuban Revolt Grows"; Apr. 4, 1958, p. 1, "Damage to U.S. Firms Mounts as Rebels Push for Showdown Fight."

saw Batista's decline as a result rather than a cause of U.S. aloofness and continued to argue for a restoration of arms shipments.[36]

Though more circumspect than the Pentagon chiefs, Ambassador Smith in Havana sustained the defense of Batista by continually suggesting that the Cuban president was willing to cooperate with the United States. Smith relayed what he described as Batista's willingness to meet the U.S. desire that he reopen the political arena if only firm backing of his regime (including weapons sales) were restored.[37] Although Smith's ignorance of the strength of the opposition to Batista had first led him to dismiss it, he now deluged Washington with evidence from Havana's police investigation files that the opposition was infiltrated by and was acting in concert with both insular and international communist organizations. Much of this evidence erased all meaningful distinction between revolutionary Marxism and the reformism and anti-tyrannical nationalism that formed the perspective of most of the opposition, the M-26-7 included. The stream of subversion traced by Havana for consumption in Washington was also muddied by the fact that many Auténticos—the conservative wing of the opposition—had past records as radicals, while the young militants around Castro, born too late to have participated in the left-wing politics of the 1930s, had less ominous-sounding dossiers. To add irony to confusion, not a few of Batista's henchmen had anarchist, Trotskyist, or Communist backgrounds. In any event, many State Department officials were by this time suspicious of all attempts by the dictator to manipulate the communist issue. The public disdain for Castro expressed by the Cuban Communist Party and the anti-communism of many 26th of July Movement activists reinforced this attitude.[38]

Some in Washington, however, *were* impressed by the charges of communism. Militant anti-communists, only recently disabused of the idea that subversives had worked their way into the State Department itself, were now very wary of foreign-policy initiatives that seemed ignorant of Soviet designs on Third World governments. Some were fiscal conservatives who worried that the United States was caving in to irresponsible demands for more economic aid because the State Department feared losing friends in

[36] DDI, 1977, #172A; 1981, #143D, #149C, #150B.

[37] R.G. 59, State Department, 611.37/8-858, Embtel. #181 and 611.37/10-2258, Emb. Desp. #429.

[38] Some of the "evidence" from Batista's police files appears in U.S. Senate, 86th Congress, 2nd Session, Committee on the Judiciary, Subcommittee to Investigate the Administration of the Internal Security Act and Other Internal Security Laws, *The Communist Threat to the United States Through the Caribbean* (U.S.G.P.O., 1960), pp. 528–630.

There were in fact some contacts between Castro and certain of the more adventurous leaders of the Cuban Communists in 1958. These are noted in Szulc, *Fidel*, pp. 327, 369, 453, and in Martín, *The Early Fidel*, pp. 174, 179–82, 186, 198, 202, 219–21.

Latin America. This might lead the United States to accommodate itself to radical regimes to keep them from being attracted by Nikita Khrushchev's new policy of building Soviet bridges to the Third World. This was indeed the case, as liberals in the State Department, reacting to the outbreak of anti-U.S. nationalism attendant upon Nixon's "goodwill" mission, fashioned their own understanding of the way to beat communism, began to promote greater U.S. aid to Latin American, and changed the official attitude toward government's like Betancourt's in Venezuela despite the fact that the new president there had once been a Communist. Responding to this shift—which in the Eisenhower years was hardly precipitate—conservatives in Congress, the military, and among retired and active government officials argued the case for backing strong military leaders, who were seen as much better defenders of U.S. interests than the potentially dangerous reformers or secret Moscow agents who might replace them.

The growing aloofness to Batista at the State Department disturbed these people. Many were still plugged into the old counter-subversive network built in the Truman-McCarthy era (FBI, HUAC, SISS, SACB), whose purpose had been to uncover "loyalty risks" in the U.S. government. Now attuned to international subversion, these agencies made their allies in Washington aware of the information coming in from Havana concerning communist infiltration of the Batista opposition. These conservative anti-communists drew even fewer distinctions between the aims of a presumed worldwide communist campaign to weaken the United States and the rhetoric of Latin American anti-Yankee nationalism. The subtle effort by the liberals to respond to a moderate Latin American nationalism in order to weaken the more radical version (and thereby the communists' ability to turn it against the United States) was considered by such conservatives as a sacrifice of the very U.S. interests that should be defended and as opening the way to radical governments that would likely become allies of Moscow.[39]

Even within the State Department some people opposed any move that might open the way for a potentially dangerous radical like Castro. In fact, the internal debate over Cuban policy stirred up the only partly interred bones of the old China debate. For those like Whiting Willauer, the U.S. ambassador to Costa Rica, and William Pawley, former ambassador to Brazil, the analogy was a strong one. Both had fought in the late 1940s for unstinting support for the Nationalist Chinese. To desert the pro-U.S. Batista and thus pave the way for the agrarian reformer Castro was to make the same error (or commit the same treason) as had the old China hands in

[39] Opposition to the liberals' policy is in *Communist Threat to the United States*, Testimony of Spruille Braden (pp. 280–95), Arthur Gardner (pp. 663–80), Earl Smith (pp. 681–710), William Pawley (pp. 711–63), Arthur Hill (pp. 793–828), and Whiting Willauer (pp. 861–88).

helping to replace Jiang Jieshi with Mao.[40] This perspective reinforced the view of Ambassador Smith that we should not abandon Batista. This view was also shared by former ambassadors to Cuba Arthur Gardner and Spruille Braden and by the current ambassador to Mexico, Robert Hill. It must have given pause to those such as Wieland, Rubottom, and Murphy, who backed disengagement from Batista, that they might one day face the charge of having "lost" Cuba.

Still, the alternative program proposed by the conservatives—restoring full military support to Batista or, if all else failed, intervening with U.S. forces—fared poorly in the State Department. Those knowledgeable about the situation in Cuba, the mood in the United States, and sensitive to the growing nationalism in Latin America suspected the great damage to U.S. interests that would result from such an action. In the wake of the demonstrations against Nixon, the State Department authorized the United States Information Agency (USIA) to monitor the degree and kind of "anti-U.S." statements coming from the Latin American media. The National Security Council began a review of U.S. policy toward Latin America.[41] Later in the year, State Department efforts to interest the Organization of American States in mediation efforts in Cuba that might finesse the question of U.S. intervention drew no satisfactory response.[42] The mood in Latin America did not suggest the practicability of the conservatives' proposal for military intervention. In the face of this dilemma, those in the State Department who opposed direct support for Batista were able to turn the anti-communist argument to their own advantage. They claimed that such support or, worse yet, direct intervention would only make more credible the Soviet charge that the U.S. role in Latin America was one of "imperialism." To State Department liberals, the mental picture of the U.S. Marines chasing Castro's guerrillas through the Sierra Maestra was nightmarish.

VII

The infighting between these two groups and the inherent cautiousness of the anti-Batista forces in the State Department stood in the way of an assertive policy toward Cuba in 1958. Moreover, because Ambassador Smith

[40] Lazo, *Dagger*, pp. 170–75; Princeton University, Seeley G. Mudd Library, Whiting Willauer Papers, Diary entries, 1958–1959; DDEL, Herter, M-Z Official - Classified(4) Willauer to Herter; HSTL, Bohan Papers, Subject File, Cuba.

[41] DDEL, WHO, OSANSA, U.S. Policy Toward Latin America(3), Memorandum for the Honorable Robert Cutler, 5/26/58, and Memorandum "Proposed Central American Visit of Dr. Milton Eisenhower," 7/3/58; CIA, Memorandum for the Secretary of State, "The Likelihood of Anti-American Demonstrations," 5/27/58. Also see DDI, 1986, #585, #984.

[42] JFKL, Schlesinger Papers, "Considerations Affecting United States Policy," pp. 100–5.

stood at the confluence of the principal streams of intelligence concerning conditions on the island, he was able for a long time to undermine the anti-Batista position in Washington. As noted above, more and more people in the department came to discount the ambassador's judgments. But this left them with only scraps of dissenting intelligence routed around Smith by lower-echelon embassy and consular staff and by the CIA station in Havana. As a friend of Eisenhower's and a major Republican Party contributor and, more importantly, as the symbol of U.S. power and policy in Cuba, Smith could not be removed without that act itself signaling a major shift in U.S. policy away from Batista. This was something that those committed to an alternative to both Batista and Castro hoped to accomplish only gradually and quietly.[43]

This stalemate continued through much of the year, compounded by the ambivalence of both groups. Since the pro-Batista forces could not take a stand in favor of dictatorship and since Batista's detractors feared the Castro alternative, neither operated with firm conviction. However, by the last two months of the year, as the pro-Batista option rapidly receded, department liberals were finally able to exert significant pressure on Ambassador Smith. They obtained authority to require him to explain to Batista how vain were the latter's hopes of restoring his fortunes through a renewal of U.S. support—something that Smith had successfully resisted doing until then.

The policy of the liberals was to convince Batista to step down and hand power to a group representative enough of the old order to reassure North Americans and yet also representative enough of the moderate opposition to satisfy Cubans. The trouble was that, by this time, the moderate opposition had been eclipsed by the militant opponents of the dictator. Moreover, Batista made it clear that he would not step aside for such people—whose blood was on his hands and who had murdered his henchmen—nor would they join any government that included pro-Batista elements. It was the Machado problem all over again.

AS THE LIBERAL policymakers became aware of this dilemma, they intensified their efforts to end Batista's regime. However, by the time their policy was approved at a higher level, it was late in November and the success of Castro's forces made it less and less likely that he could be denied power. Still, it was presumed that there were several months in which to make the policy work. Batista would be told that he had to go. He would turn over

[43] Wayne Smith, *The Closest of Enemies*, pp. 29–30, 33–34. Ambassador Earl Smith's assessment of events in Cuba in 1958 can be found in R.G. 59, 611.37/2-1958 (Progress Report), 611.37/8-858 (Embtel #182), and 611.37/10-2258 (Revision of Operations Plan).

power to a less tainted member of his regime. That person would make way for a junta composed of moderate and even militant oppositionists acceptable to the United States. It was hoped that most Cubans would go along with such an end to the dictatorship.

Ambassador Smith was called back to Washington late in November and told that he must make it clear to Batista that the latter's hope of surviving long enough to hand over power to his hand-picked successor, Andrés Rivero Agüero, in February 1959 was in vain. Rivero had been recently "elected" in balloting so rigged that it even tainted the losing candidates. It was becoming clear that there would be no electoral path out of the dictatorship. Smith was told to advise Batista that Rivero Agüero would not receive U.S. support.

When Smith returned to Havana—convinced that Batista's regime would collapse upon such news and certain that Castro was a crypto-communist—he softened the message to the Cuban president. He and Batista then came up with a counter-offer: the president would step down in favor of Rivero immediately (instead of the following February) in return for U.S. backing of the new government. Exasperated, the State Department called Smith back to Washington once again.

BY THIS TIME, even the conservatives accepted the necessity of Batista's departure. Having done so, their principal difference with the liberals was reduced to the wish that he be replaced only with the most trusted people, whereas the liberals wanted a fresh new leader who might have the popular appeal—in Cuba—to draw away some of Castro's following. In addition, conservatives were less concerned to hide the U.S. hand in ending Batista's seven-year rule.

Early in December, the conservatives made their bid to influence the termination of the *Batistato*. William Pawley, a friend of Eisenhower's and a man with investments in Cuba going back to the 1920s, went to see the president. After several meetings, he received permission to use his influence to convince Batista to step down in favor of a junta composed of people whom Pawley considered trustworthy.

Wieland and Rubottom were glad that the opposition within the U.S. government had finally agreed to Batista's departure. Still, they worried that Pawley, even if successful with Batista, would produce an interim regime tainted as a U.S. puppet and thus unable to stem the Castro tide. Pawley, for his part, suspected that Wieland and Rubottom were willing to see the communist Castro come to power.

Pawley's proposal to Batista was to include a graceful retirement for the dictator at the president's estate in Florida. It also included the promise that the new government would take no reprisals against his followers and that it would receive U.S. military aid. Pawley intended to speak as the personal representative of Eisenhower to assure that Batista took the offer seriously. This last point worried the liberals so much that they convinced Eisenhower to tell Pawley that he could speak only as a private individual. Pawley was certain that this change of plan had been plotted by his liberal opponents to assure the failure of his mission. Nevertheless, Pawley saw Batista on December 9 and included in his proposals at least the hint that Eisenhower supported them. Batista, however, was angered that the proposed junta contained his enemies. Unhappy with the proposal and uncertain as to its official status, he rejected it.

On December 10, with Smith safely out of the way in Washington, the State Department took advantage of an invitation for further discussions from Batista's prime minister, Gonzalo Güell. It ordered Daniel Braddock, chief of mission at Havana, to tell Güell that Batista's continued presence prevented a possible compromise between his successor, Rivero Agüero, and the responsible element of the opposition. Braddock suggested to Güell that *if* Batista left and *if* Rivero surrounded himself with a Cabinet drawn from the moderate opposition, U.S. recognition of such a regime might be forthcoming.

While awaiting an answer to Braddock's offer, the State Department stepped up the pressure. Assistant Secretary Murphy told Smith to return to Havana and tell his friend Batista that the United States government wanted him to leave. Smith finally delivered this message on December 17.[44] In light of all this pressure and because of the rapidly deteriorating military situation, Batista finally decided to take the money and run. Since such news would immediately panic his supporters, however, he kept his counsel. As a result, no one in Washington knew how close to the end things had come.

VIII

While the United States had been increasing the pressure on Batista to resign, it was also stepping up its search for an acceptable replacement. By now it was evident to most in Washington that a successor regime must

[44] United States relations with Batista in the last two months of 1958 are discussed in Dorschner and Fabricio, *Winds of December*, pp. 51–58, 69–73, 141–49, 152–55, 158–61, 165–67, 190–93, 245–46, 285–86, 323–24, 348–51, 481–83. Also see Philip W. Bonsal, *Cuba, Castro and the United States* (Pittsburgh: University of Pittsburgh Press, 1971), ch. 2; Earl Smith, *The Fourth Floor*, chs. 16–18; Lazo, *Dagger*, ch. 11; Thomas, *Pursuit*, pp. 1009–10, 1014–19, 1023, 1026, 1028–29. According to Dorschner and Fabricio, the junta to replace Batista that Pawley proposed consisted of Colonel Ramón Barquín, Major Enrique Borbonnet, General Martín Díaz Tamayo, and Pepín Bosch (p. 158).

have anti-Batista credentials. Nevertheless, such a regime also had to satisfy both the liberals' and the conservatives' desire to block Castro. Without the knowledge of Ambassador Smith, the CIA had been encouraging certain anti-Batista elements in the military. The agency is said to have had some kind of contact with the naval forces that revolted at Cienfuegos in 1957. Certain authors also claim that the CIA made financial contributions to elements of the M-26-7 in Santiago early in 1958. More substantial evidence indicates that the CIA facilitated the plotting, financing, and arming of several anti-Batista groups that were also anti-Castro: Auténticos, the Montecristi Movement, and the Second Front of the Escambray. It also supported the efforts of the military *puros*—army officers opposed to Batista—to free Colonel Ramón Barquín, jailed in 1956 for plotting to overthrow the dictator. All of these efforts were small scale, not only because they had to be kept secret from Smith and, of course, from Batista, but also because of the continuing liberal-conservative debate in Washington over whether or not to support the dictator. Nevertheless, the inevitable leaks occurred, and Smith went so far as to fire the CIA station chief in Havana and threaten his successor with the same fate.[45]

In the end, none of these CIA-assisted conspiracies ever threatened Batista's rule or even approached the U.S. goal of placing a cooperative anti-Batista leader in office before the Cuban army collapsed and Castro's movement became unchallengeable. The same fate awaited the State Department's search for a moderate outcome to the dictatorship. The fault, however, lay not only in bureaucratic indecision and infighting in Washington but in the irresolution and weakness of the anti-Castro opponents of the dictator. Suffering from one of the principal side effects of North American hegemony—a state of dependence in which the sufferer believed that no effort in Cuban politics could succeed without U.S. blessing—these indecisive plotters each waited for the call from their CIA contact or the favorable sign from the U.S. embassy that would give them the initiative, the resources, and the base of support that they otherwise lacked. Washington, on the other hand, looking for an alternative to Castro strong enough to stand without the prop of overt U.S. intervention, kept its sustenance modest until one of these forces could demonstrate its strength and legitimacy

---

[45] Specific CIA activities are excised from declassified U.S. documents. Indirect references appear in R.G. 59, 737.00/12–2358 and in DDI, 1985, #2139. Also see Dorschner and Fabricio, *Winds of December*, pp. 54–55, 70, 92–94, 166–67, 285–86, 311–13; Szulc, *Fidel*, pp. 427–29; Thomas, *Pursuit*, pp. 961, 1028; Kirkpatrick, *The Real CIA*, pp. 157, 159. In late November, the CIA concluded that the best outcome was for Batista to be replaced by a moderate military junta that would forestall Castro. By mid-December, the CIA felt that the army was collapsing and that the desired military junta might not be possible. See CIA, SNIE 85-58, "The Situation in Cuba," and SNIE 85/1-58, "Developments in Cuba Since Mid-November."

in Cuba. As a result, each of these efforts came to nothing, including the last, desperate one that actually placed Barquín in command of the Cuban army the day Batista fled. Worse yet, Castro's knowledge of them—his intelligence network was excellent—only confirmed his growing belief that the United States, now hedging its bets on the dictator, would become his new opponent.[46]

Batista had shaken up his high command early in December and received several large weapons shipments from Europe. Ever hopeful, the embassy in Havana reported that there was "a more optimistic attitude among the officers," and some in Washington hoped that Castro's forces might yet be held back. But by the end of the month, the rebels had surrounded Santiago and taken the city of Santa Clara. A flood of civilians joined the guerrillas or the armed opposition in the cities. Whatever the fears in Washington, it looked as if it might be too late to forestall Castro.[47]

Only at this last minute, it seems, did the full seriousness of the Cuban problem reach the highest echelon of the U.S. government. On December 23, Acting Secretary of State Christian Herter (in charge of the department while John Foster Dulles underwent treatment for cancer) sent a long memorandum on the crisis to President Eisenhower. Writing in a manner that implied his chief's unfamiliarity with the details of the subject, he told the president that "we do not believe that Batista can possibly establish his successor [Rivero Agüero] peacefully and firmly in office on February 24, 1959." He then rehearsed the arguments of the liberals for having distanced the United States from the dictator. Herter also made clear that because Castro and his movement were untrustworthy, anti-U.S., and to some extent influenced by communists, the department and CIA were still seeking ways to keep him from power.

Eisenhower was greatly disturbed that he had not previously been fully informed of the seriousness of the situation before and was surprised to learn that Castro was considered so dangerous. The president called a meeting of the National Security Council, where he was informed by Allen Dulles, director of the CIA, that "Communists and other extreme radicals appear to have penetrated the Castro movement." Admiral Arleigh Burke, Chief of Naval Operations, again spoke up for his proposal to use military force to stop Castro. The State Department defended its policy of pressing Batista to leave while looking for a "third force" solution. Eisenhower rejected military intervention and also the option of reversing course and

[46] Dorschner and Fabricio, *Winds of December*, pp. 168, 285, 431, 444, 461; Franqui, *Diary*, pp. 443, 458, 469–71, 478, 481, 487–89, 502–4.

[47] JFKL, Schlesinger Papers, "Considerations Affecting U.S. Policy," pp. 106–7. The last days of the regime are described in Dorchner and Fabricio, *Winds of December*, parts 3 and 4; Thomas, *Pursuit*, pp. 1005–34; Phillips, *Island of Paradox*, ch. 16.

renewing support for Batista. He sided with the State Department position that the United States should continue to seek a "third force" solution.[48]

As difficult as the situation appeared, no one in Washington seems to have realized that the end was at hand. The last day of December found John Dreier, the U.S. ambassador to the Organization of American States, consulting with several other OAS ambassadors about the possibility of having their nations mediate the conflict in Cuba. That same day, Assistant Secretary of State Rubottom briefed members of the Senate Foreign Relations Committee in closed session. He explained that there were no plans to intervene militarily in Cuba and that the department had "not been able to show at this stage that it [the rebellion against Batista] is a Communist-dominated revolt." Rubottom told the committee that communists would, of course, attempt to take advantage of the situation, but that the Cuban people were unlikely to "turn toward Communist blandishments." He did not mention the effort to head off Castro, but said that the department was hopeful that an "extreme showdown" could be avoided. In its last report on the military situation, the embassy in Havana cabled that an army offensive in Las Villas indicated an increased willingness to combat the rebels.[49] At the end of his New Year's Eve party, Batista and his closest allies secretly boarded a plane for the Dominican Republic.

Batista's abrupt departure in the wee hours of January 1, 1959, effectively ended the search for the elusive "third force." In Havana, General Eulogio Cantillo, left in command of the army by Batista, gave way without a fight to the *puro* Barquín, freed from prison just hours earlier. Barquín, trusted by the CIA to use the army to control Castro, soon realized the futility of opposing the popular hero. For his part, the guerrilla leader, fearing the kind of deal between the United States and moderate anti-Batista forces that had, in fact, been Washington's goal, called a general strike that shut down the island's economy. Within hours, Barquín gave way to the newly arrived M-26-7 commander, Camilo Cienfuegos. Castro, still in Oriente, then led a long triumphal march across the length of the island to Havana, stopping at numerous towns to tell the cheering crowds that it was they who had destroyed the tyrant. Castro's candidate for provisional pres-

[48] DDEL, Whitman File, Admin. Series, Herter(1) "Memorandum for the President: Subject —Cuba," 12/23/58; WHO, OSANSA, Records, 1952–61, Special Asst. Series, Presidential Subseries, Meetings with the President—1958(1), "Memorandum of Conversation with the President (Wednesday, 24 December 1958, 9:45 a.m.)" and "Memorandum of Conversation with the President (Friday, 26 December, 1958)." Also see DDI, 1981, #171D; 1983, #252.

[49] JFKL, Schlesinger Papers, "Considerations Affecting United States Policy," pp. 101–2, 107. Rubottom's testimony is in Senate Committee on Foreign Relations, Historical Series, *Executive Sessions*, vol. 10, pp. 767–800. Also see U.S. Senate, 87th Congress, Subcommittee of the Committee on the Judiciary, Hearings on State Department Security, 1961, "Testimony of William Wieland," parts 1 and 5.

ident, Manuel Urrutia, was installed in office, and the guerrilla chieftain arrived in the capital on January 8 to a popular adulation that bordered on the euphoric. On that same day, almost unnoticed amidst the jubilation, an event that had traditionally filled the center stage of Cuban politics took place: without fanfare, the United States granted recognition to Urrutia's provisional government.[50]

[50] DDEL, WHO, Office of Staff Sect., International Series, Cuba(1), Memorandum for the President, "Recognition of the New Government of Cuba."

CHAPTER 7

RADICAL NATIONALISM
RESISTS GRAVITATION

I

THE PRECIPITOUS end of the Batista era was disturbing to the U.S. government. The initial assumption that Batista's power was formidable, as well as the subsequent one that Washington could arrange a succession that excluded Castro, had both proved incorrect. Still, the most fundamental North American belief—that the structure of the relationship with Cuba could not be broken—remained initially unshaken. This confidence was demonstrated by the paternalistic approach taken toward the new Cuban leadership. Certain that the U.S. economic presence in Cuba was both beneficial and essential and that each past government of the island had accepted this, nothing more serious than renewed bargaining over the protection of U.S. interests was expected. It was assumed that once the moderates who composed the original administration realized that Washington accepted the need for reforms in Cuban society, U.S. influence would remain a prominent factor in Cuban affairs.[1]

The reality of the situation, however, was much more problematic. The new government in Havana drew much of its membership from segments of the anti-Batista movement that Washington had not favored and over which it did not have anything approaching its usual influence. Many of

[1] Washington's initial apprehensions were not that the Cuban regime might develop the strength to break its ties to the United States but rather that the new government was so inexperienced and the immediate post-revolutionary situation so chaotic that it might not be able to make the state apparatus run at all. The CIA described the provisional government as "floundering" and Castro as exhibiting "no desire to buckle down to the responsibilities of his position as Commander in Chief of the Armed Forces." DDEL, Papers as President, Dulles-Herter, Dulles, Feb., 1959, Memorandum for the Director [CIA], 2/4/59, pp. 1–2. Also see Rabe, *Eisenhower and Latin America*, pp. 122–23, 126.

these people were not only enemies of dictatorship but also part of a young generation that had absorbed important elements of the radical nationalist view of Cuban history. In this view, full sovereignty included a significant reduction in the weight of U.S. political and economic influence on the island.[2]

This shift in generational authority and in the prevailing view of Cuban history did not necessarily imply a concerted assault on U.S. investments, but it did create a greatly increased sensitivity to everything that reflected North American hegemony. Since actual U.S. power in Cuba, regardless of the care with which it was exercised, was bound to confine any attempt by Cubans to assert full independence, relations between the two states were in for a stormy episode, at the least.

If this situation was not by itself threatening to Washington, when combined with the extreme sensitivity to all opposition by the new charismatic guerrilla leader, Fidel Castro, it gained an explosive potential. During the first part of 1959, those in the State Department vaguely aware of the new ground rules expected that the fate of U.S. interests in Cuba would turn on their ability to work with moderate reform nationalists. In reality, the fate of those interests hung on U.S. willingness to accept rule over the island by someone who demanded complete independence of action and whose goal, though still inchoate, was a fundamental alteration of the social order that had been built on the island by Spanish values and governance and by the Yankee dollar and North American consumer culture.[3]

II

The first few months of the post-Batista era produced much frustration in Washington over the disorder in the new Cuban government, but no serious

[2] The nationalist school of Cuban history is discussed in Duvon C. Corbitt, "Cuban Revisionist Interpretations of Cuba's Struggle for Independence," *Hispanic American Historical Review* 43 (Aug. 1963), pp. 395–404; Robert Freeman Smith, "Twentieth Century Cuban Historiography," *HAHR* 44 (Feb. 1964), pp. 44–73; Louis A. Pérez, Jr., "In the Service of the Revolution: Two Decades of Cuban Historiography. 1959–1979," *HAHR* 60 (Feb. 1980), pp. 79–89. The dean of such scholars was Emilio Roig de Leuchsenring. See his *Cuba no debe su independencia a los Estados Unidos*, 3d. ed. (La Habana: Ediciones La Tertulia, 1960). The influence of this view of Cuban history can be found in early publications of the new Cuban government. See Republic of Cuba, Ministry of State, Public Relations Department, *In Defense of National Sovereignty* (Havana: Ministry of State Printing Office, Nov. 13, 1959). A typical Castro speech expressing this view of Cuban history is contained in his Havana television interview of Feb. 19, 1959. See Instituto de Historia del Movimiento Comunista, *El Pensamiento de Fidel Castro*, T.1, vol. 1 (La Habana: Editora Política, 1983), pp. 14–17.

[3] Castro's personality and its relation to his political actions are discussed in Casuso, *Cuba and Castro*, and Szulc, *Fidel*. Also see Herbert Matthews, *Revolution in Cuba* (New York: Scribner's, 1975), pp. 40–44, 126–27.

conflicts. The Cuban Communists seemed to have little influence, and no significant threats to U.S. interests arose. The main worry was over Castro, then not even a member of the government. From the start his unorthodox political behavior troubled Washington. He spoke publicly on all subjects, often spontaneously, and had a directness bordering on defiance when speaking of U.S.-Cuban relations, though he was also capable of apologizing for remarks that he later considered, for whatever reason, ill advised. All of these actions by Castro confirmed the State Department's long-held beliefs about his irresponsibility and inexperience. It deepened suspicions about him but in the reigning mood of confidence in Washington did not preclude faith in his ability to learn the rules of proper behavior. This latter attitude ignored not only Castro's character but the tremendous power that the charismatic leader held over the Cuban people. But then the United States had never before had to contend with such a Cuban leader.[4]

In any event, the State Department was not required at this point to deal with Castro but rather with Prime Minister José Miró Cardona, the former head of the Cuban Bar Association and a man respected in Washington. Even more comforting, Cardona was surrounded by a Cabinet most of whose members considered themselves friends of the United States— though not necessarily of past U.S. policies. Many U.S. businesses with interests in Cuba were also initially pleased with the new government. They expected to benefit from the replacement of a regime of corruption and cronyism with one that was managerially competent and willing to clear away barriers to what North Americans considered the proper development of the Cuban economy. Other U.S. businessmen were less confident but, as they had with each past administration, presumed that an inside track to the pertinent government departments could be developed by firms that carried weight in the Cuban economy.[5]

To help clear the air, Washington called home the controversial ambassador Earl E. T. Smith. This gesture also reflected the State Department's dissatisfaction with his performance and the expectation that even the moderate Havana government was likely to ask for his recall in view of the ambassador's well-known closeness to the fallen dictator. The embassy was temporarily left in the hands of Deputy Chief of Mission Daniel Braddock. Braddock's reports sustained the moderate optimism in Washington. He cabled that "the Cabinet as a whole must be judged basically friendly toward the United States and oriented against Communism." This was a reasonably accurate judgment but displayed the narrow framework that Washington employed when viewing Cuban politics. Moreover, it assumed

[4] Castro's early speeches are in *Pensamiento de Fidel Castro*, T.1, vol. 1, pp. 3–28.
[5] Padula diss., pp. 249, 286; Morley, *Imperial State*, pp. 77, 92, 99–101.

that the Cabinet would exercise real authority; such had not been the pattern of past Cuban governments.[6]

Greater concern during this early period was shown in the CIA reports, which expressed the fear—shared by many of the State Department liberals—that the new government might not exercise its authority vigorously enough. The agency reported that the provisional president, Manuel Urrutia, seemed indecisive and that many of the new government officials lacked experience. This guardian of U.S. security did take some note of an anti-U.S. tone in certain segments of the Cuban press but was much more concerned with the ineffectiveness of the new government than with the ideology of the non-governmental forces gathering in the wings.[7]

In certain respects that were reassuring to Washington, the new government acted appropriately. The Ministry of the Treasury and the National Bank, now staffed by moderate developmentalists, initiated discussions with the United States concerning the possibility of economic assistance. Treasury Minister Rufo López-Fresquet led a delegation to Puerto Rico to see how "Operation Bootstrap"—that commonwealth's development program—might be applied to Cuba. This was heartening to liberals in the State Department who were already looking for a "good" revolution in Latin America, one that with U.S. assistance might become a model of anti-communist, progressive capitalist development.[8]

THERE were disturbing signs as well, especially from the point of view of conservatives in Washington. The Cuban government requested the termination of the U.S. military mission. This was an indication that even the moderates harbored resentment for the historic ties between the U.S. and Cuban militaries. More significant was the dissolution of the Cuban army carried out by the radical guerrilla chieftains, who began to create a new institution under their direction—one dedicated to defending what they continually (though often ambiguously) referred to as the "Revolution." The United States had created the Cuban army early in the century and had slowly resurrected its influence with that body after Batista reorganized it in 1933. Without the military missions, and with the army now under guer-

[6] Braddock's remarks are in R.G. 59, 737.00/1-1559, Desp. #736 to State Department, "The First Two Weeks of the Revolutionary Government," p. 5.

[7] The CIA's remarks are in DDEL, PAP, Dulles-Herter Series, Dulles, Feb. 1959, Memorandum to the Director [of the CIA], 2/4/59.

[8] On U.S. contacts with Cuban officials concerning economic matters see Rufo López-Fresquet, *My Fourteen Months with Castro* (Cleveland: World, 1966), ch. 6. Related documents are in DDEL: Whitman File, DDE Diary Series, Toner Notes - Jan. 1959, "Staff Notes," #486 (1/16/59); Herter Papers, Chronological File, Mar. 1959 (2), Herter to Fulbright, 3/15/59.

rilla officers who had spent two years under fire from U.S. weapons in the hands of Batista's soldiers, one of the old channels of U.S. influence had rapidly dried up. Since this change was uniformly welcomed on the island, Washington was constrained from protesting publicly.[9]

The State Department, though still principally concerned about Castro's unreliability and his penchant for making unflattering remarks about U.S. past involvement in Cuban affairs, began to take note of the freedom granted the Communist PSP to organize and propagandize. The removal of Batista's ban on Communist activities occurred in what appeared to be a general opening of the political field by the new government, and as such was not easily challenged by Washington. It had always been an embarrassment (at least to Washington liberals) that the United States, which had never found a domestic consensus for outlawing its own Communist Party, had openly required such actions of hemisphere governments as a sign of their commitment to the free-world side of the cold war. Nonetheless, Washington began to watch the party closely for signs (which it soon thought it detected) of its subversion of the Cuban government—too closely, in fact, thus diverting its attention from the radicalization of Castro and his close followers, the real determinant of Communist influence in Cuba.[10]

Though partly bemused by their own belief in the special subversive propensities of Moscow-oriented Communist parties, the State Department did take the precaution of preventing the new rebel-inspired military from obtaining additional equipment. It defended its action by citing the growing tensions in the Caribbean area. These tensions resulted from the expectation that the Caribbean Legion and its supporters would take advantage of the anti-dictatorial sympathies of the new Havana government to launch another assault on the Trujillo dictatorship. Moreover, the hated Batista had taken refuge in the Dominican Republic, while Trujillo was thought to be planning his own assault on Cuba. Castro viewed U.S. motives differently and publicly contrasted Washington's former willingness to arm Batista with its reticence to fill weapons requests from the democratic government that overthrew him. Washington may have had good reason to fear the use to which a military now headed by Castro might put its new arms, but the

[9] DDEL, PAP, DDE Diary Series, Goodpaster Briefings: Jan. 21, 24, and 26, 1959. Defensive public reactions by Eisenhower and Secretary of State Dulles early in 1959 can be seen in U.S., *Department of State Bulletin* 40:1023, pp. 159ff., 162, 197. The new army is examined in Judson, *Revolutionary Myth*, pp. 225–59. The best history of the old army is Pérez, *Army Politics*.

[10] FRUS, 1955–1957, vol. 6, pp. 151–52; DDEL, WHO, OSANSA, NSC 5432/1, Policy Toward Latin America, "United States Objectives and Courses of Action with Respect to Latin America," 2/3/55, p. 9.

suspicion left by this episode, on both sides, was only part of the price the U.S. would eventually pay for having put so many of its eggs in Batista's basket for so many years.[11]

Another early source of tension was the U.S. response to the trials of the former Batista officials charged with crimes against the opposition. Some U.S. newspapers and congressmen were disturbed by what they described as the "circus-like" atmosphere of the trials—a few of which reflected the personal and political vengeance common among underdog victors after bitter social warfare. Certain of their right to require conformity to U.S. standards, they chastised the Cuban government for the failings of its system of justice. Castro, always sensitive to U.S. criticism, reacted sharply. He asked why there had been no similar outcry when the crimes now being punished had been committed.[12]

III

Castro was rapidly becoming the focus of U.S. concern, but Washington's efforts to establish what it considered constructive relations with moderates in the Cuban government were also meeting with difficulty. These moderates—often themselves influenced by the radical nationalist critique of the U.S. role in Cuban history—were trying to warn their North American counterparts about the new Cuban sensitivity to U.S. pressure. In doing so, they often perplexed and dismayed Washington officials. Braddock was surprised to discover that many of the new officials in Havana believed the United States had been a principal ally of Batista in his struggle with the armed opposition. In discussions with Felipe Pazos, Regino Boti, and Luis Bush—all considered moderates by Washington—Braddock was told that the United States must be prepared for tough bargaining and a more independent attitude from the new government as a whole. The original Cabinet supported the rent and tax reforms and the reduction of utility rates. President Urrutia defended the trials of the Batistianos, and even men destined to become bitter enemies of the regime—Manuel Ray and Huber Matos—

[11] Thomas, *Pursuit*, p. 1242; *Hispanic American Report* 12:1 (1/60), p. 601. Cuban-Dominican tensions in 1959 are examined in Robert D. Crassweller, *Trujillo: The Life and Times of a Caribbean Dictator* (New York: Macmillan, 1966), pp. 348–53. The Cuban Ministry of State's publication *In Defense of National Sovereignty* declared that Cuba was being denied arms "by the same government that furnished the former dictator Batista with all the aircraft, bombs, arms and other weapons with which his troops spread terror and death, desperation and ruin," p. 20.

[12] U.S. reaction to the trials is in Welch, *Response to Revolution*, pp. 36, 162; Thomas, *Pursuit*, pp. 1073–76, and Szulc, *Fidel*, pp. 483–84. Castro's own reaction is in Matthews, *Revolution in Cuba*, pp. 131–35.

actively promoted the initial stages of the Cubanization of industry and the land-reform program.[13]

In mid-February Washington sent its new ambassador to Havana. He was Philip Bonsal, perhaps the perfect choice to soothe the feelings of the moderate nationalists—assuming that was what was required. Like other State Department liberals, Bonsal was distrustful of Castro. Nevertheless, he sensed the heightened mood of nationalism in Cuba and the general sensitivity to criticism by the United States. He went out of his way not to act in the proconsular tradition that Cubans' had observed in previous U.S. ambassadors. He even accepted slights from Castro, who had become prime minister by this time, and he cautioned North Americans in Cuba to be on their best behavior. Nonetheless, Bonsal was himself oriented by an understanding of the healthy relationship that official North America believed had existed over the years between the two nations. He admitted past errors of judgment or decorum but rejected the nationalist contention that the United States had dominated Cuban affairs. This belief often led him into defenses of U.S. policy that at times became lectures to Cuban officials on the great benefits to both nations of close ties.[14]

Bonsal's attempt to understand how the fall of Batista had altered the framework of Cuban politics placed him in general agreement with those at the State Department like Wieland and Rubottom who realized that the United States could not go back to business as usual with Cuba—though they did not yet suspect how radically the rules of the game were to change. On the other side of the fence at the department were those who had earlier disagreed with the policy of pressing Batista to resign and who, continuing their earlier view of Castro as a subversive, now saw in Cuba a communist plot to infiltrate the new government.

In one of many confrontations, partisans of the two groups met in El Salvador in early April 1959 to discuss the situation in Cuba. Gathered at the meeting were the U.S. ambassadors to the twelve Hispanic republics of the Caribbean area, as well as Deputy Undersecretary of State for Administrative Affairs Loy Henderson, and Undersecretary Rubottom. Bonsal

---

[13] Braddock's discussion with Pazos, Boti, and Bush is in R.G. 59, 737.00/2-1359, Desp. #897. Also see Padula, diss., pp. 232–33, 259, 268, 274–81, 396, 404, 508, 537; and Thomas, *Pursuit*, pp. 1077. There is a distinct anti-U.S. tone at many points, even in the anti-Castro memoirs by Casuso and López-Fresquet. See also Montaner, *Secret Report on the Cuban Revolution*, pp. 206–7.

[14] Bonsal's sensitivity to Cuban nationalism is noted in Bonsal, *Cuba, Castro and the United States*, pp. 57, 68, 75, 80, and 140. His lectures to Cuban officials are referred to on pages 48, 51, 54, and 90. Bonsal says, "I shared a belief based upon the Cuban American experience of sixty years that the reciprocal economic interests of Cuba and the United States would exercise a stabilizing and moderating influence on developments in Cuba." Ibid., p. 29.

was there and spoke for the position of the majority, which was to let the dust settle in Havana. He admitted that the leftists Raúl Castro and Che Guevara were close to Fidel and acknowledged the hostility shown by all three to U.S. influence. Still, he pointed out that there was general agreement in Cuba with many of their comments (especially those of Fidel) and that a cautious, non-antagonistic policy was best, given the alternatives. Bonsal added that to respond aggressively to the unofficial, radical, and anti-U.S. pronouncements by these Cuban leaders would only poison the atmosphere and be taken as undue interference in Cuban affairs, making it more difficult to work even with moderate Cuban officials.[15]

The opposition to this cautious approach, led by Ambassadors Robert Hill (Mexico) and Whiting Willauer (Costa Rica), wanted to alert hemisphere governments to the growing danger of communist intrusion in Cuba by taking the matter to the Organization of American States. Hill and Willauer were convinced by the evidence, first produced in 1957 and 1958 by Batista's supporters to defame the armed opposition, that Castro had become a secret communist in his university days and had helped lead the "communist" riots that engulfed Bogotá, Colombia, during the 1948 meeting of hemisphere nations that set up the OAS.[16] From their perspective, Castro, though acting cautiously for the present, was operating as an agent of the Soviet Union. He thus represented a threat to hemisphere security as defined by the OAS resolution, pried out of unwilling Latin delegates at the 1954 Caracas meeting of that body, which declared:

That the domination or control of the political institutions of any American state by the international communist movement . . . would constitute a threat to the sovereignty and political independence of the American states, endangering the peace of America, and would call for appropriate action in accordance with existing treaties.[17]

As noted in chapter 5, the resolution had been used to justify the U.S. actions that culminated in the overthrow of the government of Jacobo Arbenz in Guatemala in 1954. Since the conservatives believed that the same situation was developing in Cuba, it would not be difficult, they thought,

[15] The San Salvador Conference is discussed in Bonsal, *Cuba, Castro and the United States*, pp. 58–61. Also see DDEL, Herter Papers, M-Z Official—Classified (4), letters from Willauer to Rubottom dated 1/27, 3/10, and 6/16/59.

[16] An account of the San Salvador meeting by Hill and Willauer appears in "Communist Threat to the U.S.," parts 12 and 13.

[17] The Caracas Resolution of the OAS. appears in Connell-Smith, *The Inter-American System*, p. 230. See also Blanch Wiesen Cook, *The Declassified Eisenhower: A Divided Legacy of Peace and Political Warfare* (New York: Doubleday, 1981), pp. 259–60.

to convince the OAS of this fact. Doing so would prepare the ground for a "legal" intervention against Castro.

The difficulty with the conservatives' program was that the mood in Latin America had shifted dramatically since 1954. Much of the evidence of communist infiltration of Cuba would not have impressed most Latin American leaders. The exceptions would have been the handful of remaining anti-communist dictators from whom the Eisenhower administration was now anxious to distance itself. If the charge would not have been persuasive, merely raising it would have embittered U.S.-Cuban relations. Most Cubans still associated claims of communist subversion of Cuba with those who wished to restore Batista.[18]

While the U.S. officials who favored a cautious approach acknowledged the generally accepted intelligence finding that Raúl and Che had Marxist backgrounds, they contended that Fidel's own background was untainted by close association with, let alone membership in, communist organizations. Moreover, up to that point, his public remarks contained no defense of communism, and he occasionally made statements of an anti-communist nature. If the State Department could not convince itself that Cuba was becoming dominated by international communism, it could not hope to convince a skeptical OAS.

In a larger sense, too, much of Washington was less nervous than usual about communist subversion at this time. By chance, the rise of Castro coincided with a period of détente in U.S.-Soviet relations. President Eisenhower and Premier Khrushchev were both steering toward a summit meeting in 1960. During much of 1959, despite continued tension about Berlin and a rising critique in the United States of a "missile gap" that (erroneously) placed Soviet ICBM development dangerously ahead, both leaders repeatedly expressed concern about the heightening dangers of nuclear war. To pave the way for the summit meeting, each modified somewhat the demon-like picture of the other common to official pronouncements. A new, amiable, and "Westernized" Soviet ambassador to Washington added to the emphasis on diplomacy rather than propaganda warfare. While Khrushchev, looking over his shoulder at the revolutionary Mao, did take verbal swipes at capitalism, they were often of the "it can't work, so why worry about it?" variety rather than the "warmongering imperialist" stance. A major psychological breakthrough occurred when

[18] Throughout the 1950s, Washington was worried about Latin America's lack of concern about communist subversion. See FRUS 1952–1954, vol. 4, pp. 81–83, 85, 90, 96–97, 107; 1955–1957, vol. 6, pp. 8, 25–26, 47–48, 55–56, 61–65, 83–89. Also see DDEL, WHO, OS ANSA, NSC 5613/1, Policy Toward Latin America (1) "Operations Coordinating Board Report," 5/21/58, Annex B (4/15/58) and Annex C (5/26/58) p. 2; "OCB Report," 11/26/58, pp. 13, 23–24; "Suggested Changes for NSC 5902/1," 12/17/60, p. 2.

Khrushchev was invited for a visit by the U.S. president in the fall of 1959. The Soviet premier was hardly humble or, at times, even gracious in his encounters with Americans, but millions followed his travels across the nation on television and saw that the gruff, frank, and engaging Russian leader was no monster. Most Americans thought the visit had been worthwhile, while the lessening of superpower tensions boosted the already high popularity of the U.S. president. Castro had the good fortune to move his program to the left just when Washington wished to avoid minor squabbles with Moscow so as not to poison the atmosphere for the discussion of larger questions.[19]

For all these reasons, then, the cautious approach toward Castro won the day. It was in this context that Washington prepared for an unofficial visit by Prime Minister Castro—now clearly the central figure in the Cuban government.

U.S. Ambassador Philip Bonsal (*right*) at his first meeting with Fidel Castro, March 6, 1959. *Wide World Photos*

[19] On the atmosphere of detente in 1959 see John L. Gaddis, *Strategies of Containment* (New York: Oxford University Press, 1982), pp. 192, 196; Eisenhower, *Waging Peace, 1956–1961*, pp. 432–49; Stephen Ambrose, *Rise to Globalism* (New York: Penguin, 1985), 4th rev. ed., pp. 166–77; Cook, *Declassified Eisenhower*, pp. 208–12.

Washington was concerned about the effect of detente on its anti-communist goals in Latin America. See NSC 5613/1 (5/21/58), p. 5.

Favorable U.S. public opinion concerning a summit meeting, Khrushchev's visit, and Eisenhower's dealings with the Soviets is registered in George H. Gallup, ed., *The Gallup Poll, 1935–1971* (New York: Random House, 1972), vol. 3, pp. 1605, 1617, 1627, 1631. Despite developments in Cuba, the president's popularity rose from 57 percent at the beginning of 1959 to 66 percent at the end. It continued to climb in 1960.

IV

Castro came to Washington in April 1959 in response to invitations by several private U.S. organizations, foremost among them the American Society of Newspaper Editors. Moderates in the Cuban government convinced him to take economic advisers with him to test the waters concerning economic aid. Castro agreed but warned them against any overt request and refused to take what he considered the position of a supplicant assumed by so many Cuban leaders before him. Since North Americans considered economic aid an act of generosity, the import of Castro's unwillingness to ask for it was missed.[20]

Eisenhower, already tiring of the Cuban prime minister's anti-Yankee

Castro meeting with U.S. Vice-President Richard M. Nixon in Washington, D.C., April 15, 1959. *Wide World Photos*

[20] Castro's trip is discussed in López-Fresquet, *My Fourteen Months*, chs. 16 and 17, and Casuso, *Cuba and Castro*, ch. 14.

barbs, arranged to be out of town. Castro did meet with Acting Secretary of State Herter and Vice President Nixon. Herter's report on his interview focused on the Cuban leader's personality—something that struck everyone who met him. He informed Eisenhower that Castro seemed immature, excitable, and almost completely ignorant about administering the affairs of state. This may have been an accurate observation but missed the most important point, which was the nature of the charismatic leader's power. In any event, this view sustained a policy of patience, waiting for Castro to calm down and learn the ropes, as Herter, backed by Rubottom, Bonsal, and others, was advising. State Department liberals were still hopeful, but, as we have seen, they were not without their own suspicions of the new Cuban leader. The department's assessment of the trip concluded that "we should await his [Castro's] decisions on specific matters before assuming a more optimistic view than heretofore about the possibility of a constructive relationship with him and his government."[21]

Nixon's interview with Castro reflected both the paternalistic attitude often taken toward Cuban leaders as well as a growing suspicion that the new Cuban prime minister bore close watching. Nixon unselfconsciously gave Castro a lecture on such subjects as democracy, capitalism, and the menace of communism. The vice president advised Castro to hold elections and attract foreign capital, suggesting Puerto Rico as an appropriate model. He concluded, in his own report on the meeting, that Castro had the makings of a strong leader and that "he is either incredibly naive about communism or under communist discipline—my guess is the former. . . . But because he has the power to lead to which I have referred, we have no choice but at least to orient him in the right direction." The vice president's emphasis on the question of communism marked him as someone receptive to the notion that the machinations of international subversive forces were the key to the Cuban situation. Nevertheless, his conclusion was in line with the paternalism of the liberals and thus compatible with the watchful approach adopted by the State Department.[22]

Perhaps the classic example of the paternalistic approach was the meeting arranged between Castro and a CIA expert on Latin American communism. What the agency hoped to achieve is unclear, but the outcome of the interview seems to have been to reinforce the view of the CIA's Board of Estimates that Castro was not a communist. The CIA National Intelligence

---

[21] The relevant documents are DDEL, Herter, Chronological File—Mar. 1959 (1), Krebs to Rubottom, 3/31/59; WHO, Office of the Staff Secretary, Department of State, 1959, Feb.–Apr. (5), Memorandum of Conversation with the President, 4/22/59; DDE, International Series, Cuba (1), 4/23/59.

[22] The Nixon interview is in Jeffrey Safford, "The Nixon–Castro Meeting of 19 April, 1959," *Diplomatic History* 4:4 (Fall 1980), pp. 426–31.

Estimate of June 1959 held to the position that Castro was "messianic," "impractical," and "impulsive," but not a communist. As late as November, the deputy director of the CIA told the Judiciary Committee of the Senate that there was no evidence that Castro had a communist background or had ever been a member of the party. He stated further that the Communist Party itself never treated Castro as a member or follower.[23] By that date, however, as we shall see, both the intelligence community and the State Department had come around to the *private* view that his regime had to be overthrown.

Fascination with communism in Cuba was a continual subject during Castro's interviews with the U.S. media during his trip. Despite the fact that he denied on several occasions—usually persuasively—that he was or had ever been a Communist, the question was posed at every turn, and Castro was privately infuriated by it. Despite his denials, he was pressed in North American public forums and in its media again and again to explain why elections were not yet scheduled, why special courts tried those accused of crimes during Batista's era, whether he had ever been offered aid by the Soviet Union, whether the Cuban government would be democratic, if he was in favor of dictatorship, and, if he would support U.S. policy in the cold war. Castro answered each of these questions more or less the way North Americans wanted them answered, but their nature and persistence revealed much about U.S. presumptions concerning its relationship to Cuba.[24]

V

One of the developments being watched most closely by the State Department was the new agrarian-reform law promulgated on May 17, 1959. Here finally was an act and not merely an attitude to which the United States could respond. Although it was later maintained by the U.S. government that the radicals administering the reform never intended to implement the document as written and that, as it stood, the United States could have lived with it, the State Department's contemporary reaction was negative. This was a result of the damage inflicted on U.S. landholdings under its provi-

[23] Szulc, *Fidel*, pp. 481–82; López-Fresquet, *My Fourteen Months*, p. 110. Cabell's testimony to Congress is in *Communist Threat to the United States Through the Caribbean*, part III, pp. 141–67; CIA, SNIE 80-59, "The Situation in the Caribbean," pp. 1–7.

[24] López-Fresquet, *My Fourteen Months*, pp. 108–10; Casuso, *Cuba and Castro*, p. 212. Press coverage of Castro's visit can be found in *New York Times*, 4/11/59, p. 1; 4/12, p. 26; 4/13, p. 11; 4/15, pp. 1 and 16; 4/16, p. 1; 4/17, pp. 1 and 5; 4/18, pp. 1 and 10; 4/19, p. 4; 4/20, pp. 1 and 5; 4/21, pp. 1 and 12; 4/22, pp. 1 and 14; 4/23, pp. 1 and 2; 4/24, pp. 1, 4 and 5; 4/25, pp. 1 and 2; 4/26, I, p. 3; IV, pp. 1–2 and 7; VI, pp. 17–22; 4/27, p. 3; 4/28, p. 18.

sions. Embassy and department officials declared their support for "sound" land reform and the right of expropriation with "prompt, adequate and effective" compensation. These, however, were classic terms (the Mexicans had heard them decades before) that made clear the limits of U.S. flexibility in defense of its property holders. With the weapon of the U.S. sugar quota bulging under his coat, so to speak, Assistant Secretary Rubottom told the new Cuban ambassador that unwise tampering with the structure of Cuban agriculture could raise questions about the island's status as a dependable source of sugar and endanger her privileged position as supplier of the U.S. market. Ambassador Bonsal, at the same meeting, added that legislation harmful to foreign investors "may well have an adverse effect on the plans of private foreign investment in Cuba in many fields other than agriculture." Such remarks indicated that the United States, however indirectly, intended to use its power in Cuba as it had in the past to orient the workings of the Cuban economy. Moreover, coming as they did from men who represented the more flexible wing of policymakers, these warnings indicated that changes in the Cuban economy much less radical than those eventually carried out would have been the source of very serious disagreement between the two nations.[25]

The State Department also inclined toward a tough stance on agrarian reform because it was under pressure from the large U.S. landowners on the island who claimed that the law's provisions for compensation were unfair. First of all, payment was to be based upon declared value—a notoriously low figure used by the owners to reduce their taxes. Moreover, the landowners complained, the government bonds offered in compensation by the Cubans were likely to be of little value.[26]

The State Department liberals hoped, however, that by demonstrating a

[25] The U.S. internal reaction to the land-reform law is in R.G. 59, 837.16/5-2759, "U.S. Misgivings with Regard to Cuban Agrarian Reform Law"; 837.16/6-359, Desp. #1353, "Agrarian Reform," Braddock to Department of State; 837.16/6-1259, "Further Exchange of Views on Agrarian Reform and Other Matters," Memorandum of Conversation Rubottom and Dihigo (Cuban Amb.).

The U.S. response even to proposals by Cuban moderates was not always sympathetic. See Washington's reaction to a request by moderates at the Cuban Ministry of the Treasury and the National Bank for an IMF stabilization loan: U.S. Treasury Department, Confidential Draft Memorandum, State Department to Havana Embassy, 1/14/59; Memorandum on the Cuban Situation, 3/19/59; Background Briefing for Castro Visit, 4/13/59. The most extensive examination of this question is in Morley, *Imperial State*, pp. 76–81.

[26] Complaints from U.S. sugar and cattle landowners to the State Department can be found in R.G. 59, 611.37/7-1559, Memorandum of Conversation, Rubottom and Lawrence Crosby, Chairman, U.S.-Cuban Sugar Council; 837.16/6-2459, Memorandum of Conversation, Herter and Robert Kleberg, Proprietor of King Ranch; DDEL, Whitman File, Dulles-Herter Series, July 1959 (2), Memorandum for the President: Recommendations of Mr. Robert Kleberg on the Cuban Situation, 7/7/59. Also see Padula diss., pp. 132–33, 142, 226–27, 233–37.

degree of flexibility on the highly sensitive land issue, it might ease nationalist pressure on the growing and more profitable non-agricultural sector of U.S. investment. The trouble with the liberals' strategy was that it never obtained the behind-the-scenes opportunity it needed to trade flexibility on agrarian reform for concessions in other areas. Castro just would not play by the old rules. Unwilling to subject himself even to indirect pressure from the U.S. embassy, he avoided all discussion of the subject. After several attempts by Bonsal to present the formal U.S. position on land reform to the prime minister, the State Department released it to the press on June 11. The department had been forced into the political arena—a sign that negotiations with the Cuban government would have to take place on a completely new basis. In the absence of what the Department considered "real" negotiations—where U.S. hegemony could be brought to bear—Washington decided to carry its side of the story to the Cuban press, much of which carried only praise of the new agrarian program. To the dismay of the liberals, what they considered a softly worded statement fell like a thunderclap on sensitive Cuban ears.

The official U.S. note to the Cuban government on the agrarian reform stated "that it is the confident hope of the Government of the United States that agrarian reform in Cuba will be so carried out as not to impair or reduce but rather to increase the productivity of the Cuban economy."[27] The Cuban reply, also public, adopted the same polite tone but nonetheless spoke in the voice of a long-repressed Cuban nationalism. Standing on the prerogatives inherent in sovereignty and proclaiming the desire of the "Revolutionary Government" to fulfill the wishes of the Cuban people, the Cuban note stated that "unless large scale landholding is abolished . . . Cuba will continue to suffer economic stagnation and an increasing rate of unemployment." It conceded the obligation in the 1940 constitution to pay for expropriated land at once and in cash. It pointed out, however, that the same constitution had long called for the abolition of large-scale landholding. The sacking of the Treasury by the Batistianos made it impossible to comply, it said, with both provisions. The note concluded with a theory of sovereignty and a tone of defiance that had never before appeared in an official communication between the two governments. It said that "the Revolutionary Government, exercising the constituted power vested in it by the overwhelming support it enjoys—the primal source of democratic legitimacy—had elected the form of indemnification which, in the circumstances alluded to, it considers the most advisable in the best interests of the nation, which interest it places above any others."[28]

[27] The official U.S. note on the agrarian reform is in R.G. 59, 837.16/6-1159.

[28] The official Cuban note is dated June 15, 1959. State Department translation #37513,

As if to underscore the new situation, the popular magazine *Bohemia*—a good barometer of Cuban public opinion at the time—said that the U.S. note "hurts national sentiment" and that its tone harked back to the days of U.S. interventionism. The magazine praised the Cuban reply and its desire "to wave the flag of sovereignty which we will not strike in the face of interference of any type."[29] It would seem that the Cuban revolution, even in its moderate and capitalist period, pressed hard against the existing form of Cuban society and its relationship with the United States. Since demands on both sides eventually became irreconcilable as the revolution took a socialist direction, it is important to remember the deep nationalist foundation on which that later stage was constructed.

IN A demonstration of the inconsistency that bedeviled those in Washington who were trying to figure out Castro's own position in this matter, the prime minister finally agreed to see Bonsal the day after the U.S. note had been made public. In the interview he demonstrated none of the nationalist fervor of *Bohemia*. While making it clear that he favored changes in the terms under which U.S. capital operated in Cuba, he said that the revolution did not desire to exclude such capital. When questioned by reporters after the meeting, Castro praised the demeanor of the U.S. ambassador and added, coyly, "We no longer live in times when one had to worry when the American Ambassador visited the Prime Minister."[30]

VI

As unsatisfactory to both sides as it was, this sparring between a cautiously wielded U.S. power and a self-conscious Cuban nationalism represented the honeymoon phase in relations. In the summer months of 1959, Castro began a process that was eventually to take his movement from radical nationalism to socialist revolution. The new government had already taken several measures that broadened its base of support considerably: it decreed a reduction in urban rents and in all utility rates; it raised the wages of sugar workers; it opened previously private beaches to the public; and its land-reform program held out the possibility of broadened land ownership. Since all of these measures struck at the holders of wealth and privilege, North

---

file number F760001-0955, Central Files, R.G. 59, N.A. The Cuban government's defense of the agrarian reform is in Oficina de Publicidad e Información de la Presidencia de la República, *Así cumple la Revolución* (La Habana: OPI, 26 de Julio de 1959).

[29] The quote from *Bohemia* is in R.G. 59, 837.16/6-1959.

[30] Bonsal's meeting with Castro is in R.G. 59, 837.16/6-1259, Emb. Tel. #1555; Castro's remarks to the press are in 837.16/6-1359, #1556.

Americans, almost all of whom were in or near this category, felt victimized. Little could be done in response, however, because the nationalist and social-justice sentiment that surrounded these actions had immense mass appeal. These measures could also be defended from a progressive and developmentalist point of view as the elimination of economic and social monopoly power so that social harmony and economic growth could be facilitated.[31]

Even more important than the early acts of the revolution was the emotional context in which they occurred. They were announced by Castro as historic victories in a hundred-year struggle for independence and justice. In the process, Castro created a unique relationship with the Cuban people. He spoke to them directly and emotionally in mammoth rallies and hours-long television speeches in which he seemed to be able to elicit and play upon their most deeply held feelings. He complemented these exercises in mass communication with a personal touch that might have been the envy of a North American ward politician. Castro drove here and there in the countryside, stopping at villages to hear complaints, comforting those in distress, or picking up a machete and wading into the cane fields at harvest time. Whatever his purpose, he soon became the voice and the conscience of the revolution. It could take no direction that he did not sanction, and it could not do so effectively without his active support.

During this period, fearing Fidel's personal power over the masses and the radical direction of government decrees, many moderates fell or were driven away from the government. Slowly, criticism of those aspects of the revolution championed by the Maximum Leader, as he was now called (but he was affectionately known to the masses as Fidel), became more and more difficult to sustain in public discussion and in state action. Dissenters still had access to that portion of the media critical of or unassimilated into the new revolutionary outlook, but the influence of these media was declining and they were beginning to face restrictions, formal and informal, from the government.[32]

As early as July, a telling demonstration of Castro extra-institutional

[31] The early mass-oriented reforms are in Padula, diss., pp. 130, 259–61, 390, 397. The reactions of Cuban businessmen to the early reforms are discussed in Padula, pp. 112–19, 191–202, 222–31, 246–51, 259–62, 346–56, 389–404.

[32] The fate of the media is discussed in Herbert Matthews, *Revolution in Cuba*, pp. 128, 148; Padula, diss., pp. 307–9, 315, 471, 580; Efren Cordova, "Fidel Castro and the Cuban Labor Movement: 1959–1961" (diss., Cornell University, 1977), pp. 214–15; Szulc, *Fidel*, p. 521. Also see Carlos Ripoll, "The Press in Cuba, 1952–1960: Autocratic and Totalitarian Censorship," in William E. Ratliff, ed., *The Selling of Fidel Castro* (New Brunswick, N.J.: Transaction, 1987), pp. 83–108, and Phillips, *The Cuban Dilemma*, pp. 147, 155–56.

power occurred when he suddenly resigned as prime minister and went on television to denounce President Urrutia for raising the issue of communism so as to provoke foreign intervention. For good measure, Urrutia was berated for his unwillingness to live on the modest salary accepted by other members of the government. Castro exclaimed that he could not work in the poisoned atmosphere created by the president and thus was leaving the government. So vehement was Castro's invective that Urrutia, his office soon ringed by crowds demanding his removal, resigned.[33] Castro could use power as well as charismatic authority and did so in October when confronted with a serious defection within the armed forces. Huber Matos, a veteran and hero of the Sierra campaign, resigned as military governor of Camaguey Province to protest the growing influence of Communists among the officer corps and the radicalism of the local administrators of the agrarian-reform program. Matos's staff resigned in support of his action. Yet even in this instance, though Castro took the precaution of occupying Matos's headquarters area with loyal forces, the coup de grace was delivered by Fidel personally as he placed an unresisting Matos under arrest.[34]

VII

Castro's growing consolidation of power in all its forms was complemented by his growing hostility toward the United States. Some of his enemies, most notably former rebel air-force chief Pedro Díaz Lanz, based themselves, like innumerable Cuban exiles of the past, on North American soil. As their raids against the island increased, Castro openly began to associate domestic opposition to the revolution with subversion directed by (or at least tolerated by) the United States.[35] By this time, many Cubans identified the revolution with Fidel. The key to his success against the power of the United States was that he had defined the goals of the revolution as the historic aims of an independent Cuba. It was not difficult to take the next step and describe the North American nation as the principal enemy of those historic aims. As a result, every effort by Washington to defend its interests or retain its power to direct Cuban society became attacks on Cu-

[33] The Urrutia affair is discussed in Thomas, *Pursuit*, pp. 1231–33; Bonsal, *Cuba, Castro and the United States*, pp. 80–81; Phillips, *The Cuban Dilemma*, p. 102; and Matthews, *Revolution in Cuba*, pp. 137–38.

[34] The Matos affair is in Thomas, *Pursuit*, pp. 1241–45; Phillips, *The Cuban Dilemma*, pp. 112–13; and Bonsal, *Cuba, Castro and the United States*, pp. 101–4.

[35] Cuba, Ministry of State, Public Relations Dept., *In Defense of National Sovereignty*, pp. 15–19.; Cuba, Instituto de Historia del Movimento Comunista *El Pensamiento de Fidel Castro*, T.1, vol. 1, pp. 18–21, 22–25.

ban independence. The State Department was slow to realize that Castro had managed to place the United States in the intolerable position of being unable to exert its power except in an imperial manner.[36]

Castro's actions naturally increased the ranks of those in the United States who considered him a communist and his revolution a danger to North American interests. During the second half of 1959, Castro and his enemies among North Americans began a duet in which each took actions to combat the threat from the other. In this way, the deepest suspicions of both were eventually fulfilled.

In the fall of 1959 the U.S. policy of cautious diplomacy came under increasing pressure from congressmen, editorialists, and the minority at the State Department who favored a strong response to Castro's angry denunciations of the United States and to the increasing role played by the Communists in Cuba. Until midyear, Castro had generally sided with the 26th of July Movement radicals whenever they became engaged in public debate over the course of the revolution with the Communist PSP. The PSP position was often more cautious than that of the M-26-7 radicals so that Castro's stance was hardly a sign of moderation. Despite the less than full support for the revolution by the Communists, however, Castro seemed careful about his attitude toward them. His decision to remove Urrutia and later Matos had come in part because of the opposition of these men to the growing influence of the Communists. Slowly, Castro began to take the position that attacks on Communists in Cuba were tantamount to attacks on the revolution itself. Anti-communism became anti-nationalism—a connection facilitated by Batista's adoption of North American-style McCarthyism during the 1950s. It is likely that Castro was now preparing for an eventual showdown with the United States and saw the PSP as a vehicle for opening doors to Moscow, the only possible counterweight to U.S. power. Whatever his motive, Castro's growing closeness to the Cuban Communists in the fall of 1959 put the heat on the State Department liberals.[37]

[36] For this period in Cuban politics see Thomas, *Pursuit*, chs. 99 and 100, and Bonsal, *Cuba, Castro and the United States*, ch. 8.

[37] Castro's relationship with the PSP in 1959 is a matter of much speculation. See Edward Gonzalez, "Castro's Revolution, Cuban Communist Appeals, and the Soviet Response," *World Politics* 21:1 (Oct. 1968), pp. 41–43, 49–53; Samuel Farber, "The Cuban Communists in the Early Stages of the Cuban Revolution," *Latin American Research Review* 18:1 (1983), pp. 72–73; Martín, *The Early Fidel*, passim; Szulc, *Fidel*, pp. 463–78. Concerning Castro and Communists in the labor movement see Cordova diss.

Fidel's own ideology is examined in Matthews, *Revolution in Cuba*, pp. 46–47, 65–67, 97–99, 124, 152–54; Welch *Response to Revolution*, pp. 11–12. An interesting, firsthand account is in Casuso, *Cuba and Castro*. Castro's own current assessment of his thinking in

The majority at the State Department who had favored a cautious policy were also becoming alarmed over events in Cuba, but for some of their own reasons. Having watched with dismay the growing hold of Castro over the Cuban people, they were far more impressed with that fact than with the growing but still modest influence of the PSP, whose public statements seemed at times to call for more restraint by the militants among the former rebel fighters. What bothered the State Department liberals was that the moderates in the Cuban Cabinet with whom they had hoped to arrange a scaling down of the scope of the original reforms so as to make them compatible with U.S. interests were now gone or without influence. As a result, Washington was forced to do business with a man who was as physically elusive as he was uncompromising. Quite simply, there was no longer anyone whom the diplomats could hope to influence. The policy of employing internal allies to protect U.S. interests, designed laboriously in the Good Neighbor years, found itself bankrupt. If conservatives began to get tough because Castro insulted the United States and was in their eyes a tool of Moscow's design to destroy democracy in the Western Hemisphere, the liberals now went to the mat with Castro because his policies and power rendered impotent the old means of exerting U.S. influence in Cuba. Moreover, Castro's growing popularity throughout Latin America forecast the possibility that declining U.S. influence in Cuba might be followed—domino-like, as U.S. officials would have put it—by a similar loss of its preponderant position in the hemisphere.

Though State Department liberals were later pilloried by U.S. conservatives as pro-Castro dupes who had allowed a totalitarian regime to be constructed on the island, as early as October 1959—before there was any Soviet presence in Cuba and while opposition media still existed—these liberals shifted policy to one of overthrowing Castro's regime. As with the "third force" policy of 1958, Washington officials again began to search for an alternative to the man about whom their worst fears had been realized. The secret policy paper formulating the change stated that "the time is now passed when it could be reasonably hoped that Castro would adopt policies and attitudes consistent with minimum U.S. security requirements and policy interests." The liberals, like the conservatives, saw Castro as a threat to the hemisphere, but without the world communist conspiracy component. "Not only have our business interests in Cuba been seriously affected," the note went on, "but the United States cannot hope to encourage and support sound economic policies in other Latin American countries and promote necessary private investments in Latin America if it is or appears

the 1950s is in Fidel Castro and Frei Betto, *Fidel on Religion* (New York: Simon & Schuster, 1987), pp. 141–42, 146, 196.

to be simultaneously cooperating with the Castro program.'' While they had decided to get tough, as the conservatives had been urging them to do, the liberals were prevented from boasting about it because they knew of Castro's tremendous popularity in Cuba and the rest of Latin America. In the words of the policy document, ''In view of Castro's strong though diminishing support in Cuba, it is of great importance, however, that the United States government not openly take actions which would cause the United States to be blamed directly for his failure or downfall.''[38] Until now, the liberals' problem had been to defend U.S. interests in Cuba without exacerbating Cuban nationalism; now they faced the even more daunting task of overthrowing the regime without seeming to assault Cuban sovereignty.

[38] The change in policy at the State Department is documented in R.G. 59, 611.37/10-3159, ''Current Basic U.S. Policy Toward Cuba,'' Herter to Eisenhower; 611.37/11-2759, Desp. #789, ''Suggested Operations Plan for Cuba,'' Bonsal to Secretary of State; DDEL, WHO, Office of the Staff Secretary, International Series, Cuba (1), Herter to Eisenhower, 11/5/59; WHO, Intelligence File, Cuba (1), ''Current Basic U.S. Policy Toward Cuba, November, 1959.''

CHAPTER 8

SOCIAL REVOLUTION
BREAKS THE TIE

I

Confronted with the task of removing Castro, the State Department had to turn the clearly illegal parts of the program over to those U.S. agencies designed to operate in secret. In December 1959 the State Department suggested that anti-Castro propaganda be turned over to the CIA. Rubottom met with Gordon Gray, Eisenhower's special assistant for national security affairs, to request that the new policy also be taken up by the Planning Board of the National Security Council.[1]

The NSC and CIA had not been inactive since the latter's failed attempt to head off a Castro victory. Indeed, during 1959, when the State Department was attempting to moderate the nationalist reforms, the intelligence agencies—despite their own uncertainty about the ideological parentage of the Castro movement—began to prepare the plans that were resorted to when the decline in U.S. influence became precipitate. The first CIA front organization (the Double Check Corporation) was set up in Miami in May. By the fall of 1959, the CIA was smuggling active opponents out of Cuba and sending arms to the first of the small anti-Castro guerrilla bands that began operating in the Escambray Mountains of central Cuba.[2]

In December 1959, when a consensus arose that Cuba was slipping out of the North American grasp, the small-scale, lower-level operations were

[1] R.G. 59, 737.00/12-2859, Kretzman to Rubottom, "Comments on the Public Affairs Aspects of the 'Action Program' for Cuba"; 611.37/12-3159, "Current U.S. Policy Toward Cuba," Memorandum of Conversation between Rubottom and Gray. John Prados, *President's Secret Wars* (New York: William Morrow, 1986), pp. 175–76.
[2] Szulc, *Pursuit*, pp. 481–82; Padula, diss., p. 547.

given official sanction by the director's office of the CIA. Detailed plans were now prepared to begin training Cuban exiles for infiltration into the island in order to sabotage sugar mills and other economic targets. Allen Dulles, director of the CIA, brought this plan to Eisenhower for his approval in January 1960. According to national security adviser Gray:

the President said he didn't object to such an undertaking and, indeed, thought something like this was timely. However, he felt that any program should be much more ambitious, and it was probably now the time to move against Castro in a positive and aggressive way which went beyond mere harassment. He asked Mr. Dulles to come back with an enlarged program.[3]

On January 18 the CIA set up a special task force (Branch 4 of the Western Hemisphere Division) composed mainly of veterans of the 1954 operation against Arbenz in Guatemala. The task force prepared a wide-ranging assault on the Castro regime. Early in March this plan was approved by the secret high-level study group that oversaw all major covert operations. The approved program was sent to Eisenhower on March 14. Three days later the president met with Allen Dulles and gave final approval to the plan. The program now included the creation of an organized political opposition from among Cuban exiles, the construction of a secret radio transmitter for "black" propaganda broadcasts, the conduct of sabotage and intelligence operations within the island, and the creation of a paramilitary force among dissident Cubans for possible use at a later date. This last element was the origin of the Bay of Pigs invasion of April 1961. A separate project to assassinate Castro and other top Cuban leaders, under discussion since December 1959, was also implemented by the CIA. Several of the actual attempts on Castro's life were carried out by the agency with the cooperation of the U.S. Mafia. All of these actions were to be complemented by a program of economic denial and, eventually, of widespread economic warfare. There was confidence, at least among the covert operators, that the Cuban government could not withstand such a multi-pronged assault.[4]

---

[3] DDEL, Gordon Gray Papers, "Gordon Gray," letter from Gray to Don Wilson, 12/3/74; DDE Correspondence, 1965–66, Gray to Eisenhower, 9/20 and 9/26/66, and Eisenhower to Gray, 9/22 and 9/28/66. Gray's quoted remarks are from his letter to Don Wilson of 12/3/74, p. 1.

[4] The plan approved by Eisenhower has never been fully declassified. Censored versions of the document—"A Program of Covert Action Against the Castro Regime"—appear in DDI, 1985, #1537; in JFKL, Papers of President Kennedy, NSF-Countries, Cuba: Para-Military Study Group, Annex 1; and in Luis Aguilar, ed., *Operation Zapata . . . The Board of Inquiry on the Bay of Pigs* (Frederick, Md.: University Publications of America, 1981), pp. 3–4.

The origins and development of the plan are discussed in Aguilar, *Operation Zapata*, pp. x, 55–57; Peter Wyden, *Bay of Pigs* (New York: Simon & Schuster, 1979), pp. 19–20, 23–

The State Department, laboring on the overt side of Cuban policy, and not always aware of the extent or exact nature of covert activities, was less optimistic. Still, throughout 1960 it dutifully worked at maintaining the dwindling U.S. official influence in Cuba. Its main task was to keep the lines of communication with the Cuban government open so as to be informed about and to blunt as best it could the growing assault on U.S. economic interests. Such contacts also, it was hoped, would demonstrate that the United States was a reasonable neighbor of the island people, open to dialogue and compromise. This latter stance was also meant to keep Castro guessing whether or not he had burned his bridges to Washington. (The Cuban leader's own occasional moderation may have been similarly motivated.) Washington's overt activity also served to dampen suspicion about U.S. interventionism in Cuba and Latin America. In doing so, however, it intensified the need to keep what was rapidly becoming the *real* policy totally secret.

Another responsibility of the State Department was to retard and, if possible, reverse Castro's growing influence in the hemisphere. In August 1959, at a meeting of the council of the OAS in Santiago, Chile, the Cubans had attempted to gather support for a broad-scale crusade against dictators. Castro had inherited his anti-tyrannical filibustering from the tradition of Cuban nationalism and had by now expanded that inheritance into a vision of himself as the Simón Bolívar of a hemisphere-wide struggle against tyrannical government. (With appropriate Marxist additions in later years, the struggle would be one against "imperialism" as well.) As we have seen, the United States had for over a decade been unhappy with the slap-dash assaults on dictators in the Caribbean area mounted by the Caribbean Legion, whose actions, in Washington's view, created instability in the region. Now that Cuba proposed a more serious effort (and actually supported a series of unsuccessful forays against unsavory regimes in the Dominican Republic, Haiti, and Panama early in 1959) the State Department had yet another reason for opposing Castro's government. In line with the cautious, public side of its policy, the United States quietly lobbied against the Cuban proposal at the Santiago meeting, with some success.[5]

25; Hinkle and Turner, *The Fish Is Red*, pp. 23–34; Prados, *President's Secret Wars*, pp. 177–81; DDEL, Oral History Interviews, Neil McElroy Interview, p. 88.

Plans for assassinating Castro and other top Cuban leaders are described in Senate, Select Committee to Study Government Operations with Respect to Intelligence Activities, *Alleged Assassination Plots Involving Foreign Leaders*, Senate Report #465, 94th Congress, 1st Session (Washingon, D.C., U.S.G.P.O., 1975); 11/20/75; Hinkle and Turner, *The Fish Is Red*, p. 34; Wyden, *Bay of Pigs*, pp. 19, 25; Szulc, *Fidel*, pp. 523–24, 672.

[5] DDEL, Dulles-Herter Series, Herter, Aug. 1959, Telegrams "For President From Secretary [of State]."

OTHER attempts by the State Department to turn hemisphere opinion against Castro were less productive. In fact, during 1959 and 1960 the Cuban leader enjoyed widespread popularity in Latin America, especially at the grass roots. His successful struggle against Batista and his current fight against social injustice made him a true hero to many Latin Americans. Castro's image in the hemisphere, like his popularity in Cuba, was a real problem for the United States. He raised the specter of radical social change in a most attractive form. This, for a time, prevented the United States from gathering OAS support for some kind of anti-Castro alliance. This was a serious problem. The United States needed Latin American support to block social revolution in Cuba. With such backing, it could employ its extensive power over Cuba under the protection of an OAS mandate. The problem was one of image as well as of law. Only with OAS sanction could the United States get around the hemisphere ban on intervention written into the charter of that organization. However, most OAS nations were loath to take action against the charismatic Castro, whose actions and rhetoric were so admired in their countries. Some of the most conservative regimes did offer to support the U.S. effort, but the United States could not openly act against Castro flanked only by the likes of Somoza and Trujillo. As always, official U.S. actions had to be taken in the name of "hemisphere democracy."

The general OAS reaction indicated why the State Department liberals resisted the conservatives' demand to take the evidence of Castro's "communism" to the leaders of the hemisphere. This evidence included left-of-center policies that were not considered subversive in Latin America; it was a generic "communism" that might have seemed subversive only in a nation like the United States that had no political Left whose power had to be respected. By the late 1950s, moreover, those with "communist" backgrounds were well represented among Latin American leaders. Two of them had been recently anointed as "democrats" by the Eisenhower administration: José Figueres of Costa Rica and Rómulo Betancourt of Venezuela. The United States hoped to use these leaders prominently in the assault on revolutionary Cuba. With such allies, Washington could demonstrate its commitment to social change while opposing only "communist" revolution.[6]

In 1960 it became clear to the State Department that OAS cooperation

[6] The attitude of the State Department toward the social-democratic Figueres, who had been active in the Caribbean Legion, is referred to in Walter La Feber, *Inevitable Revolutions: The United States in Central America* (New York: Norton, 1984), pp. 104–6. As late as May 1958, Allen Dulles had been referring to the ex-communist Betancourt as an "extreme leftist." See Senate Committee on Foreign Relations, Historical Series, *Executive Sessions*, vol. 10, p. 234.

with its policy of isolating and pressuring Castro depended in part on Washington's willingness to place similar pressure on the regime of the durable anti-communist dictator of the Dominican Republic, Rafael Leonidas Trujillo. Trujillo had his own record of trying to overthrow unfriendly heads of state, and hemisphere nations were more willing to act against him than against Castro. Informally, several Latin American governments told the State Department that they might be willing to back tough measures against Cuba if the United States would join them in acting against the Dominican dictator. Conservative friends of Eisenhower such as William Pawley and Florida Senator George Smathers (longtime allies of Trujillo) resisted any direct pressure on the dictator and instead suggested easing him out gradually by means of elections and with assurances that his immense wealth would follow him into exile. State Department liberals considered a Trujillo-controlled election a joke but had their own reasons for limiting pressure on him. They feared that the vacuum that might exist in Trujillo's absence would be filled by Castro, thus spreading rather than confining Castroism—the principal reason for pressuring Trujillo in the first place. Still, the State Department needed the OAS votes against Castro, and these might be obtained by an active anti-Trujillo policy. As a result, the department wracked its brains over some way to replace Trujillo with a pro-U.S. government resistant to Castroism. Like all searches for a democratic center in a society that had only the trace of one, the Eisenhower administration never found a safe way to remove Trujillo in order to get at Castro, leaving both problems for the Kennedy administration.[7]

By August 1960, however, Castro having by this time frightened hemisphere conservatives and disillusioned most democrats, the United States was emboldened to attempt to push through the OAS a resolution condemning Cuba as a totalitarian state. Though partially successful, it still had to settle for a general condemnation of such rule. In fact, it was not until the Punta del Este conference in January 1962 that an OAS majority was willing to act specifically against Cuba. But even on that occasion, with Castro and Khrushchev in each other's arms, the organization would sanction no *hostile* actions against Cuba, merely suspending it from the organization—a vote on which the largest Latin American states (Argentina, Brazil, Chile, and Mexico) abstained. Thus the ostracism of Cuba came too late to save U.S. interests on the island from socialist revolution or to serve as justification for the Bay of Pigs invasion the year before.[8]

---

[7] Eisenhower-era plans on removing Trujillo are in DDI, 1977, 251C; 1982, #2473; 1983, #921, #1769; 1984, #1685, #1686, #1687, #2053; 1985, #139. Also see Crassweller, *Trujillo*, pp. 354–55, 423–31; Rabe, *Eisenhower and Latin America*, pp. 153–60.

[8] U.S. actions in the OAS are discussed in DDEL, Dulles-Herter Series, Herter—Apr. 1960 (1), Herter to Eisenhower, 4/23/60; WHO, Office of the Staff Secretary, International Series,

By agreeing to a major program of economic aid to Latin America, initiated under Eisenhower and expanded by developmentalist liberals under Kennedy, the United States successfully defended itself from Castro's charge that it was a reactionary state. But on the question of intervention—the only real antidote to Castro's power in Cuba—the U.S. hemisphere program failed. Despite the growing desire in Latin capitals that the United States eliminate the revolutionary regime, the fear that direct U.S. intervention, once sanctioned, might be turned against their own nations prevented them from giving Washington the freedom of action it needed.

II

The problem of gaining Latin American support for U.S. hegemony in the hemisphere was part of the larger problem of the nature of that hegemony itself. Open domination was not only resisted by Latin Americans, it was weakened at its source as well. Liberal and conservative policymakers stalemated one another's efforts or caused the defense of U.S. interests to swing between the assertive and the ameliorative mode. This infighting reflected different understandings of the role of U.S. power in Latin America. Conservatives held such power to be a strategic necessity and considered its economic form natural and justified—certainly nothing for which the nation need apologize. Moreover, no right-thinking person could equate such power with imperialism since, in the cold-war era, that was the practice of revolutionary Marxists. Hence, opposition to U.S. influence was the work of subversive communists and hotheaded Latin nationalists. Liberals in Washington, more in touch with Latin American moderates who also resented U.S. power (though they desired certain forms of it), knew better the problematic nature, especially of the U.S. economic presence. They acknowledged, in varying degrees, the realites behind the economic, political and cultural expressions of anti-Yankee feeling. In the final analysis, however, they could not accept the idea of the United States as an imperial power—a nation whose interests prevailed in its sphere of influence only because of its power to determine the outcome of political and economic developments there. To liberals (and to most North Americans), U.S. influence was different from that of other powerful nations throughout history. It was well intentioned and in the main beneficent. Hence, the principal liberal solution to challenges to U.S. hegemony was to reform its function. United States influence that was employed properly and sensitively would

---

Cuba (2), "Status of Possible OAS Action on Cuba," Herter to Eisenhower, 3/17/60; and Cuba (3) "The Problem of Cuba in the OAS," [n.d.]. Also see Stephen Ambrose, *Eisenhower: The President* (New York: Simon & Schuster, 1984), pp. 555–58; Connell-Smith, *The Inter-American System*, pp. 168–84.

enhance its presumed beneficent effect and at the same time protect it from nationalist assault. Because of the limits of their enlightenment, however, the liberals never solved the problem of using U.S. power against Cuba legitimately. The conservatives, for their part, seem never to have understood the nature of the problem itself.[9]

III

As the United States tried vainly in 1960 to gain sanction for action against Cuba, and while the CIA expanded its sabotage raids into plans for an exile invasion, the U.S. Departments of State, Commerce, and Agriculture were wrestling with the problem of how to use the tremendous North American economic power over Cuba. The problem was to squeeze Cuba economically without seeming guilty of economic aggression and without provoking the confiscation of U.S. property, most of which, as 1960 began, was still in the hands of its owners.

Washington took a series of actions in 1960 aimed at weakening the Cuban economy: it attempted to cut off Cuba's access to foreign credits; it convinced U.S. companies to withdraw quietly their managerial personnel; and it supported the oil companies that controlled Cuba's only refineries in their refusal to refine Soviet crude oil. It also increased the secret CIA program of sabotage against important economic installations on the island. None of these actions, however, slowed the pace of the revolution; as some in the State Department feared, they became the basis for Cuban charges of economic warfare, serving to justify and accelerate the confiscation of U.S. property.[10]

The major weapon in the U.S. arsenal, and the one that most presumed would deliver the death blow, was sugar. Many of the largest mills were in U.S. hands, and the North American market absorbed more Cuban sugar than all others combined. Both the wealth and poverty of generations of Cubans attested to the powerful impact of sugar on the island's economy. This was a volatile weapon, however, because it could be detonated prematurely by U.S. beet-sugar growers or by foreign competitors of Cuban cane sugar whose influence with the congressional committees that set quotas had always made the State Department's fight for "fair" treatment of

[9] A good summary of the non-economic forces behind U.S. foreign policy is Michael H. Hunt, *Ideology and U.S. Foreign Policy* (New Haven: Yale University Press, 1987). Also see Benjamin. "Framework," pp. 91–112.

[10] DDEL, WHO, OSANSA, "Questions Concerning a Program of Economic Pressure Against Castro," [6/60]; R.G. 59, 837.2553/6-860, Memorandum of Conversation, "Cuban Petroleum Situation." Also see Morley, *Imperial State and Revolution*, pp. 76–79, 88, 95–96, 99–107. The oil weapon is discussed in Michael Tanzer, *The Political Economy of International Oil and the Underdeveloped Countries* (Boston: Beacon, 1969), pp. 327–44, and in Bonsal, *Cuba, Castro and the United States*, pp. 145–53.

Cuba an uphill battle. Ironically, now it was the State Department that wanted to squeeze Cuba. Just as surprising was the response of the domestic beet industry and its friends in the agriculture committees of the House and Senate. Like many in Washington, they believed that Castro—defying the rules that governed U.S.-Cuban relations—would not survive for very long. Thus they reasoned that any portion of the Cuban quota that they might pick up would be a short-lived windfall. Moreover, the price they were being asked to pay for it was high. The State Department was requesting that power over sugar imports be taken from the committees (and the lobbies) that set such quotas and be given to the president. Domestic sugar politics, which had long bedeviled the Cubans, now stood in the way of the department's plan. The National Beet [Sugar] Growers Federation opposed the change, as did the Democrat-controlled House Agriculture Committee. Only after Herter pleaded in secret committee session that this tool was indispensable for removing Castro did the House committee relent. In the Senate, where beet-grower influence was even stronger, the grant of presidential authority to set sugar quotas was finally accepted, but only after it had been limited to one year.[11]

With this powerful economic weapon finally in hand, the administration engaged in an internal debate over how best to camouflage its act of economic warfare. On July 6, 1960, Eisenhower announced that the remainder of Cuba's quota for 1960 was to be suspended. He explained that Cuba's agreement to sell large quantities of sugar to the U.S.S.R. had made the island an undependable supplier. Though hardly the true reason for the action, Cuba soon demonstrated its "unreliability" by arranging to sell the suspended sugar to Moscow and Peking.[12]

The last major blows in what was now a mutual economic slug match came in August when Cuba nationalized a large chunk of the U.S. property on the island and in October when the United States cut off all trade with Cuba, to which Castro responded by nationalizing the remaining U.S.-owned assets. The cycle of assault and protest, counter-assault and counter-protest was finally ended with the severing of diplomatic relations on January 3, 1961.[13]

[11] DDEL, DDE, OF 149-B-Z Sugar, "Meeting with the President on Cuban Sugar," 7/6/60; Whitman File, DDE Diary Series, Staff Notes Aug. 1960 (1), Memorandum of Conversation with the President, 8/30/60 and 10/13/60; R.G. 59, 837.235/6-1060, Memorandum of Telephone Conversation, "Sugar Legislation." Also see Morley, *Imperial State and Revolution*, pp. 108–12.

[12] *Department of State Bulletin* 43:110, July 25, 1960; DDEL, WHO, OSANSA, Suspension of Nuclear Testing and Surprise Attack (1), Memorandum of Conversation, "Questions Concerning the Program of Economic Pressure against Castro," 6/27/60.

[13] The best summary of this period is in Cole Blasier, *The Hovering Giant: U.S. Responses to Revolutionary Change in Latin America, 1910–1985* (Pittsburgh: University of Pittsburgh Press, 1986), rev. ed., pp. 182–200.

IV

When all of the economic and paramilitary smoke cleared away in the wake of the Bay of Pigs invasion in April 1961, it was astonishing for North Americans to behold that Castro was still firmly in power and that the social structure of the island had been utterly transformed. How could so much of Washington's tremendous power have been expended with no result other than the one most feared?

The U.S. decision in the fall of 1959 to attempt the removal of Castro was arrived at because the conservatives considered him a subversive and strategic threat and because the liberals had concluded that his ideology menaced traditional North American interests in Cuba and U.S. influence in the hemisphere. Whatever the wisdom or morality of these judgments, a program to overthrow Castro had to have the rationale and the weapons necessary to make it work. The rationale of the conservative position—though usually stated indirectly—was the right of the United States to a sphere of influence in the Western Hemisphere. Its weapon was military force. The trouble, as we have seen, was that there was little popular support for such a right either in the United States or in Latin America. Indeed the thrust of U.S. foreign policy after 1945, especially its condemnation of the Soviet sphere in Eastern Europe as aggression, directly challenged such a conception. The historical precedent for this anti-spheres perspective went back to the charges made against an expanding Germany and Japan before World War II—if not further back, to the heritage of anti-colonialism from the nineteenth century. The idea of preventing the violent expansion of the spheres of influence of the Axis powers had been an important element in the internationalist argument that eventually convinced a reluctant American populace to give up its preferred isolationism. Transferred to an expanding Soviet Union, this argument had become the core of a bipartisan cold-war foreign policy of containing Soviet "aggression." In Cuba, the presumed expansion of the Soviet empire into the U.S. sphere had to be opposed, but only to preserve the liberties of the island's population. Without a Soviet assault against Cuba to which it could retaliate, or at least a "free" Cuban government to whose pleas it could respond, the overthrow of the island's government by Washington would seem an imperial act dedicated simply to maintaining the U.S. sphere.

The liberals had seen this dilemma back in the 1930s. It was one of the reasons for the abrogation of the Platt Amendment and the development of internal allies through which its influence in Cuba could be more legitimately exercised. During that period also, under pressure from a growing Latin American nationalism, liberals had renounced the practice of military intervention in the hemisphere as a whole. In an attempt to forge a regional

196

alliance that operated differently from those constructed by Japan and Germany, the "Good Neighbor" diplomats had signed several inter-hemisphere pacts promising not to resort to intervention in the affairs of what it then termed its "sister republics" in the New World. The hemisphere treaties of the 1930s, of which the Organization of American States was a lineal descendant, did not in the minds of the liberal diplomats cancel out the preponderant U.S. influence in hemisphere affairs. But it did construct a means of exerting that influence which most U.S. citizens and most Latin Americans considered legitimate. The conservative program ignored this history and presumed that the ends of total cold-war struggle erased the problem of means.[14]

THE LIBERALS knew that ideological warfare in the Western Hemisphere required Latin allies so as not to seem imperial and not to endanger further the very interests that were to be protected. As it was, the liberals were in charge of policy toward Cuba (under both Eisenhower and Kennedy), and so it was they who chose the rationale and the weapons for the struggle against Castro. The liberals' banner was the "defense of democracy," and their weapons, as we have already seen, were economic pressure and covert war. The greater acceptability of their rationale and the lesser opposition to their weapons rendered their program feasible.

The task of the liberals was complicated by the fact that even their weapon of indirect aggression was outlawed by inter-American agreements. Thus the weapon had to be wielded as inconspicuously as possible. The solution to this problem was for the United States to ally itself with Cuban democrats whose open, political opposition to the regime in Havana would justify the defense-of-democracy rationale and undermine Castro's power so that the weapons of indirect warfare, modestly and quietly employed, could be effective. The success of the liberal program thus depended on a competent, broad, internal opposition to the regime and to the radical direction in which it was moving.

Like most North American observers of the Cuban scene in the period just after the fall of Batista, the liberals were confident that Cuban society was fundamentally oriented toward North America in the structure of its economy and in the outlook of its people. This view was the modern counterpart of the nineteenth-century conception that Cuba naturally fit into the North American system of states and of the twentieth-century view that Cuban and U.S. interests naturally coincided. From this perspective it followed that as Castro moved away from close association with North American interests and values he would lose support. At some point in the pro-

[14] Benjamin, "Framework," pp. 91–102.

cess his radicalism would create an opposition, fortified by the U.S. program to undermine Castro, that would lead to his overthrow. The even older North American view of Cubans as racially inferior and incapable of governing themselves survived in diminished strength into the cold-war era. Though its presumptions were very different, it led to a similar conclusion about Castro's fate: no Cuban regime could structure itself rationally and coherently enough to obtain the strength to stand against a combination of local opponents backed by the United States.[15]

V

In reality, Cuban society was structured differently from that in North America, and it responded to Castro and to the revolution in ways that Washington could not predict. The island's landed upper class did not, as in other Latin American nations, constitute a right wing, either reactionary or conservative. It was not a coherent group nor did it have a common outlook. More important, it was not powerful. It did not control land and agricultural production as did the *latifundista* sector elsewhere. The big landed estates were highly capitalized (especially in sugar and cattle raising) and had contractual rather than patrimonial relations with their workers. Moreover, a significant number of large landowners were North American corporations (or, in a few cases, families), and their presence and outlook prevented the cultural and even economic cohesion of the Cuban landed upper class. The power of large landowners as a group was also limited by a variety of countervailing groups and state authorities that had grown up in the wake of the sugar depression and the nationalist-populist insurgency of the 1920s and 1930s. Thus landowners were confronted by cane-planter organizations, by those of small-scale agricultural producers outside the sugar sector, and by strong worker organizations. Each of these constituencies had its counterpart in a government ministry dedicated to protecting that portion of agricultural wealth secured by each sector during the turbulent 1920s and 1930s. In many instances these divisions of the agricultural pie were spelled out in public laws and private contracts. Absence of hegemony in the countryside meant that the landed upper class controlled no political party, and no sector of the legislature or executive acted as its natural guardian. It had no more power than it could buy. This

---

[15] Confidence that no regime in Cuba could retain support if it challenged North American ties and values can be found in Bonsal, *Cuba, Castro and the United States*, pp. 6, 61, 78, 166–67. Eisenhower kept putting off a decision about the exile invasion, waiting for the coalescence of a popular, democratic opposition to Castro on the island. Ambrose, *Eisenhower*, pp. 583–84, 615.

was not little, but was much less than it would have exerted as a class with powerful institutions and a persuasive ideology.

The industrial wing of the upper class was relatively weak as well. Its strength and numbers were confined by powerful U.S. producers, both those with plants on the island and those situated in North America that exported to Cuba under favorable conditions arranged by Washington. Less hemmed in by populist legislation than their landowning counterparts, they were also less protected by nationalist legislation from foreign competition. They often had to deal with strong unions and with the necessity of paying for the political favors without which they could not prosper. Indeed, so tight became the tie between business and politics that both were held in low esteem as twin agents of corruption. Cuba lacked not only respected corporate leaders, it lacked, for the most part, a respected entrepreneurial tradition. Finally, because of declining profits and intense regulation in sugar, much invested capital was sunk in Havana (and Miami) real estate. These were highly speculative ventures, intimately tied to both windfall profits and to graft—so much so that an important portion of this business was in the hands of the U.S. Mafia.

In the almost puritanical atmosphere that accompanied the revolution, the old arrangements in and between the world of business and politics were seen as tarnished. The bourgeoisie and the politicians were stigmatized if not by their ties to the former dictator then by the very sources of their wealth. The new moral (and social) atmosphere was one in which the bourgeoisie could make no effective ideological or even political defense of its social function. It soon became an outcast, a role for which its notoriously conspicuous consumption and its ties to North America had unwittingly prepared it.

If men of affairs could be swept aside, would not the Cuban middle class be able to turn revolution into evolution, as Washington policymakers hoped? The island's middle sector was large by Latin American standards. Significantly, however, it was not historically an industrial-era middle *class*, with its own place in society, its own values and life-style. The middle sector aped the rich, seeing that group's wealth as both an incredibly powerful lure and a perennial affront. Jealous but not deferential, the middle sector saw the upper class not as possessing an inherent status but merely fat bank accounts and close political connections. In the absence of rigid class barriers to mobility, a segment of the middle class gravitated toward politics and, indeed, dominated that arena by the 1950s. For those members of the middle sector not on their way up through political business, parties and elections appeared as an endless series of deals between potent economic organizations and powerful politicians. This process was only occasionally challenged by political muckrakers such as Chibás and, in his early career, by his protégé, Castro. None of this seemed to change things, however, and the unconnected middle-sector elements were left with their frustrated longing for entry into the world of consumer luxuries and political favors. Under the right conditions, disaffected members of the middle sectors might decide to commit themselves to the dream of a rational and honest administration that would recognize their training and talents and reward them with a respected place in society and a chance to restore the dignity of the republic. Significantly, even this most liberal group of Cubans did not emphasize political procedure (elections and due process) but rather the idealistic conception of democracy inherited from Martí, who had seen it more a result of community than of polity.

The island's organized, urban workers were, by Latin American standards, well paid and, in some cases, well connected with government. But their overall welfare was tied to the roller coaster set in motion by the swings of the sugar economy and to the deals made with bosses and government bureaucrats by their union leaders. Despite the general health of the economy in the 1950s, union officials tended, as did government, to bargain more in their own interest than in that of the working class. Like the middle class, workers were cynical about politics. They had even fewer expectations that due process, elections, and lack of corruption would, of themselves, improve their welfare. Moreover, their lack of respect for owners of wealth was not compensated for by the hope of one day moving up to such status themselves.

At the bottom of the social pyramid were large numbers of the unemployed, swelled enormously after the end of the short sugar harvest by underemployed agricultural workers. At the bottom also were the small squatter-farmers of the hill regions among whom Castro's guerrillas had found haven. These groups were all desperately poor, but unlike the peasant masses in other parts of Latin America, they shared the culture and language of the rest of the population and were not cut off from them by high mountains or lack of roads. Indeed, electricity penetrated almost all of rural Cuba and with it the radio with its incessant reports of the politics and social life of Havana. The political system ignored these people. No politician spoke for them (and, indeed, *to* them) until Castro made their welfare the center of the revolution's goals. Free of ancient village cultures and aware of the new appeals, they readily responded.

Quite different from U.S. expectations, social revolution in Cuba confronted a weak and divided upper class that could not even slow it down. The middle sector and the union members were, for the most part, attracted to the revolution. Some sought the chance to move up by weakening the political and economic power of those above them who were now tainted by their ties to Batista and Washington. Others were inspired by the prospect of using their talents in the task of purifying the republic and sought the rewards, material and spiritual, that faith in the new order might bring. Those at the bottom, despite their less than prominent role in the struggle against the dictator, with few exceptions made a wholehearted commitment to the new order.

As a result, nowhere in 1959 was there to be found on the island a powerful group or institution clearly committed to the defense of U.S. interests. Even though the turn to state socialism and charismatic authoritarianism in 1960 alienated most of the bourgeoisie, significant elements of the middle sector, and even portions of the working class, these people went into exile, for the most part gradually and individually. As they did so, they were sustained by the belief that they would soon return to Cuba—once it had been liberated for them by North American power.[16]

VI

Despite the unfavorable historical setting, and generally ignorant of it, the United States set out to "liberate" Cuba. A key element of the State Department program was to encourage and strengthen the anti-Castro forces. Such a stance was, as we have seen, not a new one. Washington had begun to seek out such allies against Castro even before Batista fell. Despite the failure of this plan, U.S. policymakers felt confident that the opening of the political arena following the dictator's demise would bring forth Cuban leaders who commanded respect as enemies of the former dictator and who,

[16] Cuba's class structure in 1959 is examined in O'Connor, *The Origins of Socialism in Cuba*, chs. 1–4; Padula, diss., pp. 43, 52, 76, 168, 179–95, 213–26, 246–59, 588–91; Blackburn, "Prologue," pp. 52–91; Manitzas, "The Setting of the Cuban Revolution," in Barkin and Manitzas, eds., *Cuba: The Logic of the Revolution*, pp. 1–18; Nelson Amaro Victoria, "Mass and Class in the Origins of the Cuban Revolution," in Horowitz, ed., *Cuban Communism*, 4th ed. pp. 221–51; Zeitlin, "Political Generations," pp. 493–508; Thomas, *Pursuit*, pp. 1108–16; Farber, *Revolution and Reaction*, pp. 212–18.

Formal studies of Cuban public opinion in 1959–1960 are few. A notable one, the results of which were communicated to the White House, was organized by Lloyd Free, director of the Institute for International Social Research in Princeton, N.J. In April 1960 the institute prepared a survey for a Cuban firm which sampled about a thousand Cubans, mostly in or near Havana. The study concluded that most Cubans were optimistic about the future and were moderate-to-strong supporters of Castro and of the program of the revolution. Of those surveyed, only 7 percent expressed concern about communism and only 2 percent about the failure to hold elections. The results of the study cannot be attributed to investigator bias as both the Cuban and North American researchers were anti-Castro. Indeed, the report of the opinion survey concludes with an analysis of the regime's strengths and weaknesses and ponders the ways in which the latter might be exacerbated. See JFKL, Schlesinger Papers, Subject Files, Cuba-Printed Materials, 5/1/60–3/27/61, "Attitude of the Cuban People Toward the Castro Regime in the Late Spring of 1960," 26 pages. For insight into the perspective of the study see DDI, 1985, #773.

with its support, could effectively oppose any attempt at radical social change.

When the State Department gave up its hope of educating Castro in mid-1959, it turned more than before to the Cuban moderates. Through numerous official and unofficial contacts with them, Washington made clear its unhappiness with the developing situation. The chief political officer of the U.S. embassy, John Topping, recommended to his superiors "discreet contacts with those groups not now associated with the regime." The embassy reported several hopeful signs to Washington, and Ambassador Bonsal conveyed his belief that the opposition was growing. In fact, the hard line adopted by the State Department in October 1959 was based in part on the idea that Castro was *losing* support. Wieland suggested that the goal of the new program of economic denial should not be the destruction of the Cuban economy since there was good reason to believe that Castro's regime was, as he put it, "transitory." Under Secretary of State Douglas Dillon made a similar point when he suggested to Eisenhower that economic pressure would make clear U.S. opposition to Castro and would have "an encouraging effect on the dissident groups now becoming active in Cuba." [17]

The trouble with the evidence that Castro was alienating many of his former followers was that it ignored the fact that the *base* of his support was actually widening. His program was becoming social rather than political, and North Americans were, as we have seen, least prepared to understand the implications of the social composition of the island. Washington did not recognize the institutional vacuum that its hegemony in Cuba had allowed to develop over the years and within which Castro's vibrant personality and political sagacity echoed with great intensity. By the time the United States began to grasp the extent of his influence and decided to overthrow him, Castro had moved well beyond the small nationalist movement he had coordinated from the Sierra Maestra and had become the undisputed leader of a mass movement based upon the urban and rural working class. [18]

United States policymakers not only failed to grasp the source of Castro's power, they also misconstrued its form. The histrionic aspect of the Latin temperament was held to be not a cultural difference but a character defect. Public displays of strong emotion, long a sign of immaturity to the neo-Calvinists who worked their way to the top of the Washington bureau-

---

[17] R.G. 59, 611.37/11-2759, Desp. #789, "Suggested Operations Plan for Cuba"; 737.00/12-959, Wieland to Rubottom, "Suggested Course of Action Toward Cuban Expropriation Problem," 12/9/59; DDEL, Whitman File, DDE Diary Series, Staff Notes, Oct. 1960 (1), Memorandum of Conversations with the President, 10/13/60.

[18] The development of a mass base by Castro is discussed in Farber, *Revolution and Reaction*, pp. 215–23; Gonzalez, *Cuba Under Castro*, pp. 116–21.

cracy, were taken in this instance to mean that Castro was somehow deranged. His hostility toward the United States was considered pathological. Eisenhower referred to him as a "madman." Clinical terminology found its way into high-level analyses of his leadership. CIA reports referred to the Cuban leader's "erratic behavior" and to his being "under sedation and close medical attention." The chief intelligence officer of the CIA concluded that the adulation of the masses put Castro "in a high state of elation amounting to mental illness." Moreover, Castro's belief that the United States opposed his regime in 1959 "was a conclusion of his disordered mind." His later alignment with the Soviet Union was "not a function of U.S. policy and action, but of Castro's psychotic personality."[19]

VII

Just as ominous for the U.S. plan to remove Castro were the character and actions of the now alienated middle- and upper-class Cubans on whom depended the active, democratic opposition desired by the United States. By and large, this group demonstrated neither the leadership, the popularity, nor the will to oppose Castro effectively. The portion of the elite that had been associated with Batista was thoroughly discredited. The old political chieftains (Prío, Grau, Varona, Marquéz-Sterling, and Hevia) could not reinvigorate the parties they had led. Most of them were now old men who soon retired from the scene. Moreover, when those who had been in the militant opposition to Batista and had initially supported the revolutionary government broke with the regime, they tended to go into exile in the United States rather than contend with the charismatic Castro for control of the Cuban political arena. They chose exile despite the fact that until mid-1960 many political freedoms were still available to them. The media was being confined within the parameters of the offical definition of the revolution, but not all independent outlets had been silenced. The trouble was that when dissident voices called for elections, complained of state harassment, or warned of the radicalization of the government and the influence of Communists, their audience did not respond. No doubt it took courage to challenge the revolutionary leadership but, at that point in time, the political failure of the moderates was due as much to their own weakness as

[19] DDEL, WHO, OSANSA, Synopsis of State and Intelligence Material reported to the President, 1/21/59; CIA, Office of National Estimates, Memorandum for the Director, "Why the Cuban Revolution of 1958 [*sic*] Led to Cuba's Alignment with the U.S.S.R.," Sherman Kent, Chairman, 2/21/61, pp. 4–5. Eisenhower's private view of Castro can be found in DDEL, Whitman File, DDE Diary Series, Staff Notes: Jan. 1960(1) Memorandum of Conversation with President, 1/25/60, and in Ann Whitman Diary Series, July 1960(2) Desk Diary Entry, 7/6/60.

to repression. The State Department, still believing that the history of U.S.-Cuban relations had created institutional barriers to social revolution, could not understand the passivity of the middle sector (the "democratic" forces) or their inability to challenge the anti-Yankee rhetoric of the Maximum Leader. Washington just did not realize the impact of such rhetoric in Cuba. In fact, it was not even able to explain Castro's power until a consensus formed in North America a few years later around the conservatives' notion of "totalitarianism." For their part, the liberals preferred the idea of an initially democratic revolution "betrayed" by Castro and delivered into the arms of Moscow.[20]

VIII

The State Department's view of events in Cuba was clouded by its belief that dictatorship and communism could not be planted among a Cuban people who presumably hated both. The department was also confounded by its failure to realize the role played by the United States itself in undermining the opposition. Just as the United States had weakened the Cuban bourgeoisie early in the century by taking over much of its economic role and just as it had undermined the authority of Cuban presidents by depriving them of the capacity to affect important matters of state, so the great strength of the United States now led the anti-Castro opposition—sensing its own weakness in a society undergoing social revolution—into a state of dependence in which it expected Washington to remove the hated Castro for them.

PERHAPS the clearest example of this dependency can be found, surprisingly, among those anti-Castro activists who joined the CIA project to organize an exile invasion of the island. Until galvanized by the agency, the exiles quarreled among themselves and could not produce an effective coordinating body for their struggle. In their disorganized state, many were

[20] Dependency on the United States by the Cuban elite is discussed in Padula, diss., pp. 3–5, 26, 43, 111, 151, 158, 247, 266–67, 317, 588–91. Also see JFKL, Pre-Presidential Papers, Box 737, letter from Carlos Marquez Sterling dated 2/25/60. Several hundred letters to Kennedy from exiled Cubans asking him to remove Castro are in this file and in White House Central Files, Box 48.

On the old political parties see Blackburn, "Prologue," pp. 66–70; Domínguez, *Order and Revolution*, pp. 96–109, 191–94. Also see Vignier and Alonso, *La corrupción política y administrativa en Cuba*, and Sánchez Otero, "La Crisis del Sistema Neocolonial en Cuba, 1934–1952," in *Los partidos políticos*, pp. 141–268.

The revolution-betrayed thesis is best summarized in Theodore Draper, *Castro's Revolution: Myths and Realities* (New York: Praeger, 1962), and U.S. Department of State, *[White Paper on] Cuba*, Inter-American Series, #66 (Washington, D.C.: U.S.G.P.O., 1961).

attracted to the CIA recruiters who set up headquarters in Miami to find men willing to conduct sabotage against the regime. The CIA had all of the resources the exiles could have wished for, and what is more, it had plans and organization.

As the project to organize an invasion force developed in Washington, the CIA grew tired of trying to work with unwieldy, bickering exile groups. The agency decided to get around internal exile politics by creating its own organization of Cubans. It separated the guerrilla trainees from the exile community. They and their families were put on the U.S. government payroll with trainees and their families paid a monthly stipend by the agency. Later the fighters were sent to Guatemala for further instruction at a CIA-run military base. Thereafter, they were completely dependent upon the United States for their wages, equipment, operational plans, and even news of events in Cuba. The CIA went so far as to determine the political complexion of the force, at first favoring right-wing exiles and later, at the request of the newly elected Kennedy administration, adding more liberals. None of the trainees were told of the invasion plan until the day they boarded the ships for Cuba. The CIA man in charge of political relations with exile leaders spoke no Spanish and was fond of saying that he carried the revolution in his checkbook. Some exiles chafed under the strict CIA control and the barely concealed racist attitudes of certain agency personnel. Most, however, accepted the situation. Indeed, they found it comforting that the United States was finally acting, believing that this insured their success.

As unwise as it was to confront an enemy whose principal strength was nationalism with a liberation army that was the product of a foreign power, the CIA also organized the provisional government that was to follow liberation. The agency insisted that the quarreling factions form a unified political organization and name a provisional president acceptable to the United States. When the new organization, the Cuban Revolutionary Council (CRC), wrote its first manifesto, White House liberals, employing the services of John Plank, a Harvard political scientist, rewrote it. Plank eliminated references to the defense of private property and foreign capital as unlikely to command respect in Cuba and inserted the New Frontier justification for the invasion: that the Castro government had betrayed the moderate program of social change that had been the goal of the anti-Batista struggle. Subsequent pronouncements of the CRC were written by the CIA and released to the press through a New York City public relations firm. The agency moved the council members first from Miami to New York and then, as the date of the invasion approached, to an abandoned U.S. Navy airfield in Florida, where they were held incommunicado. The leaders of a free Cuba did not know of the invasion until they heard the news on the radio. What standing these men might have achieved in a post-Castro Cuba does not seem to have preoccupied their North American mentors.[21]

In the final analysis, the exiles accepted the manipulation and indignities because they had only modest confidence in their own efforts and unbounded faith in the power of the United States to control events in Cuba. They were admirers of North American society and had absorbed, as had many other Cubans, the classic North American notion that Cuba's fate would be determined by the United States. Quite different was the reaction of Castro and his followers, who relied on the strength of Cuban nationalism not only to sustain them on the island but also to fortify their belief that they could rule Cuba without U.S. blessing and, indeed, in the face of its opposition. The absence of such a belief by the anti-Castro forces was, no doubt, a key to their failure.

In the wake of the defeat of the invasion force, the incomprehension was mutual: Washington could not believe that the Cuban elite had failed to oppose socialist revolution, while that elite could not believe that Washington had allowed its massive interests in Cuba to be sacrificed.

IX

The Bay of Pigs invasion has been called a "perfect failure." It did not so much fail, however, as self-destruct. Everyone but the enemy, it seems, was deceived. The exile invaders had been led to believe by the CIA that if the hoped-for internal uprising did not occur, direct U.S. military support would arrive to aid them.[22] In fact, neither Eisenhower nor Kennedy approved direct U.S. involvement. Nonetheless, the CIA agents training the exiles feared that without such belief the Cubans might not be willing to play their part in the overthrow of Castro. Manipulation of the anti-Castro Cubans came easily to a North American intelligence institution that operated free of the requirements placed upon official acts of state. Official acts had to demonstrate the moral superiority of the United States. The assump-

---

[21] Dependency on the part of exiles is discussed in Arthur Schlesinger, Jr., *A Thousand Days* (New York: Fawcett, 1965), pp. 202–3, 213–18, 221–24, 229; Wyden, *Bay of Pigs*, pp. 31, 35–38, 53–59, 75–76, 114–19; Thomas, *Pursuit*, pp. 1357, 1359, 1364, 1368; Padula, diss., pp. 553, 583; and Aguilar, ed., *Operation Zapata*, pp. 70, 82, 92, 97, 104–5, 121–23, 127, 158, 170–71, 173–75, 191, 294–95, 300, 337, 338–41, 355–56. Also see JFKL, Kennedy Oral History Collection, Robert A. Hurwitch Interview, 4/24/64, pp. 44–49, 72–73, 102; Papers of President Kennedy, Official File-Staff Memoranda, Schlesinger, 3/61–4/61; NSF, Country Files, Cuba, General, 1/61–4/61; Schlesinger Papers, Subject Files, Cuba, 1/17/61–3/31/61 and Cuba: Background Materials, Box 5; Theodore Sorensen Papers, Classified Subject Files, 1961–1964, Cuba: General, 5/3/61–5/24/61.

[22] Lloyd S. Etheredge, *Can Governments Learn?* (New York: Pergamon Press, 1985), pp. 24, 38; Hinkle and Turner, *The Fish Is Red*, p. 82.

tion of such superiority was vital in maintaining the morale of the American people in their long cold-war struggle with communism.

Lack of moral inhibition also made the CIA the natural vehicle for preparing the murder of Castro. Agencies like the State Department were encumbered not only by their accountability to the public and to other nations but by their concern that the death of Castro might bring the rule of the more radical Che or Raúl. Some CIA and military covert planners responded to this latter concern with a proposal to kill all three. Indeed, when the foolishness of expecting an internal uprising became manifest in the wake of the debacle, some CIA people defended themselves by claiming that the actual plan rested not on the success of such an uprising but rather on the assassination of the top leadership in Havana and massive U.S. support for a Cuban provisional government lodged, however precariously, on the beaches.

Since the U.S. government did not carry out assassinations, the CIA had to pay others to do so. Despite many attempts, the hired murderers failed to do the job, and so the exile invaders faced a Cuban army led by Fidel himself. As it turned out, the beachhead was not held securely enough or long enough even to raise the issue of U.S. recognition and reinforcement. The CIA hard-liners never got the civil war in Cuba at which they had been aiming.[23]

The defeat of the invasion was swift not only because Castro survived but because all of the predictions of internal revolt and the unwillingness of the Cuban people to fight in defense of the revolution were wrong. United States military power might have compensated for these difficulties, but President Kennedy refused direct support by U.S. forces. Kennedy had told a press conference the day before the landing that "there will not be, under any conditions, an intervention in Cuba by the United States Armed Forces."[24] This refusal was not simply a public pose; it had been foretold in the original plan for the overthrow of Castro drawn up in March 1960 and set in motion by President Eisenhower. The planning document states:

> The purpose of the program outlined herein is to bring about the replacement of the Castro regime with one more devoted to the true interests of the Cuban people and more acceptable to the U.S. in such a manner as to avoid any appearance of U.S. intervention.[25]

[23] Etheredge, *Can Governments Learn?*, p. 9; Hinkle and Turner, *The Fish Is Red*, pp. 76, 80–81; DDI, 1985, #1540.

[24] David Halberstam, ed., *The Kennedy Presidential Press Conferences* (New York: Earl M. Coleman Enterprises, 1978) p. 76.

[25] JFKL, Papers of President Kennedy, NSF-Countries, Cuba, Para-military Study Group, Annex 1.

It is noteworthy that this "Eyes Only" document (the highest security classification) contained the same belief as the public rhetoric: that the new government would "serve the true interests of the Cuban people" and at the same time would be "more acceptable to the U.S." The historic assumption of mutual interest reached down even into the bedrock of North American realpolitik. Of course, the disparity between this belief and the actions being undertaken had to be veiled, hence the admonition that the deed be done "in such a manner as to avoid any appearance of U.S. intervention."

The contradiction between preferred means and desired ends set in motion an orgy of interagency wrangling, cynical manipulation, and self-deception at which bureaucratic analysts—ignoring the root cause—still marvel. The CIA had to claim the likelihood of an internal uprising despite the findings of their own intelligence reports. This was necessary not only because it fit the North American belief structure but because, as noted above, it raised the morale of the Cubans whom they were training and helped ease the fears of the State Department concerning the diplomatic fallout from an *open* U.S. intervention. Some CIA memoirists now contend that such a claim was also part of a double game (at which no doubt they were experienced): the absence of an internal uprising would leave the Cuban agents of North American democracy clinging to the beaches, thus forcing the hand of the president on the issue of direct U.S. intervention. The Pentagon, for its part, favored a no-nonsense Marine assault but never formally proposed such an attack. It retreated quietly when confronted with CIA defense of its bureacratic prerogatives and with State Department and White House opposition. The Pentagon ended up giving its cautious blessing to what it considered a Rube Goldberg operation configured by the needs of deniability. Like everyone else, they desperately wanted Castro eliminated and accepted the plan that had gained the most momentum. President Kennedy had to worry about both failure *and* success, especially if the latter came only as the result of employing U.S. power openly. He wanted a "quiet" assault attributable to Cubans alone and hoped that an initial "Cuban" success would open options for direct support of a "legitimate" Cuban government ensconced somewhere on the island. The CIA, however, becoming more and more skeptical that their Cubans could do the job despite the intense behind-the-scenes U.S. effort, wanted a noisy assault that would be more likely to demoralize the enemy and, as noted above, force the hand of the White House.[26]

[26] Documents bearing on the bureaucratic infighting are JFKL, Papers of President Kennedy, Countries, Cuba, General, Security, 1961, 1/61–4/61; Official File, Staff Memoranda, Schlesinger, 3/61–4/61; NSF, "Memorandum of Discussion on Cuba," 3/11/61, NASM #31; Schlesinger Papers, Subject Files, Cuba, 1/17/61–3/31/61, and Cuba, Background Materials.

Castro's defiance and Washington's compulsion to respond to "communist threats" backed the Kennedy administration into an action that it could neither forgo nor defend. It is hardly surprising that a government required to deceive at once the enemy, bureaucratic opponents, its own people, and, indeed, itself could not act effectively, let alone rationally. A solid structure, capable of overthrowing Castro, could not be built on the myths surrounding the nature of U.S.-Cuban relations.

X

What did Washington learn from all of this? Not much, it would seem. Conservatives were certain that they had witnessed yet another display of the timidity and ideological fuzziness of the liberals when confronted with the long-honed subversive skills of the communists. Socialism, atheism, and totalitarianism now had a foothold in "our" hemisphere. The reaction of the Kennedy liberals was hardly timid, though characterized by a certain ideological schizophrenia. The soft side of liberalism moved rapidly toward an intensification of the program for Latin American economic development that Eisenhower had been backed into. The cold-war logic behind developmentalism held that improvement in the lives of poor people made them more resistant to the appeals of communist demagogues. Economic development in turn energized a social and political modernization that promoted democracy. The liberals did not seem to have noticed that North American-style economic development had not been lacking in Cuba and that, for some reason, it had not led to a stable and legitimate system of parties and elections nor had it created a respected divide between public funds and private wealth. Finally, and inexplicably, the island's economic development had not turned the masses of Cubans into ideological enemies of communism. If Cuba was a case of communist subversion, as the conservatives believed and the liberals found it expedient to claim, Moscow had chosen a most unpromising target—one right under the guns of the North American market, North American culture, North American political and economic power, and a large U.S. naval base.

If liberals were in no mood to reassess their socio-economic program for Latin America, they did rethink the hard side of their policy—covert warfare. This, however, they did in secret. President Kennedy convened a high-level study group to explain the Bay of Pigs debacle. The group dis-

---

The relevant JCS documents are JCSM 57-61 (2/61) and JCSM 166-61 (3/61) in DDI, 1985, #1540, 1544, and 1557. Other relevant documents are in DDI, 1985, #1550–#1558.

Kennedy's insistence on a low U.S. profile is in Etheredge, *Can Governments Learn?*, pp. 13, 26, 41; Peter Collier and David Horowitz, *The Kennedys* (New York: Summit, 1984), pp. 268, 270; and Schlesinger, *A Thousand Days*, pp. 228, 241, 255, 260.

covered all manner of planning, intelligence, and operational failures. Ignoring the massive CIA effort that had underwritten the exile invasion, it concluded that the operation had been too modest to achieve its goal. At the same time, it declared that the program had been too large to keep secret and that operations on such a scale had to be treated differently from simple covert actions. Concerned principally with the surface issue of determining how to conduct covert warfare successfully, the study group did not directly address the deeper problem of the U.S. acting as an aggressor.

The study group's secret recommendations to the president were filled with tough rhetoric about there being "no long-term living with Castro." The group suggested wriggling out of the secrecy dilemma by means of a presidential declaration of a "limited national emergency" and by "the review of any treaties or international agreements which restrain the full use of our resources in the Cold War." The best it could manage concerning the lack of Latin American support was to recommend the "determination to seek the respect of our neighbors, without the criterion being international popularity." Some way out of the dilemma was imperative since "we are in a life and death struggle which we may be losing, and will lose unless we change our ways and marshal our resources with an intensity associated in the past only with times of war."[27]

A counter-insurgency program that was the moral and legal equivalent of war was sorely needed. At the time of the inquiry, the Gallup Poll recorded that while most Americans thoroughly disliked Castro, only 24 percent favored the use of U.S. troops to remove him. At that time also, a majority of OAS nations were still unwilling to take strong action against Cuba.[28] In the end, the study group failed to set out a policy for removing the political, ideological, and psychological barriers to a U.S. invasion of Cuba. It settled instead for an elaboration and reorganization of the covert-warfare bureaucracy. The study group recommended establishment of a "Strategic Resources Group supported by a Cold War Indications Center." This new apparatus was to replace the 5412 Committee that had overseen covert operations during the Eisenhower era.[29]

Bureaucratic rearrangement coincided with renewed covert assaults on Cuba—which actually accelerated in the years after the Bay of Pigs failure. These actions reflected the inability of the Kennedy liberals (and the few conservatives who had sat with them on the study group) to preach their apocalyptic rhetoric about "losing" the cold war in the public arena, except to frighten the American people. Unwilling to expose itself to the con-

[27] Aguilar, ed., *Operation Zapata*, pp. 51–52.
[28] Gallup, ed., *The Gallup Poll*, vol. 3, 1959–1971, p. 1721.
[29] Aguilar, ed., *Operation Zapata*, p. 2.

tradictions inherent in the campaign to destroy the Castro government, Kennedy's administration settled for better coordination of the expanding covert apparatus. Unable to practice the alchemy by which illegality and immorality might be transmuted into legitimacy and popular support, policymakers entered the bizarre land of "Operation Mongoose" with its fantastic attempts to poison the Cuban leadership and the well-springs of the Cuban economy.[30]

The loud cry from Washington that the island had become a totalitarian society only partly obscured the fact that U.S. policy toward Cuba was in fact what the American people expected from its cold-war enemies, not its own government. The loss of U.S. hegemony in Cuba seemed to bring America back to the same imperial dilemma that the acquisition of that hegemony had presented in 1898.

[30] Collier and Horowitz, *The Kennedys*, pp. 290–98; Hinkle and Turner, *The Fish Is Red*, ch. 4; Prados, *President's Secret Wars*, pp. 210–17.

CHAPTER 9

CONCLUSION

I

THE UNITED STATES never resolved its contradictory need both to stabilize and to change Cuban society. The defense of its economic presence required stability; yet that presence introduced great and unsettling changes in Cuba. Moreover, Washington's desire to organize Cuban politics on a moderate basis prevented the consolidation of either a conservative or a radical regime during the republican period, one that would have been better able to control the U.S. economic impact and thus actually achieve a Cuban-defined stability. Unaware of the forces, including its own, that were producing unwanted change in Cuba, the United States continually found itself allied with the old order. In 1898, in 1933, and again in 1958, Washington stood by that order as the source of stability until it was clearly about to fail. At the last moment, however, when Spain's colonial regime and Machado's dictatorship were no longer viable, the United States shifted its allegiance in time to gain influence over moderate opponents of the old regime: annexationist Creoles in 1898 and moderate nationalists in 1933. The shift away from Batista and toward the non-Castroite opposition during the period between mid-1958 and 1960 was not, however, similarly rewarded.

United States inability to find viable allies in the post-Batista era had many causes, but among them was Washington's failure to appreciate the energizing impact that its own power had on Cuban nationalism and the unhealthy influence it wielded over its political supporters on the island.

Washington realized only too late that Batista's power had been much less substantial than it appeared. Even then, however, his fall was attributed simply to corruption and repression. Washington did not recognize its own role in the failure of the old regime. The relentless impact of liberal influ-

212

ence (economic and cultural) from North America had deprived the Cuban elite of conservative doctrines and institutions. Indeed, the U.S. requirement that Cuban governments pronounce goals that conformed to the North American ideological perspective tended to remove more relevant doctrines from Cuban politics and, with the flow of dollars from the United States, helped make the purpose of such politics unusually mercenary and opportunist. In the end, U.S. influence established a patron-client relationship with Cuban governments that made them appear alien and thus helped fuel the flames of an unfulfilled social utopianism.

It was the force of this social utopianism that empowered the 26th of July Movement and made its more radical members (Castro in particular) certain of the validity of their historical mission. Perhaps the force of utopian nationalism, in other hands, might have spent itself in bombastic rhetoric and ineffectual posturing, leaving Cuba more or less within the boundaries of U.S. hegemony. But Fidel Castro wielded this tool with tremendous effectiveness both psychologically and strategically. He was a master tactician, strategist, and propagandist, at once entranced with his vision of himself as the liberator of Cuba and yet wily in the manner in which he played that role. He lived and spoke the idiom of Cuban nationalism and populism and obtained a level of mass support that gave him more power than any previous Cuban leader. His strong personality reverberated with particular resonance in the hollow institutional structure of island society. He could draw a special commitment from members of a new generation of young nationalists who leapt at the chance to end the partial nature of Cuban independence. Moreover, by appealing to the pure Martían republic, for a time he drew a large segment of the Cuban middle class and even elements of the Cuban upper class to his project.

To the educated elite, Castro held up the attractive vision of an efficient, honest, modern, and proud republic. At the same time he also preached an egalitarianism in which he spoke eloquently of the dignity of each Cuban. Moreover, he set in motion government programs that made manifest his rhetoric about the right of each Cuban to share in the fruits of the revolution. In this manner, even as he retained the allegiance of segments of the upper stratum, he forged a powerful mass base. This mass loyalty sustained the momentum of the revolution even when the upper class and large segments of the middle class and labor leadership turned against it.

In his speeches, Castro emphasized the role of the people-in-arms that the revisionist school of the island's history had set forth decades before. In this view the masses of Cubans had been the embodiment of the nation in the great struggles against Spain in the latter half of the nineteenth century and in the overthrow of the Machado dictatorship. Castro added to these honors their heroism in the anti-Batista struggle. Now, to sustain the revolution, Castro called them once again to their historical duty. The masses responded with a fervor that made his rule unchallengeable. Empowered in this way, Fidel and his followers proceeded to overturn the island's social order, defying in the process the nation that for half a century had been seen as the guarantor of that order.

II

Castro's rhetoric was powerful in Cuba because it was enriched by the deep structures of the island's history. It was also powerful in the United States because Washington was unprepared to refute it. Ignorant of the history of the island which most Cubans had learned—or which in 1959 they rushed to embrace—the United States was left with the stale references to "close cooperation" and "mutual benefits" that had become hollow Fourth of July rhetoric without its knowing it. It was with this feeble rhetoric that the United States initially confronted the most magnetic speechmaker in Cuban history.

UNITED STATES influence was not the result of natural affinity between the two societies. It derived from U.S. military power, from its proximity, from the force and structure of its huge economy, and, finally, from its intention to mold Cuban society. North American blindness to its true role in Cuban history can be found at the very outset of the relationship. The soon-to-be-infamous Platt Amendment contained not only in its intent but in its very language the contradictions that would rule U.S.-Cuban relations. The amendment appears as Article III of the 1903 treaty between the two countries and states:

> The government of Cuba consents that the United States may exercise the right of intervention.

This statement seems in obvious conflict with article I of the same treaty which states:

> The government of Cuba shall never enter into any treaty or other compact with a foreign power or powers that will impair or tend to impair the independence of Cuba.

The Humpty-Dumpty logic by which these two statements were reconciled was quite simple: the U.S. right of intervention was to be exercised, as noted in article III, "for the preservation of Cuban independence."[1]

This strange idea, that U.S. power served to assure rather than threaten

[1] *United States Statutes at Large*, vol. 21, pp. 897–98.

Cuban sovereignty, lasted through many changes of administration in Washington. On April 19, 1948, President Truman addressed a joint session of the U.S. Congress convened to celebrate the fiftieth anniversary of Cuban independence. Truman told Congress:

> The commemoration of the half century of Cuban independence recalls the valor of the Cuban patriots and American soldiers who gave liberally of their strength and their blood that Cuba might be free.

After noting that "those in quest of independence have always had the support of this nation" and that "Americans fought side by side with their Cuban allies [until] the dream of José Martí became at last a glorious reality," Truman concluded:

> From these sound beginnings, relations between the Republic of Cuba and the United States have continued through the years on a mutually satisfactory basis. I believe that few nations of differing languages and cultures have drawn so closely together during the last fifty years, freely and without duress, as have Cuba and the United States.[2]

It is significant that the language of Truman's speech made no concession at all to the widely held belief of Cubans that the United States had intervened in 1898 to prevent their true independence. Indeed, Truman took no notice in his remarks of the fact that only two years earlier the influence of this revisionist view of Cuban history had reached into the Cuban congress, which officially changed the name of the 1895–1898 independence war from the "Spanish-American War" to the "Spanish-Cuban-American War."[3]

Like many of his generation, Castro was a student of this revisionist history. In his very first speech after the victory of the revolution, on January 2, 1959, he declared:

> This time the Revolution will not be frustrated. This time, luckily for Cuba, the Revolution will truly achieve its objective; it will not be like 1898, when the Americans came and made themselves masters of the country.[4]

As if oblivious to the potential meaning of these remarks, President Eisenhower seemed at times truly perplexed by the course of U.S.-Cuban relations. During a press conference on October 25, 1959, even as the long-

---

[2] *Public Papers of the Presidents of the United States: Harry S. Truman,* 1948 (Washington, D.C.: U.S.G.P.O., 1954), pp. 224–26.

[3] Corbitt, "Cuban Revisionist Interpretations," pp. 395–403.

[4] Speech at Céspedes Park, Santiago. Cuba, Instituto de Historia del Movimiento Comunista, *El Pensamiento de Fidel Castro,* T.1, v.1, p. 3.

standing U.S. influence over the island was rapidly disappearing—but before the idea of communist subversion settled in comfortably to explain the Cuban apostasy—Eisenhower told reporters in apparent candor and exasperation that

> here is a country that you would believe, on the basis of our history, would be one of our real friends. The whole history . . . would seem to make it a puzzling matter to figure out just exactly why the Cubans and the Cuban government would be so unhappy when, after all, their principal market is right here, their best market. You would think they would want good relationships. I don't know exactly what the difficulty is.[5]

On one level, Eisenhower was genuinely perplexed. As we now know, he was also privately enraged. He referred to Castro as a "little Hitler" and a "madman." The other side of the coin of confidence that Cuba was safely within the U.S. orbit was shock that it was not. The mood swing in Washington from a sense of confidence early in 1959 to a sense of betrayal by the fall helps to explain the rapid shift from a wait-and-see policy to one of all-out political and economic warfare.

The Eisenhower administration never solved the problem of overthrowing Castro without conceding its historic view of Cuba as a dependency or dirtying its cold-war image as defender of small states from external aggression. It merely handed the problem to the Kennedy administration, which had to operate under the same conditions of deception and self-deception.

The requirements of the cold-war crusade only compounded the problem of moving Cuba back within the North American orbit. But they also served as an effective justification in North America. The imperial effort to reestablish the historic relationship between the two nations could be explained as restoring Cuba to the "free world." The fact is, however, that the decision to remove Castro came when it was clear that he had stepped outside the bounds of the old relationship. It preceded and to some extent precipitated the "national security threat" that helped North Americans justify their actions to themselves. The historic restrictions were older and tighter than the anti-communist ones, and thus Castro broke them before he chose to challenge (or was forced to challenge) the strategic imperatives of bipolar cold war. In the long run, the double betrayal of ideological loyalty and presumed historic destiny reinforced each other and led to an intense and enduring ideological antagonism.

---

[5] *Public Papers of the Presidents of the United States: Dwight D. Eisenhower*, 1959 (Washington, D.C.: U.S.G.P.O., 1960), p. 751.

III

As a progressive dominant power, the United States was flexible enough to seek a new center of authority in Cuba with which to protect its interests. But the nature and extent of those interests, the requirements of cold-war ideology, and the unwillingness to give up its historic command over Cuban affairs meant that the new center had to be located within certain prescribed boundaries. When, with something of a shock, Washington discovered that this was not possible, its confidence turned to rage and it set in motion a wide-ranging program to destroy the Cuban regime. But it was too late. Castro's power, his instincts as a nationalist, and his desire to fulfill the dream of building a new Cuba all assured that he would press against almost any boundaries that the United States tried to establish. For its part, unable to use its power nakedly, the United States relied upon its historic control over important aspects of Cuban society to exert its influence. Castro responded to this assault by joining the deep nationalist hostility to U.S. domination to a Marxist critique of capitalism and imperialism. With these weapons he broke the structures of Cuban society through which U.S. influence could be applied. Standing upon a broad base of power and committed wholly now to the anti-Yankee cause, Castro first strained the boundaries set by the United States and then broke them altogether. In the end, Cuba would not gravitate into the orbit of John Quincy Adams's empire of liberty but into that of her superpower rival.

BIBLIOGRAPHY

MANUSCRIPT COLLECTIONS
AND U.S. GOVERNMENT DOCUMENTS

Abbreviations in parentheses indicate the way in which files are referred to in footnotes.

United States National Archives (USNA)
    Record Group 59 (R.G. 59)—Central Files of the Department of State:
        Office of Intelligence Research (OIR)
        Bureau of Intelligence and Research (BIR)
        Division of Research and Analysis (R & A)
        Office of American Republics Affairs (ARA)
        Decimal File [by document #]
    Record Group 226—Office of Strategic Services (OSS)
    Record Group 263—Central Intelligence Agency (CIA)
        National Intelligence Estimates (NIE)
        Special National Intelligence Estimates (SNIE)
    Record Group 353—Interdepartmental and Intradepartmental Committees
    Lot Files [no record group number]
        Records of Harley Notter
        State Department; Office of Intelligence Research: Reports.
Seeley G. Mudd Library (Princeton University)
    Whiting Willauer Papers
University of Delaware Library
    George Messersmith Papers
Franklin D. Roosevelt Library (FDRL)
    Franklin D. Roosevelt, Papers as President (PAP)
        Official File (OF)
        President's Secretary's File (PSF)
    Harry L. Hopkins Papers
    Adolf A. Berle Papers
Harry S. Truman Library (HSTL)
    Harry S. Truman Papers, Papers as President (PAP)
        President's Secretary's File (PSF)

Merwin L. Bohan Papers
Dean Acheson Papers
Dwight D. Eisenhower Library (DDEL)
  Dwight D. Eisenhower, Papers as President (PAP)
    Ann Whitman File:
      Administrative Series
      Ann Whitman Diary Series
      DDE Diary Series
      Dulles-Herter Series
      International Series
      National Security Council Series
  Dwight D. Eisenhower, Records as President
    White House Central Files:
      Official File (OF)
      President's Personal File (PPF)
      Confidential File (CF)
    White House Office (WHO)
      Office of the Special Assistant for National Security Affairs (OSANSA)
      Office of the Staff Secretary
      Operations Coordinating Board Series (OCB)
      National Security Council Series (NSC)
    President's Citizen Advisers on the Mutual Security Program
    President's Commission on Foreign Economic Policy
    John Foster Dulles Papers
    Gordon Gray Papers
    James C. Hagerty Papers
    Christian Herter Papers
    Oral History Transcripts:
      Richard M. Bissell Interview
      Neil McElroy Interview
John F. Kennedy Library (JFKL)
  John F. Kennedy, Pre-Presidential Papers
    Senate Files
  John F. Kennedy, Presidential Papers
    President's Office Files (POF)
    National Security Files (NSF)
    White House Central File (CF)
  Arthur Schlesinger, Jr. Papers
  Theodore Sorensen Papers
  Oral History Interviews:
    Robert Hurwitch Interview
U.S. Government Publications and Documents
  Congress:
  House. Committee on Foreign Affairs. Historical Series. *Selected Executive Hearings, 1951–1956*, vol. 16. Washington, D.C., United States Government Printing Office, 1980.

House. *Congressional Record*. 85th Congress, 2nd Session.

Senate. Committee on Foreign Relations. Historical Series. *Executive Sessions*, vols. 10–12. Washington, D.C., U.S. G.P.O. 1980–1982.

Senate. Committee on Foreign Relations. *Hearings on the Mutual Security Act of 1958*. March 1958. Washington, D.C., U.S., G.P.O., 1958.

Senate. Committee on Foreign Relations. *Study Mission in the Caribbean Area*. Jan. 20, 1958. Washington D.C., G.P.O., 1958.

Senate. Committee on the Judiciary. Subcommittee to Investigate the Administration of the Internal Security Act and Other Internal Security Laws. *The Communist Threat to the United States Through the Caribbean*. 86th Congress, 2nd Session; 87th Congress, 1st and 2nd Sessions. Washington, D.C., U.S. G.P.O., 1960–1961.

Senate. Subcommittee of the Committee on the Judiciary. Hearings. *State Department Security*. 87th Congress, 1st Session. Washington, D.C., U.S. G.P.O., 1961.

Senate. Select Committee to Study Government Operations with Respect to Intelligence Activities. *Alleged Assassination Plots Involving Foreign Leaders*. Senate Report #465. 94th Congress, 1st Session. Washington, D.C., U.S. G.P.O., 1975.

State Department:

The Foreign Relations of the United States. (FRUS)
   Yearly volumes, 1941–1957. Washington, D.C., U.S. G.P.O., 1963–1987.

Department of State Bulletin. (DSB) 1958–1960. Washington, D.C., G.P.O., 1958–1960.

[White Paper on] Cuba. Inter-American Series, #66. Washington, D.C., U.S. G.P.O., 1961.

Commerce Department:
Investment in Cuba. Washington, D.C., U.S. G.P.O., 1957.

Freedom of Information Act Documents:
   Listed in *Declassified Documents Index* (DDI), published by Carrollton Press, Inc., 1975–1981 and by Research Publications, Inc., 1982–. Documents are cited by year indexed and by the document number under which they appear in that year's index, e.g., 1981, #1024.

BOOKS

Abel, Christopher, and Nissa Torrents, eds. *José Martí: Revolutionary Democrat*. Durham, N.C.: Duke University Press, 1986.

Aguilar, Luis. *Cuba, 1933: Prologue to Revolution*. Ithaca, N.Y.: Cornell University Press, 1972.

Aguilar, Luis, ed. *Operation Zapata: The Ultrasensitive Report and Testimony of the Board of Inquiry on the Bay of Pigs*. Frederick, Md.: University Publications of America, 1981.

Alvarez Díaz, José R., et al. *A Study on Cuba*. Coral Gables, Fla.: University of Miami Press, 1965.

Ambrose, Stephen. *Eisenhower: The President*. New York: Simon & Schuster, 1984.

——. *Rise to Globalism*. New York: Penguin, 1985. 4th rev. ed.

Ameringer, Charles D. *The Democratic Left in Exile: The Antidictatorial Struggle in the Caribbean, 1945–1959*. Coral Gables, Fla.: University of Miami Press, 1974.

Anglo-American Directory of Cuba. Marianao, Cuba: A.A.D.O.C., 1954–1955.

Atkins, Edwin F. *Sixty Years in Cuba*. Cambridge, Mass.: Riverside Press, 1926.

Barbier, Jacques A., and Allan J. Kuethe, eds. *The North American role in the Spanish imperial economy, 1760–1819*. Manchester: Manchester University Press, 1984.

Barkin, David B., and Nita Manitzas, eds. *Cuba: The Logic of the Revolution*. Andover, Mass.: Warner Modular Publications, 1973.

Batista, Fulgencio. *The Growth and Decline of the Cuban Republic*. New York: Devin-Adair, 1964.

Beck, Henry Houghton. *Cuba's Fight for Freedom and the War with Spain*. Philadelphia: Globe Bible Publishing Co., 1898.

Becker, William R., and Samuel F. Wells, eds. *Economics and World Power*. New York: Columbia University Press, 1984.

Beisner, Robert L. *From the Old Diplomacy to the New, 1865–1900*. New York: Crowell, 1975.

——. *Twelve Against Empire: The Anti-Imperialists, 1898–1900*. Chicago: University of Chicago Press, 1985.

Benjamin, Jules R. *The United States and Cuba: Hegemony and Dependent Development, 1880–1934*. Pittsburgh: University of Pittsburgh Press, 1977.

Bernstein, Barton, ed. *Toward a New Past*. New York: Vintage, 1969.

Blasier, Cole. *The Hovering Giant: U.S. Responses to Revolutionary Change in Latin America, 1910–1985*. Pittsburgh: University of Pittsburgh Press, 1986. Rev. ed.

Bonachea, Ramón, and Marta San Martín. *The Cuban Insurrection, 1952–1959*. New Brunswick, N.J.: Transaction, 1974.

Bonachea, Rolando, and Nelson Valdés. *Revolutionary Struggle: Selected Works of Fidel Castro, 1947–1958*. Cambridge: MIT Press, 1972.

Bonsal, Philip W. *Cuba, Castro and the United States*. Pittsburgh: University of Pittsburgh Press, 1971.

Campbell, Charles S. *The Transformation of American Foreign Relations, 1865–1900*. New York: Harper & Row, 1976.

Castro, Fidel. *History Will Absolve Me*. New York: Lyle Stuart, 1961.

Castro, Fidel, and Frei Betto. *Fidel on Religion*. New York: Simon & Schuster, 1987.

Casuso, Teresa. *Cuba and Castro*. New York: Random House, 1961.

Collier, Peter, and David Horowitz. *The Kennedys: An American Drama*. New York: Summit, 1984.

Connell-Smith, Gordon. *The Inter-American System*. London: Oxford University Press, 1966.

Cook, Blanch Wiesen. *The Declassified Eisenhower: A Divided Legacy of Peace and Political Warfare*. New York: Doubleday, 1981.

Cordova, Efren. "Fidel Castro and the Cuban Labor Movement: 1959– 1961." Ph.D. diss., Cornell University, 1977.

Crassweller, Robert D. *Trujillo: The Life and Times of a Caribbean Dictator*. New York: Macmillan, 1966.

Cuba, Instituto de Historia del Movimiento Comunista y de la Revolución Socialista de Cuba anexo al Comité Central del PCC. *El Pensamiento de Fidel Castro: selección tematica*. La Habana: Editora Política, 1983. Tomo 1, Volumen 1.

————, Ministry of State, Public Relations Department. *In Defense of National Sovereignty*. Havana: Ministry of State Printing Office, Nov. 13, 1959.

Davis, David Brion. *Slavery and Human Progress*. New York: Oxford University Press, 1984.

Domínguez, Jorge. *Cuba: Order and Revolution*. Cambridge: Harvard University Press, 1978.

Dorschner, John, and Roberto Fabricio. *The Winds of December*. New York: Coward, McCann & Geoghegan, 1980.

Draper, Theodore. *Castro's Revolution: Myths and Realities*. New York: Praeger, 1962.

Duarte Oropesa, José A. *Historiología cubana*. Hollywood, Calif., 1969. 5 vols.

Dubofsky, Melvyn. *Industrialization and the American Worker, 1865–1920*. Arlington Heights, Ill.: AHM Publishing Co., 1975.

Eichner, Alfred S. *The Emergence of Oligopoly: Sugar Refining as a Case Study*. Baltimore: Johns Hopkins University Press, 1969.

Eisenhower, Dwight D. *Waging Peace: The White House Years, 1956–1961*. New York: Doubleday, 1965.

Etheredge, Lloyd S. *Can Governments Learn?* New York: Pergamon Press, 1985.

Farber, Samuel. *Revolution and Reàction in Cuba, 1933–1960*. Middletown, Conn.: Wesleyan University Press, 1976.

Fermoselle, Rafael. *Política y color en Cuba: La guerrita de 1912*. Montevideo: Ediciones Geminis, 1974.

Fidel en Radio Rebelde. La Habana: Editorial Gente Nueva, 1979.

Fitzgibbon, Russell H. *The Constitutions of the Americas*. Chicago: University of Chicago Press, 1948.

Foley, Michael. *The New Senate: Liberal Influence on a Conservative Institution*. New Haven: Yale University Press, 1980.

Foner, Eric. *Free Soil, Free Labor, Free Men: The Ideology of the Republican Party before the Civil War*. London: Oxford University Press, 1970.

Foner, Philip S. *A History of Cuba and Its Relations with the United States*. New York: International Publishers, 1962. 2 vols.

————. *The Spanish-Cuban-American War and the Birth of American Imperialism*. New York: Monthly Review Press, 1972. 2 vols.

————, ed. *Inside the Monster: Writings on the United States and American Imperialism by José Martí*. New York: Monthly Review Press, 1975.

Foner, Philip S., ed. *Our America by José Martí*. New York: Monthly Review Press, 1978.

Fraginals, Manuel Moreno. *The Sugarmill: The Socioeconomic Complex of Sugar in Cuba*. New York: Monthly Review Press, 1976.

Franqui, Carlos. *Diary of the Cuban Revolution*. New York: Viking, 1980.

Friedlaender, Heinrich. *Historia económica de Cuba*. La Habana: Editorial de Ciencias Sociales, 1978.

Gaddis, John L. *Strategies of Containment*. New York: Oxford University Press, 1982

Gallup, George H., ed. *The Gallup Poll, 1935–1971*. New York: Random House, 1972. 3 vols.

García Montes, Jorge, and Antonio Alonso Avila. *Historia del Partido Comunista de Cuba*. Miami: Ed. Universal, 1970.

Gardner, Lloyd, Walter LaFeber, and Thomas McCormick. *Creation of the American Empire*. Chicago: Rand McNally & Co., 1973.

Gellman, Irwin F. *Roosevelt and Batista: Good Neighbor Diplomacy in Cuba, 1933–1945*. Albuquerque: University of New Mexico Press, 1973.

Genovese, Eugene. *The World the Slaveholders Made*. New York: Vintage, 1971.

Gonzalez, Edward. *Cuba Under Castro: The Limits of Charisma*. Boston: Houghton Mifflin, 1974.

Goodwyn, Lawrence. *The Populist Moment: A Short History of the Agrarian Revolt in America*. New York: Oxford University Press, 1978.

Graff, Henry, ed. *American Imperialism and the Philippine Insurrection*. Boston: Little Brown, 1969.

Guerra y Sánchez, Ramiro. *Azúcar y Población en las Antillas*. Madrid: Cultural S.A., 1935.

———. *Sugar and Society in the Caribbean*. New Haven: Yale University Press, 1964.

Gutman, Herbert. *Work, Culture and Society in Industrializing America*. New York: Vintage, 1977.

Halberstam, David, ed. *The Kennedy Presidential Press Conferences*. New York: Earl M. Coleman Enterprises, 1978.

Halstead, Murat. *The Story of Cuba: Her Struggles for Liberty*. Akron, Ohio: Werner Co., 1898.

Hays, Samuel P. *Response to Industrialism, 1885–1914*. Chicago: University of Chicago Press, 1957.

Healy, David. *The United States in Cuba: 1898–1902*. Madison: University of Wisconsin Press, 1963.

———. *US Expansionism: The Imperialist Urge of the 1890's*. Madison: University of Wisconsin Press, 1970.

Hinkle, Warren, and William Turner. *The Fish Is Red*. New York: Harper & Row, 1981.

Hofstadter, Richard. *The Age of Reform*. New York: Vintage, 1955.

———. *The American Political Tradition*. New York: Vintage, 1961.

Horowitz, Irving Louis, ed. *Cuban Communism*. New Brunswick, N.J.: Transaction, 1982. 4th ed.

Horsman, Reginald. *Race and Manifest Destiny: The Origins of American Racial Anglo-Saxonism*. Cambridge: Harvard University Press, 1981.

Howard, Nathaniel R., ed. *The Basic Papers of George M. Humphrey as Secretary of the Treasury, 1953–1957*. Cleveland: Western Reserve Historical Society, 1965.

Hunt, Michael H. *Ideology and U.S. Foreign Policy*. New Haven: Yale University Press, 1987.

Jenks, Leland. *Our Cuban Colony: A Study in Sugar*. New York: Vanguard, 1928.

Johnson, Donald, and Kirk Porter, comps. *National Party Platforms, 1840–1972*. Urbana: University of Illinois Press, 1975.

Johnson, John J. *Latin America in Caricature*. Austin: University of Texas Press, 1980.

Jorrin, Miguel, and John D. Martz. *Latin American Political Thought and Ideology*. Chapel Hill: University of North Carolina Press, 1970.

Judson, C. Fred. *Cuba and the Revolutionary Myth: The Political Education of the Cuban Rebel Army, 1953–1963*. Boulder, Colo.: Westview Press, 1984.

Kaufman, Burton I. *Trade and Aid: Eisenhower's Foreign Economic Policy, 1953–1961*. Baltimore: Johns Hopkins University Press, 1982.

Kirk, John M. *José Martí: Mentor of the Cuban Nation*. Tampa: University Presses of Florida, 1983.

Kirkpatrick, Lyman, Jr. *The Real CIA*. New York: Macmillan, 1968.

Knight, Franklin W. *Slave Society in Cuba During the Nineteenth Century*. Madison: University of Wisconsin Press, 1970.

Kolko, Gabriel. *The Limits of Power*. New York: Harper & Row, 1972.

Kutner, Stanley, and Stanley Katz, eds. *The Promise of American History*. Baltimore: Johns Hopkins University Press, 1982.

LaFeber, Walter. *The New Empire: An Interpretation of American Expansion, 1860–1898*. Ithaca, N.Y.: Cornell University Press, 1964.

———. *Inevitable Revolutions: The United States in Central America*. New York: W. W. Norton, 1984.

Langley, Lester D. *The Cuban Policy of the United States: A Brief History*. New York: John Wiley & Sons, 1968.

———. *Struggle for the American Mediterranean, 1776–1904*. Athens: University of Georgia Press, 1976.

Lazo, Mario. *Dagger in the Heart*. New York: Funk & Wagnalls, 1968.

Lears, Jackson. *No Place of Grace: Antimodernism and the Transformation of American Culture, 1880–1920*. New York: Pantheon, 1981.

Leech, Margaret. *In the Days of McKinley*. New York: Harper, 1959.

Le Riverend, Julio. *Economic History of Cuba*. Havana: Book Institute, 1967.

Lewis, Gordon K. *Main Currents in Caribbean Thought*. Baltimore: Johns Hopkins University Press, 1983.

Lewis, Oscar, Ruth M. Lewis, and Susan Rigdon. *Four Men: Living the Revolution*. Urbana: University of Illinois Press, 1977.

Linderman, Gerald F. *The Mirror of War: American Society and the Spanish-American War*. Ann Arbor: University of Michigan Press, 1974.

Link, Arthur, and William J. Leary, Jr., eds. *The Diplomacy of World Power: The United States, 1898–1920*. New York: St. Martín's Press, 1970.

Liss, Sheldon. *Roots of Revolution: Radical Thought in Cuba*. Lincoln: University of Nebraska Press, 1987

Llerena, Mario. *The Unsuspected Revolution*. Ithaca, N.Y.: Cornell University Press, 1985.

López Segrera, Francisco. *Cuba: Capitalismo dependiente y subdesarrollo, 1510–1959*. La Habana: Editorial de Ciencias Sociales, 1981.

López-Fresquet, Rufo. *My Fourteen Months with Castro*. Cleveland: World Publishers, 1966.

McFeely, William S. *Grant: A Biography*. New York: W. W. Norton, 1981.

MacGaffey, Wyatt, and Clifford Barnett. *Twentieth Century Cuba*. Garden City, N.Y.: Anchor Books, 1965.

Maestri, Raúl. *El latifundismo en la economía cubana*. La Habana: Editorial Revista de Avance, 1929.

Mañach, Jorge. *La crisis de la alta cultura en Cuba*. La Habana: La Universal, 1925.

―――. *Indagacíon del choteo*. La Habana: Editorial Lex., 1936.

Martín, Lionel. *The Early Fidel*. Secaucus, N.J.: Lyle Stuart, 1978.

Matthews, Herbert. *Revolution in Cuba*. New York: Scribner's, 1975.

May, Ernest R. *American Imperialism*. New York: Atheneum, 1968.

Melanson, Richard, and David Mayers. *Reevaluating Eisenhower: American Foreign Policy in the 1950's*. Urbana: University of Illinois Press, 1987.

Merk, Frederick. *Manifest Destiny and Mission*. New York: Vintage, 1963.

Mesa-Lago, Carmelo, ed. *Revolutionary Change in Cuba*. Pittsburgh: University of Pittsburgh Press, 1971.

Montaner, Carlos Alberto. *Secret Report on the Cuban Revolution*. New Brunswick, N.J.: Transaction, 1981.

Montgomery, David. *Beyond Equality: Labor and the Radical Republicans, 1862–1872*. Urbana: University of Illinois Press, 1981.

Morley, Morris H. *Imperial State and Revolution: The United States and Cuba, 1952–1986*. London: Cambridge University Press, 1987

Murphy, Robert. *Diplomat Among Warriors*. New York: Doubleday, 1964.

Nash, Gary B., and Richard Weiss *The Great Fear: Race in the Mind of America*. New York: Holt, Rinehart Winston, 1970.

Nelson, Lowry. *Rural Cuba*. Minneapolis: University of Minnesota Press, 1950.

Nevins, Allen. *Hamilton Fish: The Inner History of the Grant Administration*. New York: Dodd, Mead & Co., 1936.

O'Connor, James. *The Origins of Socialism in Cuba*. Ithaca, N.Y.: Cornell University Press, 1970.

Ortiz, Fernando. *Cuban Counterpoint: Sugar and Tobacco*. New York: Vintage, 1970.

―――. *La decadencia cubana*. La Habana: La Universal, 1924.

Padula, Alfred Jr. "The Fall of the Bourgeoisie: Cuba, 1959–1961." Ph.D. diss., University of New Mexico, 1974.

Partido Comunista de Cuba. *El Partido Comunista y los problemas de la revolución en Cuba*. La Habana: Comité Central del Partido Comunista de Cuba, 1933.

Partido Ortodoxo. *Doctrina del Partido Ortodoxo*. La Habana: Editorial Fernández, 1951.

Paterson, Thomas G. *American Imperialism and Anti-Imperialism*. New York: T. Y. Crowell, 1973.

Payne, Stanley G. *A History of Spain and Portugal*. Madison: University of Wisconsin Press, 1973. 2 vols.

Pérez, Louis A., Jr. *Army Politics in Cuba*. Pittsburgh: University of Pittsburgh Press, 1976.

———. *Cuba Between Empires, 1878–1902*. Pittsburgh: University of Pittsburgh Press, 1983.

———. *Cuba Under the Platt Amendment, 1902–1934*. Pittsburgh: University of Pittsburgh Press, 1986.

———. *Intervention, Revolution and Politics in Cuba, 1913–1921*. Pittsburgh: University of Pittsburgh Press, 1978.

Petras, James. *Class, State and Power in the Third World*. London: Zed Press, 1981.

Phillips, Ruby Hart. *Cuba: Island of Paradox*. New York: McDowell, Obolensky, 1959.

———. *The Cuban Dilemma*. New York: Ivan Obolensky, 1962.

Pike, Fredrick B. *Hispanismo: 1898–1936*. South Bend, Ind.: University of Notre Dame Press, 1971.

Porter, Glenn. *The Rise of Big Business, 1860–1910*. Arlington Heights, Ill.: Harlan Davidson, 1973.

Porter, Robert. *Industrial Cuba*. New York: G. P. Putnam's Sons, 1899.

Portuondo, José A. *El contenido social de la literatura cubana*. México City: El Colegio de México, 1944.

Poyo, Gerald E. *With All and For the Good of All: The Emergence of Popular Nationalism in the Cuban Community of the United States, 1848–1898*. Durham, N.C.: Duke University Press, 1989.

Prados, John. *President's Secret Wars*. New York: William Morrow, 1986.

Pratt, Julius W. *Expansionists of 1898*. New York: Quadrangle, 1964.

Public Papers of the Presidents of the United States. Washington, D.C.: United States Government Printing Office, 1954 and 1960.

Rabe, Stephen G. *Eisenhower and Latin America: The Foreign Policy of Anticommunism*. Chapel Hill: University of North Carolina Press, 1988.

Ratliff, William E., ed. *The Selling of Fidel Castro*. New Brunswick, N.J.: Transaction, 1987.

Riera Hernández, Mario. *Cuba republicana, 1899–1958*. Miami: Editorial AIP, 1974.

Rippoll, Carlos. *La generación del 23 en Cuba*. New York: Las Américas Publishing Co., 1968.

Roig de Leuchsenring, Emilio. *Cuba no debe su independencia a los Estados Unidos*. La Habana: Ediciones La Tertulia, 1960. 3rd ed.

Roig de Leuchsenring, Emilio. *Los problemas sociales de Cuba*. La Habana: Imprenta El Ideal, 1927.

Rout, Leslie B., Jr. *The African Experience in Spanish America*. London: Cambridge University Press, 1976.

Ruiz, Ramón Eduardo. *Cuba: The Making of the Revolution*. Amherst: University of Massachusetts Press, 1968.

Rystad, Goren. *Ambiguous Imperialism*. Lund, Sweden: Scandinavian Books, 1975.

Sánchez Otero, German. *Los partidos políticos burgueses en Cuba neocolonial, 1899–1952*. La Habana: Editorial de Ciencias Sociales, 1985.

Schlesinger, Arthur M., Jr. *A Thousand Days*. New York: Fawcett, 1965.

————, ed. *A Documentary History of United States Foreign Policy, 1945–1973*. New York: Chelsea House, 1983. Vol. 3, part 1.

Schwartz, Jordan. *Liberal: Adolf A. Berle and the Vision of an American Era*. New York: Free Press, 1987.

Schwartz, Stephen, ed. *The Transition from Authoritarianism to Democracy in the Hispanic World*. San Francisco: Institute for Contemporary Studies, 1986.

Scott, Rebecca J. *Slave Emancipation in Cuba*. Princeton, N.J.: Princeton University Press, 1985.

Seers, Dudley, ed. *Cuba: The Economic and Social Revolution*. Chapel Hill: University of North Carolina Press, 1964.

Smith, Earl. *The Fourth Floor*. New York: Random House, 1962.

Smith, Robert F. *The United States and Cuba: Business and Diplomacy, 1917–1960*. New York: Bookman Associates, 1960.

————. *What Happened in Cuba?* New York: Twayne Publishers, Inc., 1963.

Smith, Wayne. *The Closest of Enemies*. New York: W. W. Norton, 1987.

Snow, Sinclair. *The Pan American Federation of Labor*. Durham, N.C.: Duke University Press, 1964.

Spalding, Hobart, Jr. *Organized Labor in Latin America*. New York: Harper & Row, 1977.

Stampp, Kenneth M. *The Era of Reconstruction, 1865–1877*. New York: Vintage, 1965.

Steward, Dick. *Money, Marines and Mission*. Lanham, Md.: University Press of America, 1980.

Suchlicki, Jaime. *Cuba, From Columbus to Castro*. New York: Scribner's, 1974.

————. *University Students and Revolution in Cuba, 1920–1968*. Miami: University of Miami Press, 1969.

Szulc, Tad. *Fidel: A Critical Portrait*. New York: Morrow, 1986.

Tanzer, Michael. *The Political Economy of International Oil and the Underdeveloped Countries*. Boston: Beacon, 1969.

Thomas, Hugh. *Cuba: The Pursuit of Freedom*. New York: Harper & Row, 1971.

Tomkins, E. Berkeley. *Anti-Imperialism in the United States: The Great Debate, 1890–1920*. Philadelphia: University of Pennnsylvania Press, 1970.

Truman, Harry S. *Memoirs by Harry S. Truman: Years of Trial and Hope, 1946–1952*. New York: Signet, 1965. 2 vols.

Van Alstyne, Richard. *The Rising American Empire*. Chicago: Quadrangle, 1973.

Vignier, E., and G. Alonso. *La corrupción política y administrativa en Cuba, 1944–1952*. La Habana: Editorial de Ciencias Sociales, 1973.

Wallich, Henry C. *Monetary Problems of an Export Economy: The Cuban Experience, 1914–1947*. Cambridge: Harvard University Press, 1950.

Weinberg, Albert. *Manifest Destiny*. New York: Quadrangle, 1963.

Welch, Richard, Jr. *Response to Revolution*. Chapel Hill: University of North Carolina Press, 1985.

Westin, Rubin F. *Racism in U.S. Imperialism*. Columbia, S.C.: University of South Carolina Press, 1972.

Whitaker, Arthur P. *The United States and the Independence of Latin America*. New York: W. W. Norton, 1964.

———. *The Western Hemisphere Idea: Its Rise and Decline*. Ithaca, N.Y.: Cornell University Press, 1954.

White, Trumbull. *Our New Possessions: A Graphic Account, Descriptive and Historical, of the Tropic-Islands of the Sea That Have Fallen Under Our Sway*. . . . n.p.: Trumbull White, 1898.

Wiarda, Howard, ed. *Politics and Social Change in Latin America: The Distinct Tradition*. Amherst: University of Massachusetts Press, 1982.

Wiebe, Robert H. *The Search for Order, 1877–1920*. New York: Hill & Wang, 1967.

Wilkins, Myra. *The Emergence of Multinational Enterprise*. Cambridge: Harvard University Press, 1970.

Williams, William A. *The Roots of the Modern American Empire*. New York: Random House, 1969.

Wisan, Joséph E. *The Cuban Crisis as Reflected in the New York Press, 1895–1898*. New York: Octagon Press, 1977.

Wyden, Peter. *Bay of Pigs*. New York: Simon & Schuster, 1979.

Zeitlin, Maurice. *Revolutionary Politics and the Cuban Working Class*. New York: Harper & Row, 1970.

ARTICLES

Ameringer, Charles D. "The Auténtico Party and Political Opposition in Cuba, 1952–1957." *Hispanic American Historical Review*, 65:2 (May 1985), pp. 327–51.

Auxier, George. "Middle Western Newspapers and the Spanish American War, 1895–1898." *Mississippi Valley Historical Review* 26 (March 1940), pp. 523–34.

———. "The Propaganda Activities of the Cuban Junta in Precipitating the Spanish American War." *Hispanic American Historical Review* 19 (1939), pp. 268–305.

Benjamin, Jules R. "The Framework of United States Relations with Latin America in the Twentieth Century: An Interpretive Essay," *Diplomatic History* 11:2 (Spring 1987), pp. 91–112.

BIBLIOGRAPHY

Benjamin, Jules R. "The Machadato and Cuban Nationalism, 1928–1932." *Hispanic American Historical Review* 55:1 (February 1975), pp. 66–91.

———. "The New Deal, Cuba and the Rise of a Global Foreign Economic Policy." *The Business History Review* 51:1 (Spring 1977), pp. 57–78.

———. "Scholars and the Good Neighbor Policy." Paper presented at the convention of the Organization of American Historians, Minneapolis, April 1985.

Blackburn, Robin. "Prologue to the Cuban Revolution." *New Left Review* 21 (October 1963), pp. 52–91.

Blasier, Cole. "The Elimination of United States Influence." *Revolutionary Change in Cuba*, edited by Carmelo Mesa-Lago, pp. 43–80. Pittsburgh: Univ. of Pittsburgh Press, 1971.

Corbitt, Duvon C. "Cuban Revisionist Interpretations of Cuba's Struggle for Independence." *Hispanic American Historical Review* 43 (August 1963), pp. 395–404.

Crahan, Margaret. "Religious Penetration and Nationalism in Cuba: U.S. Methodist Activities, 1898–1958." Paper presented to the Yale conference on Cuban history and society, Seven Springs, Connecticut, October 1977.

Dominguez, Jorge. "Seeking Permission to Build a Nation: Cuban Nationalism and U.S. Response Under the First Machado Presidency." *Cuban Studies* 16 (1986), pp. 33–48.

Erb, Claude. "Prelude to Point Four: The Institute of Inter-American Affairs." *Diplomatic History*. 9:3 (Summer 1985), pp. 249–69.

Farber, Samuel. "The Cuban Communists in the Early Stages of the Cuban Revolution." *Latin American Research Review*. 18:1 (1983), pp. 59–83.

Foner, Eric. "Reconstruction Revisited." *Reviews in American History*. 10 (December 1982), pp. 82–100.

Fox, Geoffrey. "Race and Class in Contemporary Cuba." *Cuban Communism*, edited by Irving L. Horowitz, pp. 309–330. New Brunswick, N.J.: Transaction, 1982. 4th ed.

Fry, Joseph. "William McKinley and the Coming of the Spanish-American War: A Study of the Besmirching and Redemption of an Historical Image." *Diplomatic History*. 3:1 (Winter 1979), pp. 77–97.

Gage, Nicolas. "The Little Big Man Who Laughs at the Law." *Atlantic* (July 1970), pp. 62–69.

Gonzalez, Edward. "Castro's Revolution, Cuban Communist Appeals, and the Soviet Response." *World Politics* 21:1 (October 1968), pp. 39–68.

Hennessy, C.A.M. "The Roots of Cuban Nationalism." *International Affairs* 39 (July 1963), pp. 346–58.

Hispanic American Report 12:1 (January 1960), p. 601.

Kapcia, Antoni. "Cuban populism and the myth of Martí." *José Martí: Revolutionary Democrat*, edited by Christopher Abel and Nissa Torrents, pp. 32–64. Durham, N.C.: Duke Univ. Press, 1986.

Lernoux, Penny. "The Miami Connection." *The Nation*. (February 18, 1984), pp. 186–98.

Malé, Belkis Cuza. "Reflections on Radio Martí." *The Transition from Authori-*

tarianism to Democracy in the Hispanic World, edited by Stephen Schwartz, pp. 131–42. San Francisco: Institute for Contemporary Studies, 1986.

Manitzas, Nina. "The Setting of the Cuban Revoluton." *Cuba: The Logic of the Revolution*, edited by David Barkin and Nita Manitzas, pp. 1–18. Andover, Mass.: Warner Modular Publications, 1973.

Morley, Morris. "The U.S. Imperial State in Cuba, 1952–1958: Policymaking and Capitalist Interests." *Journal of Latin American Studies* 14:1 (May 1982), pp. 143–70.

Ortiz, Fernando. "Los Responsabilidades de la E.E.U.U. en los males de Cuba." *Revista bimestre cubana* 33:2 (March–April 1934), pp. 232–50.

Padula, Alfred. "Financing Castro's Revolution, 1956–1958." *Revista Interamericana* 8:2 (Summer 1978), pp. 234–46.

Pérez, Louis A., Jr. "In the Service of the Revolution: Two Decades of Cuban Historiography, 1959–1979." *Hispanic American Historical Review* 60 (February 1980), pp. 79–89.

———. "Toward Dependency and Revolution: The Political Economy of Cuba between Wars, 1878–1895." *Latin American Research Review* 18:1 (1983), pp. 127–42.

———. "Vagrants, Beggars and Bandits: Social Origins of Cuban Separatism, 1878–1895." *American Historical Review* 90:5 (December 1985), pp. 1092–1121.

Pollard, Robert A., and Samuel F. Wells, Jr. "1945–1960: The Era of American Economic Hegemony." *Economics and World Power*, edited by William R. Becker and Samuel F. Wells, Jr., pp. 333–90. New York: Columbia Univ. Press, 1974.

Poyo, Gerald. E. "The Anarchist Challenge to the Cuban Independence Movement, 1885–1890." *Cuban Studies* 15:1 (Winter 1985), pp. 29–42.

Rabe, Stephen. "The Elusive Conference: United States Economic Relations with Latin America, 1945–1952." *Diplomatic History* 2:3 (Summer 1978), pp. 279–94.

Ripoll, Carlos. "The Press in Cuba, 1952–1960: Autocratic and Totalitarian Censorship." *The Selling of Fidel Castro*, edited by William E. Ratliff, pp. 83–108. New Brunswick, N.J.: Transaction, 1987.

Rogers, Daniel T. "In Search of Progressivism." *The Promise of American History*, edited by Stanley Kutner and Stanley Katz, pp. 113–32. Baltimore: Johns Hopkins Univ. Press, 1982.

Safford, Jeffrey. "The Nixon-Castro Meeting of 19 April 1959." *Diplomatic History* 4:4 (Fall 1980), pp. 426–31.

Sims, Harold D. "Cuban Labor and the Communist Party, 1937–1958: An Interpretation." *Cuban Studies* 15:1 (Winter 1985), pp. 43–58.

Smith, Robert F. "Twentieth Century Cuban Historiography." *Hispanic American Historical Review* 44 (February 1964), pp. 44–73.

Stokes, William S. "The Cuban Parliamentary System in Action, 1940–1947." *Journal of Politics* 11 (1949), pp. 344–50.

Swan, Harry. "The Nineteen Twenties: A Decade of Intellectual Change in Cuba." *Revista Interamericana* 8:2 (Summer 1978), pp. 275–88.

Trelles, Carlos M. "El proceso y el retroceso de la República de Cuba." *Revista bimestre cubana* 18 (1924), pp. 313–19, 345–64.

Victoria, Nelson Amaro. "Mass and Class in the Origins of the Cuban Revolution." *Cuban Communism*, edited by Irving L. Horowitz, pp. 221–51. New Brunswick, N.J.: Transaction, 1981.

Wexler, Alice R. "Sex, Race and Character in Nineteenth Century American Accounts of Cuba." *Caribbean Studies* 18:3 and 4 (October 1978/January 1979), pp. 115–30.

Whitaker, Arthur P. "From Dollar Diplomacy to the Good Neighbor." *Inter-American Economic Affairs* 4:4 (Spring 1951), pp. 12–19.

Wright, Theodore P., Jr. "United States Electoral Intervention in Cuba." *Inter-American Economic Affairs* 13 (Winter 1959), pp. 50–71.

Young, Mary B. "American Expansionism, 1870–1900: The Far East." *Toward a New Past*, edited by Barton Bernstein, pp. 176–201. New York: Vintage, 1969.

Zeitlin, Maurice. "Political Generations in the Cuban Working Class." *American Journal of Sociology* 71:5 (March 1966), pp. 493–508.

Zoumaras, Thomas. "Eisenhower, Dulles and the Preservation of Pan Americanism, 1957–1958." Paper presented to the convention of the American Historical Association, Washington, D.C., December 28, 1987.

———. "Eisenhower's Foreign Economic Policy: The Case of Latin America." *Reevaluating Eisenhower: American Foreign Policy in the 1950's*, edited by Richard Melanson and David Mayers, pp. 155–91. Urbana: Univ. of Illinois Press, 1987.

INDEX

ABC (party), 83, 87
Adams, John Quincy, 8, 9
Agrarian Reform Law (1959), 179–81
American Sugar Refining Company, 66
Annexation of Cuba: North American attitudes toward, 15, 25, 40, 46, 62–63, 74
Arbenz, Jacobo, 134, 189
Atkins, Edwin, 35
Auténticos, 105–6, 108, 115–16, 118, 157

Barquín, Ramón, 163, 165
Batista, Fulgencio, 93–96, 102–4, 119–28, 142, 148–53, 161–62
Bay of Pigs invasion, 206–7
Beaulac, Willard, 117
Betancourt, Rómulo, 191
Beveridge, Albert, 61
Bonsal, Philip, 173–74, 180, 182, 202
Boti, Regino, 172
Braddock, Daniel, 162, 169, 172
Braden, Spruille, 159
Burke, Arleigh, 149, 164
Bush, Luis, 172

Cabot, John Moors, 125
Caffery, Jefferson, 89
Calhoun, John, 8
Calhoun, William H., 46
Cantillo, Eulogio, 165
Carribean Legion, 116, 172, 190
Castro, Fidel, 131, 132, 142–45, 154, 168–69, 171–72, 177–79, 182–85, 190–91, 202–3, 213–15
Castro, Raúl, 144, 149, 174
Chibás, Eduardo, 126, 131, 141, 143
CIA. *See* U.S. Central Intelligence Agency
Cienfuegos, Camilo, 165

Clay, Henry, 9–10
Cleveland, Grover, 33–39
Creoles. *See* Cuban sugar bourgeoisie
Crowder, Enoch, 77–78, 82
Cuban class structure: middle class, 79, 83, 199–201; unemployed, 200; upper class, 70, 127–29, 198–99; working class, 112, 129–30, 153, 200
Cuban *colonos*, 21
Cuban Communist Party, 83–84, 94–95, 102–3, 106–7, 111–12, 126, 146, 185
Cuban Confederation of Workers (CTC), 107
Cuban constitution (1940), 96–97
Cuban culture, 79, 100–2, 198. *See also* North American cultural influence in Cuba
Cuban independence movement (1890s), 24, 25, 32, 34, 42–44
Cuban military, 90, 124, 170
Cuban nationalism: Creole, 22–23; early, 12–14; elite vs. mass, 14–15, 20, 25; farmer and worker, 22, 24; twentieth-century, 67–68, 70–71, 82–83, 85–87, 91, 99, 104–5, 108–10, 124, 127, 132, 142–43, 168, 172, 181–82, 213
Cuban political system, 71, 80, 93, 97–98, 108, 126, 128, 203
Cuban Revolutionary Council (CRC), 205
Cuban slavery, 12–13; consequences of, 24–25; North American attitudes toward, 10–13
Cuban sugar bourgeoisie, 11–13, 20–23, 42, 70

Díaz Lanz, Pedro, 184
Dillon, Douglas, 202
Dreier, John, 165

233